"HEY 'ADAM,' "WHERE YOU AT"?"
TAKE A STAND AND BE THE MAN!

(PART ONE: 3RD EDITION)
"THE RATED-R REBIRTH"

KAREN D. REID (PH.D. CANDIDATE)

authorHOUSE®

AuthorHouse™
1663 Liberty Drive
Bloomington, IN 47403
www.authorhouse.com
Phone: 1 (800) 839-8640

King James Version (KJV)
Public Domain

Published by AuthorHouse 03/31/2017

ISBN: 978-1-5246-8581-2 (sc)
ISBN: 978-1-5246-8582-9 (e)

Library of Congress Control Number: 2017904750

Print information available on the last page.

This book is printed on acid-free paper.

ACKNOWLEDGEMENTS

PASTOR RUBEN SHANNON

WHOSE PRICELESS DEPOSIT WAS THE SEED
THAT BIRTHED THIS BOOK

1951-2011

MR. LESTER KERN
OF KERN DESIGN STUDIOS

WHOSE LEGACY CONTINUES ON THE
FRONT COVER OF THIS BOOK, EVEN IN DEATH

(PERMISSION GRANTED BY LESTER KERN, III)

"A Divine Connection for Spiritual Expressions"

1955-2010

CONTENTS

INTRODUCTION

With all of the things that I have encountered and as much as I have been uncovered most of my life, if you didn't know by now, you will see soon enough that my main focus is certainly not grammar. Even as I am matriculating through my doctoral program, I have nothing to prove and only One to please. Incidentally, since this is the introduction, this may be a good place for me to go ahead and give you a "heads-up." My dissertation mentor and one of my editors have advised me to write with less words and more simplicity, but that's just not my style.

Disclaimer: I am a very descriptive writer, and by nature, I cross every "t," and I dot every "i." So if you are looking for a quick, generic read, you've got the wrong writer. If you are in a hurry for me to get to the point, stick to the point, or get past the point, this won't be the book for you. It's kind of hard to draw you into the world of my story by being simple and vague. So, since I have no committee members or review boards to report to, CAN I JUST BE FREE TO BE ME?"

You know what; you don't have to answer that. I have just taken the liberty to release this edition first, as an uncensored, unfiltered, and uncut, "Rated R-Rebirth" (the death of a dream and resurrection of a seed). I feel such an edginess and urgency to give birth to this "baby" again, that even if it has to be "incubated," I'm going to push this one out, "AS IS" and make it a trial run and a "buy at your own risk" edition. If you are not ready for a "raw and in-your-face, blood-pumping-Rebirth," you may "wanna" go back and ask for a "re-fund" and wait for the "re-mix." Or, here is the compromise: maybe we can "agree to disagree," and come to a mutual resolve for the forthcoming "Remix." Your feedback is welcomed.

Whereas I have approached the previous, two editions with dedication and determination, here, I am more concerned with putting things in the proper context. This final attempt is not an academic project with "bullet points." It is a project of obligation that has allowed my creative niche to bring me into a round of expression to gain them that are under the law. You will grasp better, later, what I mean when I propose: When the roots are not dealt with, the weeds keep growing. Whether the root is generational or environmental, genetic or demonic, we tend to judge people by their fruit. But if you want to understand the Black man's plight, you must understand that the fruit is **what** they do; the root is **why** they do it.

"Some things have the appearance of evil, but the root of it is bathed in iniquity. If the source of the fruit is from an evil tree, then the fruit can only bring forth death when eaten" (Thomas, 2017). The only way to fix the fruit for future generations is that you must fix the tree and make sure that it's yielding the right kind of fruit. According to Matthew 7:18: good fruit does not come from a bad tree, and bad fruit does not come from a good tree. No matter what you teach your child, if they came from a bad tree, their fruit will be a reflection of what's on the tree. *"Either make the tree good and its fruit good, or make the tree bad and its fruit bad; for the tree is known by its fruit"* (Mt. 12:33).

Do you know what happens when you apply wisdom to wickedness? You create thieves, robbers and future killers of America. You produce dead-beat dads and "turnt-up" moms. You can tell what kind of tree you're dealing with by the fruit it bears. Ask me why. The fruit is a direct result of the tree. If your child is out there "boot-clapping," or having babies at 14, or drugging or drinking, you need to investigate the family tree; your children are a reflection of that tree. Do you understand why some children and adults "cut-a-fool" and act like demon seeds that make you wonder what happened to the birth control method? Since they were determined to show up, be just as determined to command those demons to come out, **and** leave quietly.

The crux of the matter is that the tree gave seed after its own kind. One way to break curses is to apply the Word and go through deliverance. "Lest Satan should get an advantage of us" another way is to avoid being ignorant of his devices (2 Cor. 2:11). It follows that the purpose for this book is to "lay the axe [Word] unto the root of the tree" (Mt. 3:10). Whether it is by divine revelations, personal transformations, human observations, or other folk's evaluations, this book is intended to "bring it" with boldness and blackness, and with clarity and transparency. *"Whereof I am made a minister, according to the dispensation of God which is given to me for you, to fulfill the Word of God. Even the mystery which hath been hid from ages and from generations, but now is made manifest to His saints"* (Col. 1:25-26).

Even as the fullness of the book title has continued to emerge, strands and tangents of it have complicated an articulation of a manageable and specific question. Yet, the process of permitting aspects of the title to enter into awareness is essential in the formation of a core question that will remain viable and alive throughout this investigation (Moustakas, 1994). Here again, the question of emphasis is: "Adam, MAN, 'where you at'?!?" Would you **please** allow me to write this book the way I'm really feeling it, and in conjunction with the title? Undoubtedly, you will be able to identify with my request as you proceed with the process.

A common assumption is that Adam was preoccupied with hiding his sin and lacking transparency in exposing himself to God. However, there is another plausible reality that is much more complex than what meets the eye. Could it possibly be that he was literally engaged in covering the woman that **God** made to be his help meet? After all, did he not say in Genesis 3:12: ... *"The woman whom Thou gavest to be with me, she gave me of the tree, and I did eat."* At the risk of losing your support on this proposal, allow me to illustrate my personal perception. "For Adam so loved his wife that he gave up eternal life in Paradise, that whosoever was willing to perish for the love of a WOMAN was predestined to conform to restricted life outside of the garden" (1 Karen 3:16).

In some eccentric way, this book is especially rewarding for the reader who values the fact that Adam was the type of HIM who was destined to come. Throughout this journey, it is important to remember Romans 5:14 (with emphasis added), as the evidence when scrutinizing my investigation: *"**Nevertheless death reigned from Adam to Moses, even over them that had not sinned after the similitude of Adam's transgression, WHO IS THE FIGURE OF HIM THAT WAS TO COME.**"* More of a correlation than a comparison, my <u>ultimate</u> goal is to correlate what Adam did for Eve to what Christ did for the Church.

Considering the substantive significance of this important caveat, my objection is to present a clear discussion of a deeper revelation. Hence, a good jumping-off point leads to a questionable conclusion, which proposes that because Eve was the weaker vessel, Adam took the fall and **willfully** gave up his immortality to become her covering. Why? So that there would be no record on Earth suggesting that the world was in sin because of her transgression. Romans 5:19a solves the ambiguity of this conclusion: *"**For as by one man's disobedience many were made sinners**"*...

After reading the previous edition, C.O.G.I.G. Bishop Nathaniel Bullock informed me that the book made him recognize that my probe does matter. He acknowledged that he was able to view the content from a progressive theology vs. the traditional theology. He adds, "You will press buttons." Along these lines, go ahead and prop yourself up and prepare for some "big bang theories." I am fully persuaded that neither death, nor life, nor angels, nor principalities, nor powers, nor things present, nor things to come, nor height, nor depth, nor any other creature, was able to separate Eve from the love of Adam.

Here is my most recent example of a real, genuine love connection. Unfortunately, when the deadly tornado came through Joplin, MO in 2010, it barged its way into the home of Don Lansaw who gave his life to save his wife, Bethany. The crux that validates my conclusion is this: for the love of a woman, the fatal wound in Don's back was the ultimate result of covering his bride. We hear people say all the time: "I love you to death." But do they really? Loving someone to death indicates that you are willing to literally put your life on the line for that person.

The father who unsuccessfully attempted to wrestle his son from the grips of the Disneyland alligator is another "larger-than-life" example of true love on display. Can you think of anyone in your life who really thinks that you are worth saving? Can you think of anyone in your life who really thinks that you are worth keeping? If not, then why would you go crazy over someone who would not be willing to die for you? On the other hand, how can you live life without the One who gave it? "Ooops," that was "a come to Jesus" moment. My point is: do not allow folks to write checks with their mouths that their actions can't cash.

In the earlier illustration, Don expressed the most tangible epitome of loving Bethany to death. Moreover, Jesus thought we were to die for, so He sacrificed His life (Anthony Brown). If His death proved that He loved us, then, our lives should prove that we love Him. Later, my intention is to demonstrate to you that Adam apparently thought Eve was to die for. Above and beyond the scope of this book is the reality that the fatal decision that he made to counteract the fatal attack by the enemy on Eve, was the definitive consequence of covering his bride.

Although Eve is often blamed for the fall of man, man would not be in existence without the seed of this woman. To put it another way, it was the fall that was instigated by the enemy that resulted in the atonement by the blood. To simplify what I see as an actuality, Jesus would have had no other reason to die, except the woman's seed had bruised the enemy's head. The truth of the matter is that it was the man's disobedience (not the woman's vulnerability), which God manipulated to overthrow the enemy's deception.

In the scheme of things, God's basic retort was as it was with Joseph: "What Satan meant for evil, I meant it unto good, to bring to pass, as it is this day, to save much people alive" (Gen. 50:20). As Eve was being confronted by the serpent, it might lead one to conclude that for particular purposes, she could have easily asked, "Hey Adam, where you at? I see you standing here beside me (Gen. 3:6), but where are you in your logic? Where are you in your judgment? Are you where God expected you to be in this life or death situation? Adam, since you have been given dominion over all the earth and everything in it, is your head in the right place to use your authority and bring this serpent under your rule?" In the context of these questions, the significant outcome can be interpreted as an illuminating observation that God already knew where Adam would be.

To put this in a modern-day perspective, a very important part of the equation to consider is that if every moment of our lives has been recorded, absolutely nothing catches God by surprise. Writing backwards, He sees the end from the beginning. Considerably, the effect of the fall leads us to presume that as salvation was God's victory over Satan, the first "bailout plan" allowed the first Adam to go, "MIA" (missing in action), so that the last Adam could go, "CIA" (Christ in action).

To illustrate even more precision, Adam was not left defenseless. Had he **chosen** to, he could have easily interrupted the conversation between Eve and the serpent. However, if Adam had conquered Satan in the garden, there would have been no need for Jesus to conquer him on the cross. Watch this: no cross, no crown – no story, no glory – no Him, no you. *"For if by one man's offence death reigned by one; much more they which receive abundance of grace and of the gift of righteousness shall reign in life by one, Jesus Christ"* (Rom. 5:17). From the day Satan was evicted from Heaven, God had a plan for his plot. With "razor-sharp" consistency, "that's my story, and I'm sticking to it."

Now then, for the context of this book and the widespread reality of a universal rationale, allow me to offer a more extensive investigation of the "Adamic sin." Disclaimer: "In my shrewd analysis of the fall of man, this eye-opening exploration is what I have **personally** accepted as a prudent account of the fall of man." Actually, by the time that I was finalizing the 2nd Edition, I met another Genesis "buff," who even offered another twist on the topic. So, in view of the fact that there are different interpretations of the Genesis account of Adam and Eve, I humbly request the opportunity to challenge your ideas and beliefs with my progressive insight of another intriguing revelation. ... *"He that hath ears to hear, let him hear"* (Mk. 4:9b).

Since I have already exposed who I **was** in my previous writings, do not delight in my scorning. Please permit me to reveal what I have learned as a result of what I did. The last time I checked, the only way to expel the ramifications of ignorance is to bring light or knowledge to darkness. *"How long, ye simple ones, will ye love simplicity? And the scorners delight in their scorning, and fools hate knowledge?"* (Prov. 1:22). Given that wisdom is the principal thing, get wisdom, and with all of your getting, get understanding (Prov. 4:7). Hereafter, if you would be open to delve thoughtfully and thoroughly into the content of this groundbreaking book, it will provide a better perspective of the events of my entire Trilogy – *From Mistress to Ministry.*

CHAPTER ONE

BEHOLD, I SHOW YOU A MYSTERY

After I took the time to <u>comprehensively</u> focus on the Genesis account of Adam and Eve with Pastor Shannon, I concluded that although Satan injected a desire within Eve to digress from the purpose for which she was made, God had placed something in her that Adam could not resist. She knew exactly how to flaunt her fruit to make him comply with the serpent's conspiracy. The only thing that she had to do was put it in his face and allow him to taste it; and ladies, we have been following suit ever since (☺). And since the day that Adam failed the "acid test," most men do not have the power to resist fruit that's put in his face.

How did Esther survive in the presence of the king? She avoided telling him the whole story in one night. "Sweat-Pea," since my challenge in arising at such conclusion is so monumental, my first point is: don't give up the goods on the first date! I'm not sure where I borrowed this from, but "Dating is for data – not mating. No covenant, no cookie!" All the same, I needed to begin this chapter with a little, spiritual foreplay and the first "oral transaction," which took place between Adam and Eve. My intention is to allow your "juices" to start flowing a bit before I flirt any further with the sensation of your consciousness.

During the inevitability of writing one of my "final" revisions and initially as a chapter in my Trilogy-Part One, I hastily felt compelled to contact Pastor Shannon to explore the inconsistency of Eve being referred to first, as a help meet and later, as a wife. While we had not actually conversed in over two years, he imparted some final wisdom into my spirit that made it difficult for me to maintain my composure. I felt like a "woman-gone-wise." Endeavoring to beat a deadline at that time, I was stuck with figuring out how to tie this additional information to an already controversial chapter that was on its way to the press. Behold, I show you a mystery.

"When God originally decided that it was not good for Adam to be alone, why did He initially refer to Eve as his help meet in Gen. 2:18 & 20?" I inquired of Pastor Shannon. In the process of creation, when there was nothing else more suitable for man to relate to (not the animals, and surely not another "male-man"), this is how it happened according to Genesis 1:26-27. *"And God said, Let us make man in our image, after our likeness: and let them have dominion... So God created man in His own image, in the image of God created He Him; male and female created He them."*

I concur with Bishop Craig Baymon that there was no need for an umbilical cord because God did not connect with "them" in the flesh. After the first surgery with no anesthesia, Adam (the first man to give birth) woke up and was pleased to call his help meet, "WOMAN." Why? Worthy to be him (unlike the beasts of the earth), she was the first man that was created with a womb. If you scrutinize the veracity of the Scripture above, you will see the mystery! I believe that God initially called her his help meet because they were both created one man, sharing equal dominion.

If properly translated, "Let us make [one] **man**...and let **them** [equal] have dominion." The first "equally-yoked" couple, can you see that as being translated into one man having equal dominion? Behold, I show you a mystery. What this translation boils down to is that in the very beginning, Eve was equal to Adam in knowledge, power, and wisdom. Can you see what we see? While some people will and some will not, Pastor Shannon and I perceived that she was not less than him; they were one and the same! *"And the rib, which the LORD God had taken from man, made He a woman, and brought her unto the man"* (Gen. 2:22).

It's no wonder that Adam said: ***"This is now bone of my bones, and flesh of my flesh: she shall be called Woman, because she was taken out of Man"*** (Gen. 2:23). Even the word, "wo-**man**," pinpoints the fact that she was just another man that God "pre-fixed" with a lot of "**wo**" elements that are most befitting for a **fe**male. For instance: **wo**rn-out, **wo**unded, **wo**rthy, **wo**rdier, **wo**rrier, **wo**rker, **wo**nderful, **wo**rshiper; she is just a **wo**rldwide **wo**nder-woman with a lot of "wo"(s). "**WOW**," **wo**man! Can you not see your **wo**rth? It's not what your "M.O." is; it's all about your "WO!" "Girlfriend, you better ask somebody!"

I suppose that one of the reasons that the woman was taken from the rib is that the rib is the closet bone to the heart, which is the part of man that compels him to be loving, caring and protective. Whereas the two arms protect the rib, whatever is closest to a man's heart might force him to say, "If loving you is wrong, I don't 'wanna' be right." Hey "Adam," "where you at?" I understand now, that "where your treasure is, there will your heart be also" (Mt. 6:21). Here was my original point: the woman was taken out of man's side because she was equal to him.

If this whole scenario is properly interpreted, Eve (as his help meet), was a man like Adam, except she had a **wo**mb. Then, a reasonable question might be: Why would God create a man for Adam and like Adam, but with a womb? Since God wrote His own script, He must have known how the story would end. Although it was God's original desire for Eve to be Adam's help meet, He must have gone ahead of Himself and designed them where they could ultimately leave the garden and be husband and **wife**. ***"Therefore shall a man leave his father... and shall cleave unto his wife"***... (Gen. 2:24). Under normal conditions, you create things with your helper, but you procreate children with your wife. Did you get that?

An increasing awareness that captures much of my attention is that they were initially created to ascertain that Paradise functioned as a replica of Heaven. Because Adam was the created son of God, he was to run Earth like Jesus (the begotten Son of God) runs Heaven. Just as there is no procreating in Heaven, there was no other job for them in Paradise but to enjoy creation and **assist each other** in creating things and taking dominion over God's Earth. Nowadays, both Pastor and Co-Pastor are equal in authority **and** dominion. However, Eve was more like an "Assistant to the Pastor." Rather than being totally equal in authority or **HEAD**ship (since the head was created first), she was more equal in taking dominion. Soon, I will conclusively explain this equal element.

In this process of becoming one man with equal dominion, the very essence of Adam's substance was wrapped up in Eve's identity after his bone was joined to her body. Since everything in the man is in the bone, she was now him, as he was in her. In God's mind, Eve was designed to be Adam's soul mate before she was ever built. In Genesis 2:7, the elements of the soul were activated. Connecting with her assignment, she was taken from his **side** to be interactive with her soul mate's mind, will, emotions, imagination, and intellect. She was designed to act as Adam's EQUAL (to equally assist in caring for the things of God); yet, not taking the lead. The results of her lead role with Satan prove that God never made a man with two heads.

Until now, I had not given as much consideration to the radical philosophy that maintains this expression: "The woman was made of a rib out of the side of Adam; not made out of his head to rule over him, nor out of his feet to be trampled upon by him, but out of his side to be equal with him, under his arm to be protected, and near his heart to be beloved" (Matthew Henry). Now, I am convinced that the true identity of a real man is insinuated in this notion. While the man's duty in the relationship is to respect, protect, and never neglect; behold, let me show you the mystery that I have painstakingly tried to prepare you for.

Initially (BEFORE THE FALL), God **never** proposed to make Adam the HEAD (the "H.N.I.C."). He proposed to make them one, but because of Eve's decision, the order changed. I guess in God's mind, there needed to be somebody whom He could rely on for making better decisions. Weighed in the light of this mystery, man is not higher in being; he is only higher in authority. As the man and female were created equal, they were both classified as a man. However, the two sexes were ultimately broken down to make a distinction between the head and the help.

Indeed, Eve used her dominion to become domineering; as a result, she made the dominant, life-altering decision that would cause man to die. Yet, as a topic of order, Adam was still higher in authority. Your boss or your bishop is no more of a man than you are. His title and the fact that he secured the role before you did, only makes him higher in authority. "Come on somebody!" Have you ever heard the term, "heads first, tails you lose?" Even if Adam was not **initially** created to be the woman's head, the fact that the head came first makes him higher in authority.

When the authority does not come from the **head** down (the heaviest part of the body), men are born breeched! The woman's mindset becomes breeched! Decisions are breeched; choices are breeched. Laws become breeched due to government officials being breeched. Leaders are born prematurely from the elevated risk of breeched and unhealthy leadership. Thus, churches are started in the breeched position. In simple terms, everything is just coming out "ass-backwards" – out of control and completely out of order. Why? The HEAD failed to move into the right position prior to "delivery." While this country is overdue for some major changes and life or death declarations, the procedure becomes more difficult as the "due date" gets closer.

Accordingly, our head leaders produce dysfunctional men that perform as "breech babies." In a breeched position, our men allow the tail and the feet (the last parts of the body) to come out first and be on top. The woman being head of the household, or the pastor of a church, or the President of the United States is not the divine order of God! So it bears repeating that since the head was formed first, Adam became the head that God needed to take charge and make better decisions once Eve "breeched" the divine order. "Hey 'Adam,' 'where you at?' Take a stand and be the man!"

STOP THE PRESS!

No, I mean literally, STOP THE PRESS! Why? My homework is incomplete! Whereas I failed to search for an editor to review my previous revision, God divinely set it up so that Timothy L.

Griffith, of Miami, Florida, could walk into the project at the end of its completion. Even though I was conscious of the fact that I always need a second opinion; in my exhaustion, I failed to subject myself to that rigorous process. Had I taken a chance on my own editing skills for that particular edition, it would have been gross professional negligence on my part.

All I know is this: when God ordains the vision, He will definitely make the provision! As a matter of fact, the publishing of this book was actually delayed for two months, due to this strategic intrusion. While I apprehensively waited for the editor's edits, I would text and ask: "Hey 'Adam,' where you at?" Of particular concern, his intimidating response would go like this: "Hey 'Eve,' what have you done?" The whole time I was like: "Really, God?" Just as I was not up for a negative review at this point, I literally went into full-blown depression after receiving one of the editor's text messages. Wow, the power of words.

Afterwards, I was too afraid to ask for his overall opinion. Although there were three "great" chapters with absolutely no changes/ corrections, I literally crashed as a result of this revision. Oftentimes, when something is newly-born, uncommon or controversial, most people insist on waiting for someone else to embrace it before they are comfortable with accepting it. Trust me; I totally understand the logic. Even so, once I received the final edits, it was not as dreadful as I had anticipated. After making an informed decision to go forward, I concluded that Evangelist Tim Griffith contributed important information to my effort and pointed out some things that certainly needed "laser-sharp" clarity.

The sacrifices and the negative effects were offset by the advantage of being able to dig even deeper in my effort to feel more comfortable and satisfied with the end results. Because of this intervention, I have the confidence, peace and assurance that revising this 2nd edition will not be a manageable task but a responsibility that I cannot ignore. While this happened to be the chapter under scrutiny that provided a major challenge for Tim, his first legitimate debate was: if Eve was equal to Adam in Genesis, why does the Bible say that the <u>woman</u> is the weaker vessel? "Indeed, Tim, I am really glad you asked."

First of all, if the woman was given to Adam to reproduce of himself or to produce again, would that not make her equal to him, or a perfect duplicate of the man that equally reproduced her? While that response did not really yield to my qualitative pondering, further guidance can be found in my strategic explication of 1 Peter 3:7: ***"Likewise, ye husbands, dwell with them according to knowledge, giving honour unto the wife, as unto the weaker vessel"...*** Obviously, Peter was not talking about women here, in general. For all of my meticulous readers who Tim adequately represents, he was talking about Christian marriage and how God expects the husband to treat his wife.

Hear Olar's (2000) illumination of this passage of Scripture (with emphasis added). "Peter did not say give honour to the wife, **who is** the weaker vessel; he said, **as to** the weaker vessel. That little word **as** means that something is similar to some other thing – not that it is identical to it. And to what specifically does the phrase, 'as to the weaker vessel' refers to? To women? To wives? No, it refers back to the verb and object, GIVING HONOUR. In other words, it tells us **how** husbands are to give honor to their wives. Of supreme importance, the only reason the words, 'weaker vessel' appear in the Bible is to draw a picture to help husbands see how God expects them to treat their wives." Brethren: "where you at?"

Olar (2000) also wants us to consider this: "If 'weaker' meant 'inferior,' why would a husband give any honor at all to his wife? If a potter threw a fire porcelain vase which was virtually without flaw, but then later that day, out of fatigue, threw a vase which came out of the kiln, lopsided and lumpy, to which of those two vases would he give honor? What human, possessed of all of his reasoning faculties would give honor to an 'inferior' vessel? Inferior vessels are tossed in the trash and destroyed.

Logically, if Peter expected husbands to give honor to the wife as to the 'inferior' vessel, then, he must have intended them to abuse and dishonor, even to kill their wives. Granted, almost every day we might encounter men who seem to think that is what God intends. Yet, we can be sure that emotionally, unstable and violent men are not the kind of husbands that Peter had in mind. No, he is talking about the kind of men who would pray with their wives, not men who brutally assault and torment the women for whom they vowed to God that they would lay down their very lives if called upon to do so."

Another analogy that Olar (2000) used as an excellent illustration of Peter's words, *weaker vessel* is this: "A cast iron skillet is used to cook food while using great heat. It is strong and can take extremes of temperature. But would anyone give honor to a skillet? Use it, take care of it, sure – but honor it? Contrast that to a fine, crystal wine glass. It is used in elegant dinners and looks beautiful and delicate. If one were to drop a cast iron skillet on the floor, it would produce a loud noise, and the impact might even crack a floor tile. But if one were to drop a crystal glass, it would simply shatter to pieces. Now then, which vessel is the weaker of the two? The wine glass, obviously. But which is inferior? I would never use a wine glass to fry eggs on a stove, anymore than I would expect my guests to drink champagne out of a skillet.

In the same way, I have no sense of frustration or resentment either toward God or toward the human race as a result of the fact that I am incapable of breastfeeding my son. On the other hand, neither do I mind moving heavy boxes and furniture around while my wife carries items of lighter weight. So, I trust that it is evident that weaker vessels are not necessarily, inferior vessels. The weaker vessel merely has a different purpose. In the family, the wife is something like a fine and lovely crystal wine glass – fragile, perhaps (or perhaps not, depending on the woman), but certainly designed by the Creator, God, for a special place of honor.

While 1 Peter 3:7 has a total of 35 words, it seems that Christian men have focused most of their attention on two words (weaker vessel). If one wishes to select just two words out of this verse and place special emphasis upon them, why not look for the verbs? The Church of God should begin to lay extra weight upon the words, 'dwell with' or 'giving honor.' Or best of all, let us finally start to live by every Word of God, and put away once and for all, every misogynistic prejudice" (Olar, 2000).

Oh my! I had an "aha" moment upon discovering this significant element. That one debate validates the fact that Tim and I ended up right where God intended (in Ft. Lauderdale, Florida, at a Pastors and Leaders' Summit, in the middle of December, exhibiting side by side). It is something about Florida that has always impacted my destiny; it gives me a quiet and soothing nook to write up my observations. In a later chapter, I will literally prove to you that the power of environments has divine relevance.

Well, as having equal value, we may as well go ahead and address the editor's other, major concern. Again, if Eve is equal to Adam in Genesis (as I proposed earlier), why do we find in 1 Corinthians 11:3 that man is the head of the woman, after I suggested initially that God never intended to make Adam the head? Rather, I concurred that before the fall and before any of us came into the picture, she was designed to be by his side to be equal to him and not out of his head to rule over, or as the head as in headship.

Here, Zibani (2012) examines this headship issue that many male chauvinists happen to have with women. "In the Jewish and Christian cultures when the Bible was written, there was a concept called, 'Federal Headship,' which indicated that the male is the one who represents his descendents. Proof can be found in Hebrews 7:8-10. Likewise, we see the concept of Federal Headship in the fall. It was Eve who first sinned. Nevertheless, sin entered the world through Adam, not through Eve. Why not? Adam represented humanity and creation (read Rom. 5:12, 15). When Adam fell, we fell. That's why 1 Corinthians 15:22 says: *'For as in Adam all die'...*

According to Genesis 2:24, when a man and woman get married, they become one flesh. Even as there is a unity between them, the man is the head of the family, which is why the Scripture says that the man is the head of the woman. Some may think that this was a cultural notion that snuck in the Bible, but Paul makes it clear in 1 Corinthians 11:8-10 that the headship is related to the **created order**. It was because Eve listened to the devil that the issue of order and hierarchy in the marriage relationship has had to be raised and explained.

This headship is not about having the upper hand, nor is it to mean that a woman has no rights or is a second-class citizen (read Eph. 5:25-27). Thus, the headship issue is an issue of order, not of who is better or more important. The husband is the head of the wife in the family and has the responsibility of guiding his family to a closer relationship with the Lord, which God will require of him on the day when all of our deeds are judged by God" (Zibani, 2012).

Whether or not you are determined to read more into this element of headship than what it really is, at least, as far as the Word is concerned, the order of creation has universal application in the family. Even as there may be legitimate issues of denominational biases or cultural prejudices with many of these viewpoints, the only thing that I will ever expect from you is that you "eat the fish, and spit out the bones." In other words, ***"Prove all things; hold fast that which is good"*** (1 Thes. 5:21). All things considered, I am truly grateful that God divinely ordered my path to cross with that of the editor's so that these prayerful changes could shed light on the interpretation of Scriptures and the remaining chapters of this intriguing revelation.

Now, in view of everything that has already been shared and that which will later be expounded upon, I see **no**where in the beginning of Genesis that God designed man to rule over the woman! The cardinal rule was: whatever Adam knew, Eve was supposed to know. Whatever he could do, she could do. Specifically, how was she created to help? ... ***"And let them have dominion over the fish of the sea, and over the fowl of the air, and over the cattle, and over all the earth, and over every creeping thing that creepeth upon the earth"*** (Gen. 1:26). Not yet divided into two sexes as we are now, when He told them to be fruitful and multiply and replenish the earth in Genesis 1:28, as one translation of multiply is actually "Rabbi," this commandment can be interpreted as an instruction to master, not procreate.

So as Adam's help meet, I see that Eve's role was to: "Help me" to dress the garden." "Help me" to master every living thing that moveth upon the earth. "Help me" to take dominion over God's creation. "Help me" to preserve our Paradise. "Meet" with me to discuss how we can be successful in obeying the God of all creation. If God had called her a help **mate** at first, she would have been more responsible for mating and breeding than meeting and assisting. Together, they were equally-yoked and created to establish the very first, equal employment opportunity, with no possibility for <u>discrimination</u>. As marriage and sexual intimacy was the **end** result of the fall, Genesis

10

3:16 suggest that **if** Eve could have brought forth children before the fall, it would have been **without** sorrow, pain and suffering, or even, without being ruled over by the man.

Nonetheless, she gave up the power that made her equal by accepting an alternate purpose than what God had originated. You may have heard of God's perfect will as opposed to a permissive will. Well, even though Eve had access to everything she needed, she lost what she had, trying to be greedy. In the midst of God's provision, evil is always present (Rom. 7:21-23). But if we learn to be grateful and not greedy, what we have will often deter us from going after what we don't need. Wow; that was "stellar!" By giving her allegiance and dominion to the serpent, she had to become **subject** to Adam because now, God saw her in a different regard. Now, in sorrow, she must bring forth children, **and her desire shall be to her husband, and he shall rule over her** (Gen. 3:16).

After she lost her rights and fell to a **lower** state of being (wife) than what God intended, He never again referred to her as a help meet (equal). As long as you are walking in alignment with God's perfect will and plan for your life, you retain a unique resemblance of Him, and He maintains a higher esteem for you. Am I saying that God has favorites? Grace and mercy is when God operates with integrity and faithfulness to His Word, but He has to overlook you to do so. Holiness/obedience is when your lifestyle attracts His stare, and you can say like Job: ***"Thou hast granted me life and favour, and Thy visitation hath preserved my spirit"*** (Job 10:12).

That is to say, once your role changes and you accept a different design than what He had in mind, He makes a distinction in your identity. Of course, you are still His child, and because of justification, He loves you just as if you never sinned. But perhaps, you become a "special-needs child" like me who requires grace, mercy, **and** favor (J). Since Adam did not initially have rule over her until after the fall, when and why do I assume that Eve's title or identity changed? Behold, I show you another mystery. Eve did not only obey the voice of the serpent. With her actions, words, **and** influence, she altered the first, perfect man, which caused him to become less than God's original intention for his purpose in the garden.

11

In Genesis 3:17a, Adam hearkened unto the **voice** of his wife. Both Eve **and** Sarah are proof-positive that women are not only the man's weakness. Their **words** are the power source that can either make a man, or break him! Therefore, a man's **ear gate** is the way to his heart. Even Samson, who went after the heathen women, can validate this truth in Judges 16:16-17a; watch this: ***"And it came to pass, when she pressed him daily with her words, and urged him, so that his soul was vexed unto death. That he told her all his heart"***... Girlfriend, it is not your cooking **or** your sex; now mind you, both are good! But if the power of life and death is in your tongue, then surely, the power of a seductress is NOT a woman's body. IT'S HER TALK! Proverbs 6:23b-24 says: ... ***"And reproofs of instruction are the way of life: To keep thee from the evil woman, from the flattery of the tongue of a strange woman"***

What's on a woman's tongue can completely poison a man's entire system; his system is his soul, which incorporates his mind, will, emotions, and intellect. As I mentioned in another project, her words of worship will lure a man **into** her "gates," while her expressions of praise will entice him to enter into her **"courts"** (intercourse). "Real talk." Listen, man of God, this wisdom right here comes to "deliver thee from the strange woman, even from the stranger which flattereth with her words" (Prov. 2:16). If you are interested in more depth than is available here, read further about this topic in Trilogy-Part One.

In moving forward and staying on point, man was given unconditional authority in the earth. The devil knew that if he could get them to submit to his lie, he could take that authority and wreak havoc for thousands of years to come. He did not tell the perfect Adam and Eve that he had God's footprint on his back because he had been kicked out of Heaven. The truth is: every sin is attached to the lust of the flesh, the lust of the eye, and the pride of life. Therefore, Satan was trying to feed Eve with the same temptation that he had been overcome with. Just because your daddy did it doesn't mean that you should do it. It's time to break the curse!

When Eve ate the fruit first, in Pastor Shannon's interpretation of events, her knowledge became superior to that of Adam. You have the right to consider this idea as an eisegesis (an analysis of the interpreter's own ideas). But if rightly unraveled, even if for a mere moment, Adam must have felt inadequate because Eve knew something that he did not know – both good AND evil (fleshly propensities). Because the scales fell off of Eve's eyes first, it seems that the woman has been able to outshine the man across many of life's settings. How many men do you know that can surpass a woman when it comes to cooking, cleaning, conceiving, creating, cussing (J), caressing, care-giving, child-bearing, child-rearing, baking, "blinging," budgeting, shopping, sewing, saving, scheming, seducing, typing, "tripping," nursing and nurturing? Very few – right?

Since I will give the man his props in a later chapter, allow me to say that the woman is multi-tasking, multi-talented, multi-purposed, and multi-faceted at **any** rate. If for only a mere moment, I concur that her knowledge exceeded that of the man. As a consequence of Adam's fall and Eve's desire to be "fast," we must now submit our knowledge and skills to the man. Taken from Adam's side, becoming as gods and knowing (first) **both** good and evil (Gen. 3:5), it's no wonder that women started fighting over equal rights. I see this thing now! It has been a part of our make-up all along because we were originally created equal in the eyesight of God! Now you know!

Sadly, there are races of people who still feel that they were born superior. If they have any common sense at all, they should understand more that no matter what their race, creed, color, or pedigree is, God only made one human culture with the same color blood (see Acts 17:26). "Ya heard?" I will show you later that He may have favored or chosen one nation over the other. Yet, in a kingdom of different nationalities and billions of inhabitants, where everybody is related (Mk. 3:34-35), we all have the Spirit of God. That makes us Jews and Gentiles a part of the **same** family.

Here, take note to some pure unadulterated substance: Every Black man is not your friend; every White man is not your enemy. What it boils down to is, Mark 12:31: ... ***"Thou shalt love thy neighbor as thyself. There is none other commandment greater than these."*** While deep-seated racism still lies dormant in American, Manwell Faison held the truth that, "Racism is a sin problem – not a skin problem. So preach the hell out of!" Deductive reasoning says: "No matter how big your house is, how recent your car is, how big your bank account is, our graves will be the same size. Stay humble" (origin unknown). Although I agree that the White man believes that he defines what America is, here is some breaking news. No matter what color you are, your money is no better than the country who issues it. Our trust must be in God!

My initial point was this: the day of equal rights may be hypothetically over for the women, but as far as being an offspring of Adam and a child of God, we are still equal! God initially intended for the woman to be the man's help meet and know only the good side of being a complete spiritual equal. Even so, once Eve became discontent with God's provision and desired to be more than what He intended, she knew both sides: the good (intimacy with an Almighty God in an eternal element) and the evil (commitment and submission to flesh in an earthy environment).

Wife, the evil or negative side is that "your desire should be to thy husband (not totally to the things of God). And he shall RULE OVER thee" (Gen. 3:16). Not because you are inferior to him; he is simply higher in authority and is now the HEAD of your household! If you still have a compulsion to know more than the man and find it hard to **submit** to him, do NOT get married! One major trouble in marriages today is that the woman does not want to recognize her head. She wants to be in control and be the head!

Here is another "big bang" theory – a man can rule over his wife to a much greater degree than he could his helper. A helper can take it or leave it, or tell you to either "like it or lump it." Some will tell you to go to hell! In contrast, the wife has to be both submissive **and** intimate as she comes into compliance with the Word of God. God only says what He means and means what He says! To be intimate implies that you have an obligation to be "**into**-mate." Never marry with motives outside of the Word. It's difficult to be intimate if you have a problem being submissive. And it's hard to be submissive if you have a problem being intimate. "My-my-my!"

Once Eve lost her place as a helper **to** her mate, God had to institute the law of **submission** to prevent the woman from usurping the authority that she was given in the garden. Clearly, if you do not

submit to the man that is now your **head** (female apostles, pastors and bishops); you will eventually yield to the hand of the enemy. Oh no, God, why are You taking me here when I am only hours away from another resubmission? I promise you, this topic was **not** intended for this series. Actually, since this remaining discussion is becoming so extensive, allow me to go ahead and insert a new chapter here.

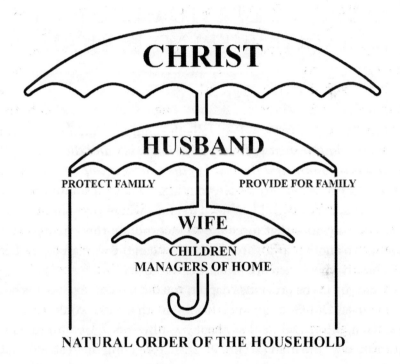

CHRIST

HUSBAND

PROTECT FAMILY · PROVIDE FOR FAMILY

WIFE

CHILDREN
MANAGERS OF HOME

NATURAL ORDER OF THE HOUSEHOLD

CHAPTER TWO

HEY FEMALE PASTOR: I JUST NEED TO KNOW WHERE YOUR "HEAD" IS

In 1 Corinthians 11: 3, Paul tells the church: ***"But I would have you know, that the head of every man is Christ; and the head of the woman is the man; and the head of the Christ is God."*** Ma'am, what are you doing? Where are you in your logic? I have absolutely nothing against you, personally; I just need to know where your "head" is. Oh well; not only does that force me to incorporate this chapter, but it leads me to another awkward query. How can the woman be the head of a church where men are under her authority?

I told you in the previous chapter; you did not come out of his head to rule over. Did God not specifically say that man would rule over thee (Gen. 3:16)? Did Paul say that he suffer not a woman to usurp authority over the man (1 Tim. 2:12)? After giving the restriction, he follows it by saying that Adam was formed first, then Eve (vs. 13). The previous questions were intended for a different "quiz." Now that I'm in a "tailspin" and I can't pull myself out of it, I will go ahead and "flip the script" at the risk of losing my female supporters. Please don't get upset this early; try and pace your anger over the whole book. Moving forward, I will try to approach the topic with caution.

"For Adam was first formed, then Eve. And Adam was not deceived, but the woman being deceived was in the transgression" (1 Tim. 2:13-14). I support Graham's (2010) belief in his explanation that stated: "By taking us back to the beginning, Paul precludes any arguments that might arise concerning women usurping the authority over men as being a cultural issue of that society. Paul's admonition was not a cultural issue then, nor is it now; it's God speaking through Paul." Likewise, *"For if a man know not how to rule his own house, how shall he take care of the church of God?"* (1 Tim. 3:5). That's a "shade-free" Scripture; how did we get it twisted? The genetic component is that fathers are the gatekeepers to the home, just as the man is to take care of the church of God! Did you notice the question: "How shall **HE** take care of the Church of God?"

Clearly, some of my discussions are personal convictions and other folks' opinions, I do admit. But since there are absolutely no "shades of gray" here that Paul was restricting the care of the church to the "male-man" (he and not she), hear my question. Have we chosen to work within the boundaries of Scripture, or the methods of men? Methods change, but principles never change. Prophet Floyd A. Barber, Jr., corresponds in this way: "Of the five-fold offices, Prophet, Evangelist and Teacher are open to women. The offices of apostle and pastor are restricted from women, and the Book of Acts and the Epistles of the Apostles support this point of view. The restriction by God is NOT chauvinistic but paternalistic." Woman of God, don't be deceived! I just need to know where your "head" is.

Since the New Testament is our blueprint for designing our actions, is it truly the order of God or even, a biblical pattern for you, *Shepherdess*, to LEAD the man whom God has created to be your head? Don't "throw me under the bus," but those same male leaders who condone it would probably not allow you to lead them. Perhaps, I can see a woman praying out a church and then, stepping back to allow a shepherd to take a stand and be the man. Why? God will never circumvent the chain of authority! Did you ever hear of female shepherds leading actual sheep to the slaughter? Incidentally, I have not.

Even in the Old Testament, all of the shepherds that were chosen and appointed by God were male. Abraham, Isaac, Jacob, Joseph's eleven brothers, Moses, and David were all shepherds, but they were all male. *"And I will set up one shepherd over them, and he shall feed them, even My servant David; he shall feed them, and he shall be their shepherd"* (Eze. 34:23). How many times did you notice the word, he? "PJW!" And since the Godhead is all male, the angels are male, the Head of God's Church is male, the first human species was male, and even Satan is referred to as male, it just seems natural and logical to me that the head of the local church should also be male.

I am aware of the instance in the Old Testament (Numbers 27) where Moses was giving out awards to families whose fathers had passed on. There was one father who did not have any sons, and his daughters approached Moses for his inheritance. *"Why should the name of our father be done away from among his family, because he hath no son? Give unto us therefore a possession among the brethren of our father"* (Num. 27:4). Today, that inheritance may have included his estate and his ministry. The man had no sons, so what did Moses do?

He took their cause before Jehovah, and He allowed the inheritance of the father to pass unto the daughters (vs. 7). Even though this is a foundational principle for a woman's right to the inheritance of her father when there is no son, it is not the same as being granted pastoral obligations. I can have a right to my father's estate, but it is the obligation of the courts to carry out the will of my father. I don't care who died and left you in charge, is it really the will of the Father for you to take over the church? Jeremiah 3:15 says: *"And I will give you pastors according to Mine heart, which shall feed you with knowledge and understanding."* Clearly, He did not say that He would give us pastors based on inheritance. "PLW" again! Just because your father or husband died, it does not give you the right to feed God's people with knowledge and understanding. And if you have no "feed," you have no reason to lead. "Get over it!"

One school of thought claims that it was God's original intent to make the human species all male, but He modified that intent for Adam's sake, when He saw the need for companionship. As a very feminine and reserved woman of God, together with the fact that He saw that it was not good for Adam to be alone, I would rather be cuddled and pampered over than to have the responsibility of ruling over the man that was designed to cover and rule over me. I realize that this is a "hot button" topic for some of you, but woman of God, I just need to know where your "head" is. Now I see why Trilogy-Part

One was appropriately entitled: *God, Why Didn't He* [the man of God in my life for that season] *Cover Me?*

Besides, what REAL manly-man wants a woman leading him around, unless he's blind or disabled? You may want to bookmark what I am about to say, but at some point in time you are bound to take on some of the feminine traits and emotional characteristics of the female that's leading you around. If a man is quick to hold on to a grudge or will completely cut you off over something that is totally frivolous and emotionally-founded, check out his foundation. Do you ever wonder why some men are stuck in an emotional time warp? Have you seen men who simply shut down and stop communicating because they suddenly "get into their **feelings**?" Likely, there is a dominant female influence lurking somewhere in the background. "Man-up!"

My prediction from my theory is supported by subsequent data; and that is: whatever is in the head is transferred to the body! Man of God, can you imagine yourself leading a congregation, or making major decisions, or treating your members like your female pastor did when she was having an emotionally bad day because of P.M.S.? Who wants to be in a personality-driven ministry? Nothing personal intended, but can I elaborate? Through my own experiences, I know the working signs of P.M.S. **and** the warning signs of menopause! I am guilty of **all** charges! And I would not have wanted to be in a pastoral position on any of those days when I may have felt like cussing out my members! "Oh snap," I meant: trying to cover my members (wink-wink,-),-). Bottom line: women primarily lead with their emotions. Why? We are emotional beings!

Not that we are inferior as women; we simply have a different purpose. Whereas the man submits to the woman's need, our purpose is to submit to his LEAD. Consequently, it started with Eve, so it is in our nature to resist male authority and change the order of God in the home and in the House of God. Even in a natural sense, unless I am lesbian, it would feel unnatural to have another woman trying to cover and protect me. In both a natural and a spiritual sense, a woman was not made to do that; that's the man's job! On the other hand, if you are a real man, it should feel spiritually-awkward to have a woman leading you around like she's the head.

19

I wrote a section in Trilogy-Part One that is entitled, *Cover your Head*. I repeat: "The importance of sitting under **strong,** godly leadership is that **a seed can only bear after its own kind.** The irony of this truth is that you cannot be much stronger than the spirit you worship under" (Reid, 2014). Man of God, I would prefer to believe that you are stronger than the Woman of God that's covering you – not by default or by accident but **by intention and design**. The man should cover his head with strong, MASCULINE leadership and be accountable to someone that is **higher in authority**. The oil runs down from the **head**! What's on the head determines what's on the body. "Like people, like priest"... (Hos. 4:9).

Alternatively, woman of God, you should cover your head, who is your husband, with sexual intimacy and by stroking his ego. Since 1 Corinthians 11:15 says that your hair was given to cover your physical head, I have never for the life of me understood how wearing a cloth or a veil protects your head. Since your man is your covering, the protection is in the covering, not the cloth! While God created man to be the Priest, Provider and the Protector, the woman was <u>ultimately</u> pulled out of him to make passionate love to him, feed him healthy and wholesome meals, support his endeavors and celebrate his victories, and to respect his authority and submit to his headship, as he follows Christ. I may be a "hopeless romantic," but if you are a real woman and really want to cover your man, the Spirit just gave you the right antidote.

Another way to cover your husband is by making him ACCOUNTABLE! I'm coming straight down the "turnpike" with this one. If Mrs. Cosby would have held Bill Cosby accountable by asking him questions like: "Hey 'Adam,' 'WHERE you at';" "WHO you wit';" and, "WHY aren't you home?" Accountability may have eliminated some of the accusations. I tried to tell you in the Introduction that I was not going to be "foot-footing" around with you Black folks! When you become one, not only does the woman's body belong to the man; his body belongs to the woman. So the woman has a responsibility to cover her husband too! No woman would be able to come to my house to visit my man unless I was home to ANSWER THE DOOR! "Where they do that at?"

Sidebar: You may be infuriated by this truth; yet, I have treasure in my earthen vessel that must be covered by the armour of God. Even as I am single, the Anointing demands that I be covered to keep hell from damaging the contents. Thanks to my Bishop whose covering me. As I am walking in obedience, I have taken the shield of faith and am equipped to quench the fiery darts of the wicked. Yes, I have often been underrated, unannounced, unanticipated, unnoticed, and unappreciated. And of course, I am affected by criticism; otherwise, I would not be human.

As I am aware that this will be a radical approach to ministry that will be criticized on many levels, for 16 years I have managed to remain strong while continuing to expand my ideas. Finally, I am learning to respond with silence to all those critics who held on to their own ideas and saw only the weaknesses and inadequacies of my goal and thinking processes. I thank you for your objective input, alternative explanations, practical considerations, and both philosophical and epistemological perspectives. While there are no simple benchmarks, the trade-off is, only a writer steeped in the text can make a final judgment.

Okay, I'm back! I felt compelled to stop and address the "rabble-rousers." Yes, I certainly know that the Gifts of the Spirit are not gender specific. At the same time, I agree that the power gifts are restricted! Although many women may be spiritually or more intellectually-developed than some men, God did NOT **emotionally** design us to intrude into senior (spiritual) leadership positions. Were you not paying attention to what happened with Eve? Because Adam allowed her to take charge, not only is the Church in trouble; the whole, entire world is chaotic!

Prophet Floyd Barber and I share a common understanding that: "Because of a woman's emotional make-up, she oftentimes needs her husband to protect her from herself, i.e., from the destructive consequences of her oftentimes impulsive decisions based on emotion." That sums it up! If you can't see that, it's not because you're blind. You may be rebellious and determined to operate the same way Eve did – out of order. While the Church has allowed this error of female leadership to escalate, there are many well-meaning women in these positions whose intention is to serve God with all their hearts. I applaud you, but in my estimation, you are well-intended but terribly misguided.

What happens to the majority of women who defy this divinely-imposed restriction? They eventually lose their femininity. Femininity is a value given to women that should not be rejected! Contrarily, there are those other women who <u>intentionally</u> bypass the clear exegetical rendering of Scriptures to pursue these offices. Ask me why. They are power tripping and have a strong desire to be in touch with their "masculine side." And for those of you who are "in-the- know," God is going to hold you accountable for being partakers and participators in their dysfunction.

Naturally speaking, when anyone has the proclivity or inclination to be the head, that person feels the need to rule over the woman – whether in a heterosexual relationship or in a lesbian relationship. In a later chapter, I will reveal the actual Bride of Christ, so stay with me. But since the church is styled **as** the Bride of Christ, He does not need a female trying to lead His "Woman." Repeat after me: "Out-of-order!" As "Mr. Brown" said on Tyler Perry's Meet the Browns; "I just stepped in something that 'ain't' my shoes!"

Ironically, or should I say by divine appointment, as I was completing this *Rebirth* edition, I was given an extensive editing assignment from Bishop Donald L. Thomas who has written a five-volume series on the Book of Genesis (Chapters 1-50). God "be hooking a 'sistah' up!" In conjunction to my investigation of Adam and Eve, the man and the woman, the Church and the Bride, I invite all Genesis enthusiasts to partake of this forthcoming collection, entitled, *A New Perspective of Genesis*. He's got my back; what I don't cover in this book, I can promise you that he has it covered within this series.

Even as I was already overwhelmed with completing school obligations and my own personal projects, I totally understand why I **had to** accept this assignment. Just as we embrace many of the same revelations, here is profound must-share that I felt compelled to borrow. "When 1 Timothy 2:15 says: *... 'She shall be saved through childbearing,'* it denotes that she shall be saved in the administration of her proper function or in performing that which she has been called to do. The message that the Apostle Paul leaves with the Church is not directed to the woman only, but to the Church at large."

Toward that end, "the same thing that the woman is commanded to do in the home for her husband and children, is what the Church is commanded to do in the Kingdom for her husband, Christ. And that is to bear children. If we fail in that administration or function of the Body, then, our Body is deformed, and the children are aborted. What an awesome responsibility is laid upon the woman and the Church. The apostles and prophets have always called upon the woman in times of barrenness. Today, the Church must heed to what the prophet, Jeremiah, commands of her. See Jeremiah 9:16-21" (Thomas, 2017).

Bishop Thomas comments that if you read his books, he's going to extend you more grace than what I have extended. LJL At any rate, my argument still has merit. If God says that man is the head of the woman and the Church is styled as a **bride** (female), then, how can the woman be the head of the Church when she has been saved through childbearing? "Yikes!" Just as I was tweaking this book for the final time, I was just presented with some "raw footage" in my ear. A female pastor trying to rule over God's Church is resemblance of being the "stud" in a lesbian relationship.

It is one thing to be missing a rib, but it is literally impossible to walk around with the wrong head and function as a balanced body. You don't have to like it, but I know I'm right about it! If the Church is the Bride (female), then, her head should be a male. I wish that we would just learn to be who we were created to be. When women lose that feminine touch or that desire to stay in a woman's place, it can usually be traced back to the absence of a dominant, **male** role model, whether it was physically, spiritually, or emotionally. Check the record! If you are surrendering the sacredness of femininity to satisfy masculine tendencies, you need DELIVERANCE! "Be thou Delivered, already!"

Someone has already made the comment that a bishop is just an overseer, but when the Word teaches that the bishop should be the *husband of one wife*, we should maintain the balance of mutual respect for both genders without violating the Scriptures in the process. Hey female bishop, where is your "head?" In basic terms, women were built to carry the weight of their children – not the weight of the Church! Why? If and when the man falls backwards, she was not built to catch him. Why? The man was built with the stronger backbone, so if he is sitting under the leadership of a woman, it is reasonable to assume that he has a weak backbone.

I now have a personal problem with the male leader who authorized this dysfunction. Here is my reality: Why would you put somebody over me that you would never allow over you? That makes me question your authority and your motives. Always judge your actions by this one question: Would I want to be exposed to the same thing that I impose on someone else? It is apparent that the majority of our storefront churches and many of our established churches have leaders with zeal, and like the children of Israel, it is not according to knowledge (Rom. 10:2).

They have no training or a clue about what they have supposedly been ordained to do. *"For they being ignorant of God's righteousness, and going about to establish their own righteousness, have not submitted themselves unto the righteousness of God"* (Rom. 10:3). Put a "bookmark" right there. God used to wink at our ignorance, but He's going to hold you men in authority, accountable for some of this foolishness. Adam proved that when the man is out of position, the whole world falls short, and the Church suffers accordingly. Believe it or not, if the Black man alone would realize who he is and take a stand to be the man, the world would operate much the way God intended it. Also "bookmark" that for a later chapter.

In any regard, the man cannot build the Church until he becomes the head of his home. Furthermore, the man cannot make up the hedge for the nation unless he stands in the gap for the Church. To build this argument, Ezekiel 22:30 (with emphasis added) is the "game-changing" Scripture: *"And I sought for a man among them, that should make up the hedge, and stand in the gap before Me for the land* [not a woman but a man], *that I should not destroy it: but I found none."* Rooted in reality, this is another Scripture that leaves no margin for error. When God wanted to get a job done that affected destiny, who did He send? A MAN! Ask the 11 apostles who God chose when He wanted to replace Judas and promote a strong leader of the New Testament Church. For starters, they had chosen two **men**, but God's final choice was Saul who became Paul. A woman was NEVER in the equation. "In business be MEN!" (Prov. 22:29).

HEY CO-PASTOR
GOD DID NOT FORGET ABOUT YOU!

Just as I mentioned in another project, it bears repeating here; just because your wife is in ministry with you is no indication that God ordained her to be your Co-Pastor. I know that it is the new normal and may challenge the foundation that spawned this view. It may be Black, but that "ain't" Bible! Maybe there was no Co-Redeemer or a Co-Adam, or even Co-pastors mentioned in the Bible because God recognized that there could only be one head at a time. God, who is emphatically described as one God, exists in THREE DISTINCT PERSONS (the Father, Son, and Holy Ghost), who are one God. Yet, they make up THE Godhead, and do not refer to themselves as having more than one head.

Brother Pastor, you cannot say that you are the head of your house, and have a co-pastor in position at the same. It suggests that you have two heads at the same time. I know that you may be powerful and all, but you cannot exist in plurality because you are not God. As far as you are concerned, there can only be one head per body. Sadly enough, some of these women don't even aspire to be in these created positions. If they would be honest, they would tell you that they were called by their husbands. Besides, how "in the hood" did both of "y'all" receive the same calling from the same voice at the same time for the same church? "Stop the madness!" Pastor, MAN-up and stop trying to hide behind the woman. You need to make a decision as to whether you were called to be THE pastor, or no. And if the woman was called first and then called her husband, you really do have issues!

Let me get this straight. Two heads for one church, and then, you'll turn around and say you have one church in multiple locations. That's another one of the *50 Shades of Ignorance in the Black Church.*

You church folks sound like Ms. Robbie's grandson, Charles, on *Welcome to Sweetie Pie's*. Before getting on a roller coaster ride at an Amusement Park ride, instead of simply praying in Jesus' name, he prayed: "Lord Jesus, John, Holy Ghost in Christ." "What the what?!?" That couldn't have been scripted! He "jack'd" up that prayer worse than we mess up numbers. But Pastor, you should know how to count by now, or better yet, just tell the truth! You are trying to pastor three churches in three different locations, at the same time.

I'm just trying to get some clarity. Even though you are one as husband and wife, the man is still THE head. Am I right or wrong? So for the woman to be the Co-Pastor of a church, you may as well say that she is co-husband/head in the marriage. The author just felt a cognitive disconnect with the reader. %-) But here is something else to consider. The Vice-President does not have the same authority as the President of the United States because there is only ONE President at a time – two separate positions and two different levels of authority. The Vice is there to assist and take over the lead in the event that the head is unable to function. If the big White House has only one President at a time that is responsible for the whole United States of America, what in the world do you need with two pastors, running one church, at the same time?

First Lady, we will still honor and respect you if you stay in your place and operate in the area of your Anointing. Indeed "Eve," we definitely need you; there is a place for you in God's garden, but "don't get it twisted!" We need you to be the MOTHER of the living and not the head of God's Church. You don't have to change the "wo" to a "co," in order for us to recognize your "M.O." Seriously, contemporary culture will have you adding things to the church structure that God never intended. Native to Black folks who do the most because they have been mishandled and emasculated for so long, we literally become addicted to titles and positions.

Therefore, WE SEEK REPARATION THROUGH RECOGNITION. How do we do it? WE START A MOVEMENT TO MAKE A STATEMENT! Wow! That was good! Then, we **make up** titles that epitomize the spirit of entitlement. When you do not know your purpose, you're fed by positions. Except in the church, the only time that you will see such "**co**nfoolishness" – **co**nfusion and foolishness "on steroids" is among clowns in the circus. When will the Church refrain from entertaining "three-ring circus" activity? It's analogous to a "clown" with two heads that's trying to take directions from the "ring leader." "Hey Pastor, 'where you at'?" Or, should I ask the Co-pastor if she knows where her "head" is?

Obviously, the conspiracy of the enemy is to pervert the order of God and to establish twisted relationships to make sure that the man is out of place, rather than where God called him to be. The enemy is so subtle; sometimes he is just as inconspicuous and silent as the b is in the word, subtle. He often comes in a bathing suit with big legs, or as a "drag-queen" with a beautiful face. In this chapter, we see that he even comes as a woman who wants to be headstrong. Instead of wearing a headpiece, she wants to wear the title, co-head. That was likely one of my poetic platitudes that was "boo-worthy." Whatever! What about the female pastor who refers to her husband as the "first man?" "What in the 'hood' is this?!?" It was only in the animal kingdom that an animal did not know its head from its tail. Now we see it in the church, of all places.

If that were not enough, we have even entertained the idea of voting in a female President. I know that this book won't be published until after the election, but I wonder, will it be the lesser of two evils, or will God allow a necessary evil, whom I consider as the man notorious for devaluing and dehumanizing women and minorities? In the first place, I'm still trying to wrap my mind around how America reduced its standards, terms and policies to allow someone without a military background or any political experience to run for election. Nonetheless, here is why I am not worried? Psalm 75:7 says: ***"But God is the Judge: He putteth down one, and setteth up another."*** Also, Romans 13:1 maintains this reckoning: ***"Let every soul be subject unto the higher powers. For there is no power but of God: the powers that be are ordained of God."*** Either way, He is about to show America who's really in charge.

If a Twitter account activity can set off the President, can you imagine what our country has to look forward to? God may have just set us up for the "main event." "Warning comes before destruction," but *"Before destruction the heart of man is haughty"* … (Prov. 18:12a). However, Dr. R. A. Vernon said that if God can make a donkey talk, He can make a Trump pray. Even as Mr. Trump has outdone himself and surprised many of us; *"There are many devices in a man's heart; nevertheless the counsel of the LORD, that shall stand"* (Prov. 19:21). In other words, His plans always prevail.

On the whole, here is the crux of my argument. Even though the Trump supporters knew that he is a racist, sexist, and a bigot at the core, and they elected him anyway, can we touch and agree that Hilary Clinton was not built for the oval office? My theory is that some men who voted for President Obama may not have voted for Hilary, just because of her GENDER. Real men do not take orders too kindly from women. By divine design, the man that was created as the head of the woman was built to have the final word and make decisions that affect destiny. Fortunately, she would have had former President, Bill Clinton to cover her!

When Eve was pulled out of Adam, the woman did not have to deal with any trouble (personally, socially, systemically, or universally). Alternatively, ever since man has been coming out of the woman (the head out of the tail), he has been **full** of trouble after only a few days (Job 14:1). It is more than just an idea; it is a well-established theory that enables us to explain the fact that order was divinely created to come from the man. God pulled Eve out of Adam, not so that he could submit to her, but so that he could look at her and say that without the man, you could have never had life. But due to the fall and Adam's prosperity being given the sentence of death, God had to bypass the man and breathe directly into the womb of the woman. Now he has to submit to her (Eph. 5:21) because without her, he would have never had life.

Isn't it ironic though that even from the birth canal (unless it's breeched) the "head" still comes out first? All the same, when what comes from the "tail" is allowed to usurp authority over the head, the man is in trouble! Whereas man sinned in the garden and must now come out of the woman and be subjected to an alternative order, it gives me reason to believe that this is why the world is so "plucked" up. It follows, therefore, that the head is coming out of that which was supposed to submit to the head! The terrible preponderance is that our days would be long and NOT full of so many troubles, if we had not changed the divine order of God. In the family, the church, politics, or whatever, it is NOT the divine order of God for the head to take orders from its "tail." That's an oxymoron! I'm not trying to sound facetious; I'm only trying to bring forth clarity to a Church that is in a state of emergency.

On further reflection, this is how the Jezebel spirit (anarchy, control, and witchcraft) has crept in and attempted to take over the Church. It is the Jezebel spirit in a woman who does not respect the order of God. Equally, it is an Ahab spirit in a man that makes him "jelly back" and too weak to take the lead. I don't have the time and space to write a substantial correspondence on the complexities of these spirits. However, one of the dominant attributes of the Jezebel spirit is to destroy the leader's fruit and prevent him from producing real sons and spiritual daughters.

Clearly, women, in order to stay in our place, we must use our femininity to stay submitted to male authority. More important in this concept is that we cannot continue to blame the first Adam because the second Adam who carries the blood of God and who was predestined to become a much better example, has shown up via the virgin birth. What is adapted from my Trilogy-Part One provides a useful summary of some foundational principles: "To begin with, Jesus was NOT just another man! Then, we should be able to determine by our own flesh that flesh is certainly not the best example or even a good example for anyone to follow.

'Which were born, not of blood, nor of the will of the flesh, nor of the will of man, but of God' (John 1:13). Thus, if Jesus' blood had been contaminated by flesh (Joseph), and He had been born like any other man rather than the perfect and unspotted Lamb of God, then certainly, He could not be both God and man. Since Jesus was already God that <u>became</u> a man, it required a virgin birth. Why? Simply stated, spirit cannot be born of flesh (also read John 3:6). Did you get that, my Muslim friends? If humanity had not met up with the divine, and Jesus had been born with Joseph's blood, Jesus could not have made a good example, especially when Paul says, 'In the flesh dwelleth no good thing!' (Rom. 7:18).

29

Because of His **pre**-existence, He had to take on the likeness of human flesh so that He could become sin and take our place. The fundamental nature of Allah says die for me, but Jesus said, 'I will die for you.' In order to die for us, He had to become like us. If He had not become God in the flesh (uncontaminated), man could not have been redeemed, and none of us would have an example to follow. Please refer to Luke 1:35" (Reid, 2014). While it still may be easy to confuse an objective observation with a subjective interpretation at this point, I repeat: a seed can only bear after its own kind. Therefore, it can be said here that only real men can reproduce real men; and, only true fathers can reproduce sons.

How can you make a sweet potato pie without the main ingredients (potatoes)? Only **men**tors can appropriately teach the benefits of son-ship and positively influence our sons to become real **men** (the strong, masculine side of God). Only fathers can give their sons true identity. Thus, parents are making babies that never got corrected because they did not have consistent father figures in their lives. And now, in a breeched position, they are experiencing a major identity crisis. Any suggestions to the contrary unfairly disprove Proverbs 4:1: *"Hear, ye children, the instructions of a father, and attend to know understanding"* (Prov. 4:1). God's got my back on this! I hope that you will keep reading as the identity crisis will be tenaciously illuminated in some later chapters. Meanwhile, "W.O.G.," I just need to know where your "head" is. We live beneath our privilege when we do not tap into our purpose!

What does a big, strong Black man look like allowing a woman to lead him around like a puppet on a string, and instructing him on how to be a father and raise his sons? Does she really know what it means to be a man? Can she truly demonstrate to him how to fight like a man? No, absolutely not! Whether you like it or not, a female pastor simply can NOT reproduce masculine men of God! It is the spirit of Absalom that wants to take the father's place! Now it's clear why there are sterile churches around the world and few sons being produced in the house. It's been the strategy of Satan since the Garden of Eden.

Satan knows that if he is going to kill the Church, he has to take out her womb and make sure that she doesn't know how to produce sons. He's not intimidated by female pastors because he knows that they don't understand how to reproduce sons. He probably laughs at our praise dancing and our hopping and skipping around the church; he definitely knows that there is no power in that. He knows that your armourbearers and religious butlers are not going to reproduce sons. In fact, he's not even intimidated by the sudden shift to apostles and prophets who do not comprehend the concept of reproduction. Revival does not scare the devil either; **reproduction** does. Reproducing real sons is the seed that's going to bruise the devil's head.

Paraphrasing him in his assessment and evaluation, Jones (2015) estimates that what has happened is that we have created a system where the women have pampered our men. And instead of allowing them to be the man, we have committed to taking care of them. "Oh baby, you just sit down, and I'll see you when I get off work." "What in the 'hood' is this?" Are you saying that you will see him later, while he's sitting there in your house, eating a bowl of fruit loops at your table, drinking up all of your orange juice, charging up your electric bill, watching your television, and sucking up your air?

The reason he refuses to do anything and has his stinky feet upon your sofa is that you have become his "sugar-mama." In reality, as long as you have half-a-man, a piece of man is better than no man at all. But oftentimes, that piece of a man is in another man's butt, and when that is not the case, he's in your girlfriend's butt. And all of this is taking place while you are at work taking care of him, while he's spending the day watching television, Lion King, rappers, and R&B artists who are renting the stuff they're riding.

Do you want the truth, or not? Well, controversial, Talk Show Host, Thaddeus Matthews, ask these questions: You "gotta" worry about how your light bill is going to be paid, and you sleeping with a man? You worried about whether the repo man will find your car, and you call yourself having a man? #welfare-syndrome He said that you're a damn fool if you give your income tax check to your unemployed man. According to Pastor Thaddeus, you would do better to pleasure yourself than to let a man play with your mind. "You won't have to cook it 'no' breakfast. You won't have to give it none of your EBT card, and it won't have to lay up in your Section 8." #PastorRaw

31

Herein is the dilemma. Because we have made excuses and pampered our men in their laziness, slothfulness, idleness, and lethargies, we have built a psychological, demonic profile in their mentalities. As a result, the woman has risen to a place where she never belonged. While our Black men are walking the streets with their "cracks" out and pants hanging low, they are misleading the Black children who have no role model because their parents are divorced. While the man continues to have babies and not take responsibility, our children are being led to the streets.

But even worse, some parents give them to the church on Sundays and Wednesdays. This is so that they can have a couple of free hours to themselves to be with "Pooky," hoping that "Pooky" will stay. Then, when "Pooky" does not stay, the woman has to step up and be both, the man and the woman, the wife and the husband. Since adolescence is when a child's identity tends to get locked in, sons don't just need to see bras and panties. I heard the widely respected, Dr. R. A. Vernon say, "They need to see drawers and 'wife-beaters'!" Evidence proves that the Black woman's womb is certainly under attack because Satan is after the Black man's seed.

Do you ever wonder why so many of our men are twisted in their mentalities and why so many of our young males have feminine tendencies? Let me tell you why. The one that should be training them are absent and totally out of order. Even at the cost or detriment of himself, a real man takes responsibility (Jones, 2015). Although she may be forced to, no woman should have to raise and train a boy by herself, any more than a woman needs to be the head of a church, especially without a covering. "Hey 'Adam,' 'where you at'?" Are you a masculine man that is committed to catching your brother **before** he falls? Or, are you already a fallen brother with a broken mentality that has allowed your son to fall? ***"For the earnest expectation of the creature waiteth for the manifestation of the sons of God"*** (Rom. 8:19). For the sake of the family and the error that the Church has allowed to escalate: "Take a stand and be **the** man!"

Just as Galatians 3:28 is often manipulated to preclude the fear of condemnation and defend these female positions, Paul was speaking about salvation. May I elaborate? I will anyway. Since I am the author,

I really don't need permission because I have editorial privileges (☺). Indeed, when it comes to salvation, God does not discriminate against Jew or Greek, prisoners or non-prisoners, nor male or female. Rather, He offers salvation to all! Thus, the subject under discussion in Galatians 3:28 is not ministry gifts but salvation! At any rate, the need for a title should never exceed the desire for the job. Never mind; let's table that for another moment because as the evil day is rapidly approaching, we don't need to seek positions. We need power!

At the end of the day, here are some certain, basic questions that are sure to arise: Since Deborah served as a senior leader of ancient Israel, have I just made a query of antiquated ideas? If God calls on Esther to lead, should we hide the scepter from her? Is it the equality of the Holy Spirit to give spiritual gifts to "each one" (1 Cor. 12:11), not according to gender, class or race, but simply according to God's choice, especially since He chooses whom He will and does not qualify us based on human criteria? While the hour is late and our spiritual enemies are attacking, aren't both Deborah and Barak needed on the battle field? In other words, if the man of the house fails to take leadership, should it find its way in the women?

Simply, my answer is this: **IF** "Adam" takes the stand to be the **MAN**, there would be no need for us to be out of place or deviate from the divine order that God originally had in mind. That's why I continue to ask: "Hey 'Adam,' 'where you at'?" In the final analysis, the fact that Adam did sin, and predictably knowing that "Eve" would be deceived, I personally believe that God's **conclusive** plan for the woman was that she would ultimately become the man's deliverer – not his pastor, apostle or bishop. Talmage (2010) clarifies yet, another profound revelation that was written so well and succinctly that I could not paraphrase it without weakening it.

Precisely: "In Hebrew, the two words that 'help meet' are derived from are the words, 'ezer' and 'k'enegdo.' The word 'ebenezer' in 1 Samuel 7:12 is used to describe the power of God's deliverance. 'Eben' means rock and 'ezer' means 'help' or 'salvation.' Ebenezer therefore means 'rock of help' or 'rock of salvation.' The root 'ezer' is the same word that God used to describe to Adam who Eve was. She was not intended to be just his helper or his companion; rather, she was intended to be his savior, his deliverer. The other part of the term, 'help meet,' which is commonly translated as 'meet for' or 'fit for,' is the word, 'k'enegdo.' It is hard to know exactly what the word, k'enegdo means because it only appears once in the entire Bible."

Whereas kenegdo has been explained as being "exactly corresponding to," as when you look at yourself in the mirror, Talmage (2010) continues: "Eve was not designed to be exactly like Adam. She was designed to be his mirror opposite, possessing the other half of the qualities, responsibilities, and attributes which he lacked. Just like Adam and Eve's sexual organs were physically mirror opposites (one being internal and the other external) so were their divine stewardship designed to be opposite but fit together perfectly to create life. Eve was Adam's complete spiritual equal, endowed with a saving power that was opposite from his.

I've pondered a lot about this clarification of Eve's role and how it is that she has been given a saving power equal but opposite to Adam's saving power. As I've thought about it, I realized that while women do much to help and assist men in their stewardship, they have been given a stewardship that is uniquely theirs and which is every bit as important as men's stewardship. Women are 'saviors' to men by the fact that they give them life and nurture them toward the light of Christ. By conceiving, creating and bearing mortal bodies, women make it possible for God's children to start on their mortal journey and have the opportunity to become perfected.

Without women, there would be no gateway into this world and no opportunity for progress or exaltation. In addition, by being willing to sacrifice (their very lives if necessary) to bring children into this world, women demonstrate the true meaning of charity. From the very first breath a child takes, he or she has been the recipient of charity and unconditional love... Each woman, regardless of her ability to give birth, is a savior to mankind when she loves men and nurtures a child closer to Christ" (Talmage, 2010).

"Even so ye, forasmuch as ye are zealous of spiritual gifts, seek that ye may excel to the edifying of the church" (1 Cor. 14:12). Despite my dissertation on the topic matter, you must personally establish whether or not you may have missed your calling, or whether

your gift truly edifies the Church. Indeed, it may be that when the man does not take the stand, women feel forced to take charge. I still believe that it is not the divine order of God, but at the end of the day, what He allows for you is between you and Him. My basic conclusion is this: don't go out with your "head" cut off. And do not proceed with demonic motives, or with the wrong mindset, or with a take-over mentality. Not limited to, but that would include being stubborn, bullheaded, overzealous, and dominating.

A good reason to look inwardly is to examine directly and deliberately, one's conscious motive. Then, if you are determined to be somebody's covering, ascertain that you, yourself, have a covering. In the Old Testament, Deborah was a prophetess and a courageous judge because of her wisdom, but she never went to war without the counsel of Barak. Where was her head? It was in Barak. The pattern of Scripture suggests that women in ministry must have a covering. The only time where I have read that the woman covered a man is in Judges 4:18: Sisera covered Jael with a mantle (a garment). And when he was thirsty, *"she opened a bottle of milk, and gave him drink, and covered him"* (vs. 19).

"Fast-forwarding" to the New Testament, isn't it ironic that out of the six instances that shed light on the teaching team of Priscilla and Aquila, the only time that Aquila (the man) was mentioned first in word order is in 1 Corinthians 16:19? Here, it just so happens to be where the church met in their house. "Hmmm," does that not send a message to anyone else other than me, or did you miss that? The data may be insufficient to support its weight, but pay close attention to the biblical paradigm to explain the pattern of this male-dominant culture. Could it be that it was due to the "teaching" Anointing on her life that the word order of their names, Priscilla and Aquila, in the other five instances of the New Testament made her first? And the only time that Aquila came before Priscilla was when God gave the man the responsibility for the pastoral ministry in 1 Corinthians 16:19? Where was her "head?" It was in Aquila.

Women of God, nobody wants us to be silent in the church; there would be no church without us. We're here now, so the man has to acknowledge us. Yet, we must be determined to act like a lady, even

35

when we have to think like a man. When Paul said that he suffer women to be silent in the church (1 Tim. 2:12), he was really talking to women in a particular church who were being unruly and out of order. However, this stipulation was given so that there would be order to the whole process of women being last in the creation and first in the transgression. When women are subject and avoid exercising dominion over the man, it should cause him to exercise his authority with gentleness, tenderness and affection.

There have been women who have escaped into ministry because they were mistreated, either by their husbands or someone in ministry. Because there are not many requirements to minister or start a church, they did not deal with their hurt. Now a prisoner of their past and trying to be somebody's pastor, they've allowed their pain to be louder than their experience. Some of them bash men and fight marriages because they are using the pulpit to make a comeback to get back at the folks that gave them a set-back. That "ain't" God! You have a zeal without knowledge.

And just because you draw the kind of people with the same mentality, and you're able to maintain a congregation, it is no indication that God's hand is on it. The common thread that knits you people together is ignorance! Part of getting to the next level is that you must deal with what you cannot change – whatever it was that caused your pain. This is one of the reasons why Black folks have churches on every corner, and some of them with six members and four carrying the same, last name. "Come on now." Before Jesus preached one text, He gathered 12, and said: "Follow Me." You can't even say you're like Jesus until you have at least, 12 disciples.

This is for you folks who have been laboring in storefronts for years and justifying it with, "Where two or three are gathered together in My name." NO! That Scripture was in reference to prayer meetings. You need to pray for another revelation because you're just having family reunion! And the wife and children are looking like my mother and I did when my dad forced us to attend his storefront, years ago: "Why am I here; I did not sign up for this." And the other two or three are just there to be the "big fish in a small pond." People that have a need to feel needed, breed other people with voids. The majority of these glorified daycare centers and puffed-up community centers are likely established with wrong motives by strange people who are out of order. And you, member, you cannot be a deliverer feeding into other folks' dysfunction.

Just as I mentioned years ago, in Trilogy-Part Three, we need to activate "church consolidations." Literally, here is the most recent example of my contention; today is New Year's Day, 2017, and this manuscript goes to the publisher tomorrow. I prayed about whether or not to write this, and since I couldn't shake it, here we go. In Dallas for the New Year, I did not stay with the tradition of attending Watch Night Service for New Year's Eve. So, for New Year's Day, I really felt the urge to attend a church that an acquaintance had invited me to. Exhausted and in a bad headspace, "I really needed a little more Jesus" and was really hoping that the pastor's gifts and discernment were in operation that day.

When I drove up to the storefront, there were five cars there, 30 minutes after the service was scheduled to start. So I'm like: okay, it's small and intimate; maybe I can get some "one-on-one." In this really wonderful set-up, there were a total of 11 people, including men, women, children, and me. Later, I found out that eight of them carried the pastor's last name. That left two other people and the one visitor. After I had given my sister, "Shannon Brown," a synopsis of my visit, she said that maybe some of the members had a hangover from the night before. Later, I found out that Pastor was in the process of rebuilding, so that explained it all.

When I told her that he had been the pastor for 13 years, "Shannon" was like: "Wait a minute; let me get this straight... Oh my God; I can't even wrap my head around that." She went on to say: "God must have sent you there today. And this is the first of the year too; you can claim your position. With all of your skills, maybe you can be the secretary, and even be over the building fund." Then I told her that the pastor had invited her to come with me next time. After she had referred to the ministry as a "starter kit," she was like: "No." No offence; unlike me, she prefers larger churches.

"No-nonsense-Shannon" is way too funny. "Shannon Brown" is the alias that she gave herself when her identity was stolen. It is especially convenient when we visit a church and fill out a visitor's card. Even though I consider myself an introvert, we differ in the aspect that she guards and monitors her space much better than me. By nature, I'm not a controversial person; so, many times I internalize my emotions until they become explosive. Obviously, my pen is my weapon, and if you come into my space, you **always** take on the likelihood to become a character in my book. And if you are a bad character, I sometimes use the "street-edge" to avoid giving in to the irritation to cuss you out in with my weapon. Nor really; even though I tend to "go postal on paper," really my goal is #damage control. I may be related to David more than I am to Moses, Elijah Noah, Enoch, or Job, but at least, I'm transparent (unlike most church people).

"Shannon Brown," on the other hand, is probably, more related to Peter. If you **look** at her the wrong way, you will get the evil face (>:D/ >=D-->). And if she catches you stalking her, she'll cuss you out **to** your face and may be ready to "cut your ear off." She has been subject to a military environment for over 27 years. "Ha!" No, I'm not suggesting that she has PTSD because her experience was a positive one. She simply says that I'm too friendly; she likes to stay "under the radar." One Saturday, I asked: "Why you 'gotta' be so mean to the Jehovah's Witnesses?" She goes: "They should have respected the 'No Soliciting' sign on the door." I see now that I may need to eventually put "Shannon" over my security team.

After first arriving at my New Year's service, I had thought of getting up to go down the street to check out the other storefront. Rather than planning my escape and trying to figure a way out, the music was so **anointed** that I decided to stay and see what would happen next. In the meantime, I went ahead and got into the worship, but the wife and daughter were looking just like I said my mother and I looked when we were being forced to attend my dad's storefront. Then, the pastor requested the daughter to sing, what I used to call, the "sermonic selection." She sang: "What God has for you, it is for you," and it broke me down. That song was for me. It resonated and ministered to my soul and spirit so much that I couldn't stop crying. The pastor had a good Word too, and I received every prophetic utterance that I felt was for me. Ultimately, I felt like the push to go was worth the persistence to stay.

After coming home and taking a long, power nap, I contacted the "recruiter" that had invited me, so that I could give her my feedback. With concern, I mentioned the attendance. Can you guess what she text back? "Where 2 or 3 are gathered together in His name. Are you going back?" Ironically, I had just added the two or three element to the earlier paragraph. By now, I'm thinking to myself, "If this ministry is worth inviting me to, 'why you at' Bishop Jakes' church, where technically, nobody knows you, sees you, misses you in your absence, or cares if you even show up? Why aren't you over here where God and 'yo' cousin can really use your services, your gifts, **and** 'yo' presence?" This is just my thought pattern; and by now, you should know how "cray-cray" that can get.

After all, she claims the offices of apostle, prophet, and evangelist, and had mentioned that God has called her to the office of pastor. Granted that she can really see, in a couple of my books, I documented a prophecy that she gave me over 16 years ago that was absolutely phenomenal. Thus, it seems to me that her cousin's church would be a great place to assist and exercise her gifts. And instead of "two or three," she can make it "four or five." No; I don't mean a bit of harm; I'm just doing what I do, and that's writing what I hear. I'm sure that she is on a different assignment, and it is none of my business! I'm not claiming that **every**thing I hear proceedeth out of the mouth of God; every now and then, I do give in to the flesh. So that makes my book imperfect for imperfect people. Nevertheless, it's on purpose for people with purpose. Anyway, I'm writing backwards, but that's how I spent the first day of 2017.

At least, the church was "headed" by male leadership, and they were not on the beggars' list. Even though I noticed that both pastor and wife were driving Mercedes Benzes, I intentionally left a sizeable offering. Why? It was obvious to me that they believe in working and being self-sustaining, unlike some of the other, regrettable contacts I had made. Consequently, I had been (past tense) the target of financial abuse and accustomed to being drawn to helping needy people who seem to read "cash cow" written across my forehead. Here is the "kicker;" as soon as they got "grounded and on their feet," their actions conveyed: "Depart from me; I know you not!" "Really?" How can they dodge and delete you, when they owe you? These are the kind of guys who have had so many enabling people around them that it made them both lazy **and** selfish. It's a spirit, and it operates the same, exact way in every guy who has taken advantage of my kindness.

Despite them, there was such a purity from this last group of people. And as a result of this experience, I pray for them that they are allowed to rebuild, or, that God will show them His perfect will for their lives and ministry. Sharing this scenario, I just wanted to show you how people think, and how some "starter-kit" ministries really look from the outside in. Nothing personal intended; this is just the nature of non-fiction authors; they write about real-life experiences. Where was I before I became distracted? I was still on the topic of female pastors.

Even as the woman is considered the "weaker link in the chain," thank God for His permissive will and the precious grace that He allows many of us to operate outside of our created purpose. Here is my assessment of Matthew 22:14: ***"For many are called, but few are chosen."*** Brace yourself. Now you know that if God used an ass, He will use anything and anybody to present, provoke, or to project His Word. You know that by looking at me. If truth be told, I am not an astute Bible Scholar, or an assiduous Bible student, or even an "avid" Bible reader, but neither was Balaam's ass. In fact, he couldn't read or write. My point exactly: just because He uses you does not indicate that He called you.

I have an anointing or the grace on my life to write, but I wouldn't dare start a church. I don't even have a desire for a public speaking ministry. Writing is my gift, and I am at my best and in my zone when that's all I'm required to do. The ass had an impractical, one time assignment, but he was not called to prophesy to anyone else (that I know of). Then again, God could have possibly called you because He already knew that you were going to change His plan and "volunteer" to do something that He had not chosen for your life. Like the ass, He uses you and gives you the grace to get a job done because He knows that either way, the glory belongs to Him. Thus, MANY are called (in season **and** out of season). But FEW are actually chosen in the position and the season that they were actually called for.

According to Thomas (2017), "God calls all men to repentance, but we are chosen when we **respond** to His call. If you do not act on God's Word, it becomes a dead Word to you. The servants were the messengers of God, the prophets and the apostles. But upon their refusal, it opened the door for the 'whosoever will,' the Gentiles. In the Book of John 1:11-12b, se see this more clearly: *'He came unto His own, and His own received Him not. But as many as received Him, to them gave He power to become the sons of God'*." Since I am a novice when compared to Bishop Thomas, I see better now why you may or may not have been chosen.

Either way, the ability to disagree with what I called your "in-season or out-of-season calling," does not give me a right to disrespect protocol or ignore the grace of God. So work your grace, and allow me to write mine out! Whereas you may be troubled by my obedience to write what I feel God is saying, hopefully, we can still remain sisters and wear our grace, gracefully. While I will not allow my theological position to impact my personal attitude toward female pastors, nothing personal was intended; you just can't pastor me. In pursuing truth and wrestling with the data in a very candid approach, I trust that I have conducted this section with dignity. One thing to keep in mind is that the cause of Christ and His Kingdom is never, really served when truth takes a backseat to our presuppositions. "Done with that!"

As a final assessment, it seems that all of the work which God created and made was good until the day He formed man and gave him a JOB. *"And the LORD God said, it is not good that the man should be alone; I will make him an help meet for him"* (Gen. 2:18). All things considered, can I get a "KISS?" "**K**eep **I**t **S**imple, '**S**weetie'!" HE MADE US THE HELP – NOT THE HEAD! Even "Adam" would likely agree here that as women of God, we were built to love our husbands, nurture our children, and take care of our homes – not to establish a church, or run the country! Now that I have established my storyline, behold, the mystery is, "it is what it is."

CHAPTER THREE

WHY GOD GAVE MAN THE ABILITY TO FALL AND A FREE WILL TO COMMIT SIN

In continuing this investigation, a significant reflection that you may want to keep in mind while reading this book is this: when God looks at us, He sees Jesus. Here is the clincher, when He looked at Eve, He saw Adam. Now that we have established that fact, let's continue. Believe it or not, once Eve gave in to the serpent, Adam never gave God the opportunity to uncover her. Ask me why. He was the man that took the stand. After they ate from the Tree of the Knowledge of Good and Evil, they hid <u>themselves</u>. Ask me why again. This tree represented condemnation; and now, because of the <u>consciousness</u> of sin, immortality ended!

At the outset, when God walked into the garden in the cool of the day, He called unto Adam – not Adam along with his help meet or his "side-kick." After all, was it not <u>Adam</u> that He commanded not to eat of the forbidden fruit, **before** he went to sleep and reproduced of himself (Gen. 2:17)? In other words, God did not give the law to Eve; He gave it to the MAN. When you don't know the Word for yourself, it is easier to doubt the truth and believe a lie. That's why a woman needs a real man who has her back and can cover her head with the right Word.

By not questioning Eve initially, was God recognizing the position that had been given to man to **cover** the woman? Is it possible that

Adam was being given an option by which to take responsibility for **her** rebellion? If so, then, why was it ultimately necessary for Adam to <u>cover</u> Eve in her **sin**? When all's said and done, aren't we to submit to our husbands as they follow Christ? Taking this into consideration, one of my readers suggested that the covering should have taken place **before** Eve ate the fruit. Well, according to the Scripture that preceded the garden scene, she was taken out of man, and they were both naked and not ashamed (Gen. 2:23 and 25). Anybody that is wearing the glory of God is already covered. If Adam had known that she would be deceived in her glory state, would he have taken measures to reinforce security?

A more reasonable question would be: What effect would Adam and Eve's decision have on the rest of humanity? I'm in harmony with Dr. Kamilah Stevenson who yielded some rich data regarding the mystery of iniquity. Since Satan could not stop God from speaking, he went after trying to pervert what He said. Thus, he introduced the concept that Adam and Eve could be more like God by eating from the Tree of the Knowledge of Good and Evil. However, there was no need to be more perfect than they already were. Even as iniquity tends to creep in whenever there is lack and need, there was never a moment where they had a need for anything to be added to them. Yet, the snake was able to convince Eve that they were not perfect and that something was missing.

How can you become more like someone when you were created in their image and likeness? The seed of iniquity was planted when she began to believe the hype. As this was also the door to iniquity for Satan, there was a need for him to become more than what he was created to be. Let me "park" here for a quick research moment. Did you know that God lives on top of a mountain in Heaven? When you go to Heaven, the angels and the saints live in the valleys and in the flatlands of Heaven, records Prophet Barber. As highly exalted as They are, the Father, the Son and the Holy Ghost live atop a mountain. This is what Lucifer was referring to when he said: ... ***"I will sit also upon the mount of the congregation, in the sides of the north"*** (Isa. 14:13b). The congregation that Lucifer was referring to here is the Holy Trinity – the Father, Son and Holy Ghost.

I see that this is the mountain (Mt. Sinai) where God commanded Moses to present himself. After referring back to a Facebook post from the prophet, my own search ensued and included such references as: Exodus 24:12, 34:1-3; Psalm 48:1; Ezekiel 20:40; Micah 4:2; Habakkuk 3:3-6; and, Revelation 21:10. I learned that Lucifer, when he was righteous, had unlimited access to the Throne Room of God, which was located atop this mountain. But when he insurrected against the Trinity, the Father permanently barred his access, thundering: ***"Therefore I will cast thee as profane out of the mountain of God"*** ... **(Eze. 28:16b)**. This is how you know that many people who claim to have gone to Heaven and were given access to the Throne Room are actually lying about their so-called out-of-body experience. How is it, when re-telling their accounts that they forget to mention that they had to first ascend a huge mountain in order to get to the Throne Room of Jehovah, asked the prophet? Know your Bible!

With respect to the subject of iniquity, all of a sudden, Satan said: "I will be like the Most High." For instance, if you were created to be an evangelist, why are you trying to start a church? If you were created to be the help, why are you trying to be the head? When you have a false void or a need to be something different than what God intended, you open the door to iniquity. The mystery of iniquity is that you may prosper for a while, but you will never come into your true experience. You will eventually start doing something against God's original plan for your life and end up missing the mark.

Be careful that you don't intrude into the wrong calling, or the wrong office, or the wrong profession, even. Once that seed of iniquity is planted, you feel like the power is in your hand. Then, your destruction becomes the manifestation of your disobedience. Once you have entered into that door of iniquity, what is good and what is evil is in complete sync with Satan's plot. Now you get to CHOOSE if you want to abort your baby. Now you get to CHOOSE if you want to be a homosexual. Now you get to CHOOSE to fornicate and justify it. That's what happens to a mind that is not renewed; it ends up going into those open doors of iniquity.

When humans/politicians become their own gods, they get to decide what's good and what's evil; what's accepted and what's not, what's wrong and what's right. While everybody is right in their own eyes, the root of iniquity says: this is how I feel; this is what I believe. With all of these opinions and humanistic ways, we have now become our own gods, whereas the Word of God is no longer allowed to dictate what we believe. We dictate what we want we want to do and adjust Scriptures to make them say what we would rather believe.

Dr. Stevenson is further accentuated in her observation that the birth of religion was created from that point, when man started doing what was "right in his own eyes" (Prov. 16:2). Now that we find it hard to allow the Word to be the final authority and the adjustment door of iniquity, our opinions and way of life and the deception that we are our own gods have led us into cultic religions. Oh, by the way, if your interpretation of grace is pushing you away from God to satisfy your flesh and compromise your faith, you need to go back to the altar. You need a visitation and a wake-up call; it's called deliverance. Please make sure that your philosophies are being shaped by the Word of God; otherwise, you open the door to iniquity.

Wow; that was profound. I am always intrigued and side-barred by an open and fresh approach to the Book of Genesis and anyone who makes related observations on the topic of Adam and Eve. Anyway, as I started to say way back when, it is apparent that Eve who was on the inside of Adam and taken out of him had already eavesdropped on the conversation that banned him from the tree. Obviously the first woman with "TMI" (too much information), she came here already knowing that this particular tree was off limits. Ask me why. She recited the order of God back to the serpent: ***"We may eat of the fruit of the trees of the garden: But of the fruit of the tree which is in the midst of the garden, God hath said, Ye shall not eat of it, neither shall ye touch it, lest ye die"*** (Gen. 3:2-3).

My questions are: "Eve, who asked you to speak anyway?" Why did the man standing beside you not man-up and do the talking? Moreover, **if** God knew that Eve would be tempted and cause the man of God to fall, why did He choose to create her when Adam's world was picture-perfect? **If** God still had power over Satan in the garden **before** they sinned, why would He even allow the serpent to converse with Eve while Adam passively stood beside her? My cross reference,

Bishop Thomas (2017) adds the following perspective. Before the law came, man had no knowledge of sin (Rom. 7:7). Wherefore, their only defense was incorporated in their obedience and trust in what God had said to them. Having no knowledge of evil, could this be an innocent act on the part of innocent people? Could this be why they failed to challenge the enticement of the serpent?

Since Eve could not recognize sin, she likely considered the serpent as just another innocent beast of the field. "Hmmm"… I've been trying to tell you that it was a set-up! Despite how or why they did it, in the garden is where iniquity started. And now you have humanism and a man and woman who have **opened** themselves up to the knowledge of good and evil. At the end of the day, they have now become their own gods, and they can make decisions in their lives as to what is good and what is evil. Before, God made the decision to what is good and what is evil. Since God had already established equality by this time and given them dominion in the earth, would it have been an inopportune time or an inappropriate decision for Him to circumvent the fall? My next question: How could He possess omniscience and not have known that the both of them would die in the first place?

Well saints, since they sinned at the beginning of what we know as creation, does not the fact that the Lamb that was slain from the world's foundation reveal that the redemption was not an afterthought? Revelation 13:8 suggests that it was already in the mind of God that sin would enter the world. Whereas this overall revelation is open to criticism, the commonalities and uniqueness of the above probing questions are still influenced by other critical variables. Like so, was this not God's ultimate plan for salvation from the foundation of the world, or at least, after Satan's dishonorable discharge from Heaven? I really don't know what happened in the world before Adam and Eve; I'm still being confounded by the Book of Genesis. But would this not make His redemptive work of grace already be in motion, at least, **before** they sinned?

Another valuable question to be considered before I open the next "can of worms" is this: Was it really God's intention to make one man and leave him alone in the garden forever (without sin)? If so, then, why would He suddenly come up with the idea of a help meet that would tempt the first man beyond his power to resist? Equally, it brows my curiosity as to why it was predicted that Eve's seed would bruise the enemy's head, **if** they were predestined to remain immortal? Allow me to ask a more logical question. Since God already had one Son (the only begotten Son) who most definitely consisted of His perfect will, why would He take a chance on leaving Adam in the garden with the ability to fall and a free will to commit sin, **if** He had no plan to eventually create an extended family?

What good is a father without children? Even as the Son of God indicates a family relationship (Mk. 3:34-35), could it be that even in His permissive will He wanted relations? From the very beginning, God implies expansion of His community when He says, "Let us," indicating that a community already existed. In keeping with this point of view, God was forming an extended family for His Son to rule so that afterwards, He could turn everything over to His Father (see 1 Cor. 15:28). Thus, the actual creation of Adam and Eve and placing them in the garden was never intended to be an end of itself but a necessary step at the beginning of a process to expand the community.

Now, I will revisit the initial suggestion. If Adam was responsible for keeping and dressing the garden, why didn't he ascertain that the garden was secure and guarded so that Eve was covered from the serpent. Or, why didn't he make an attempt to protect her when he noticed that she was initially being deceived? Well, if the fall had been circumvented, what other reason would God have had for **not** immediately and completely destroying Satan when he evicted him from Heaven? After all, He had the power to do so, right?

Even though I am the author, I do not have the answers to each and every one of these questions. And since Pastor Shannon is gone, I'm doing the best I can with what I have. Perhaps, this is why God frequently allows me to draw from others what He wants to reinforce through me. As I am very sensitive and receptive to what God is speaking, some of my research was derived from contacts with experts on the topic (like Pastor Shannon), conversations with people who typically share their experiences, a few references in books written by others, AND the wisdom that I have discovered through revelation knowledge.

I was literally in one pastor's audience when he preached an entire message from my Trilogy-Part One. It's not unique for preachers to preach other preachers' sermons. Even a Grammy Award Winning, Detroit Gospel Recording Artist, admitted to me in the airport, one day: "The book is so powerful that before I left it on the plane, I was actually preaching from it! There is so much Word in there that I can't understand why you're not preaching!" Whereas the pastor did acknowledge that his message (title and all) was coming from **"one"** of the members who had written **a** book, I was baffled as to why he refused to acknowledge me sitting right there in his face. Since my pursuit had never been promoted there, the least he could have done was give my book a "15-second elevator pitch," to allow the members to support my ministry.

Even as I still feel very invisible in my world, this is the kind of non-support that I have had to cope with for years, in trying to get my some help from the sanctuary. This is not to even mention the kind of royalty checks that I will be transparent enough to share with you in a later chapter. And it is because of my transparency and the reality of my truth that I have not had exposure. In God's timing and according to Proverbs 18:16, I will have my turn. As a matter of fact, after two weeks of publishing delays, I haphazardly listened to a man of God deliver a prophetic Word for 2017; this could not have been by accident. He said that for the influence that we struggled to get inside the "house," there's a harvest coming from the heathen. Since the church has no clue what to do with us, those of us who have not been celebrated inside are about to be received by creation (Stevenson, 2017).

That blessed me, and I received it! In Chapter 13, you will see where I embraced this same (personal) prophecy from Apostle Lawrence Braggs, almost a year ago. At the same time, rejection does not mean that something is wrong **with** me; it could mean that you don't have the capacity **for** me. "Seeing that man's rejection is oftentimes God's promotion, before you can expect acceptance from the world, you must experience rejection from your family. Jesus Himself testified that a prophet hath no honor (belief or acceptance) in his own country. 'He came unto His own and they received Him not'" (Reid, 2014).

The most important point to me as an author and as a reservoir that shares what I collect with others is that there is really no copyright on a Word when it comes from God. While we often pride ourselves in being the messenger; we are just as "beside the point" as mail carriers who deliver time-sensitive packages in bad weather. God is really His own Messenger; we are just the carriers who can't get a Word without going through the Messenger. Really, when God said it, it doesn't matter who else says it, and when He's doing the talking, it doesn't matter who the speaker is. When He needs a mouthpiece, He will use something as inconsequential as Balaam's ass. As a matter of fact, we are just a simple mouthpiece who was obedient enough to get chosen. So while people are taking ownership of their gifts and getting all "puffed up" and copyrighting the rhema, it's really not yours to copyright.

You know what; I have one more point that needs to be made while I still have the "floor." I realize that often, my point of views don't always come out in the best tone or with the most appropriate words. Honestly, recycled, disgruntled "churchy folks" really get on my nerves. Jesus got so tired of 'em that He took a boat ride and went to the other side. L☺L! Still, I try to keep in mind that there is always the right way to make a bad point. According to Winston Churchill, "Tact is the ability to tell someone to go to hell in such a way that they look forward to the trip." That's really my objective for this book.

So let me say this as tactful as possible for those of us who have been called to spread the Gospel. Our main concern should be making sure that we are qualified with knowledge to be a mouthpiece in wisdom. Can I go ahead and lay out this tapestry for what it means to be wise? You can't preach what He said and not know **how** to say it; it takes having the spirit of wisdom. Yes, wisdom is a spirit; it has a tone to it. Read Exodus 28:3, Deuteronomy 34:9, Isaiah 11:2, and Ephesians 1:17.

Wisdom definitely does not come with age; wisdom and knowledge come from God. The older some people get, the "unwiser" they become. I learned that grey hairs in the Bible mean glory; they do not mean wisdom. Moses hair was turned because he saw God, not because he was wise; otherwise, he may not have missed the promise.

God told him to lay hands on Joshua so that the spirit of wisdom would come. Moses demonstrated to us that you need the spirit of wisdom, particularly, when you are dealing with Black folks!

That was well-put; here is where I need to take Churchill's advice. How are you going to be a mighty missionary and do exploits in the Kingdom making statements like: "We is, and they is, and people is?" Under normal circumstances, we learned subject-verb agreement in the 2nd grade, but you claim to have a High School diploma. You have to wonder, from where? These are the kind of people that you get a rise out of for simply trying to bring clarity or correction. And because they are in denial and consider themselves well-learned, well-traveled, and "well-everything" else, their defensiveness makes you afraid to help them.

Balaam's ass spoke better grammar than that, and he never went to High School or Sunday School! He just opened his mouth and spoke what he heard. God is way smarter than you. So if He said it, it's not going to come out not making sense, or grammatically unseemly, or with erroneous punctuations. Okay? Some of these people have the nerve to refer to themselves as, Dr. "So-and-so," and don't even have an Associates degree! That's one of the "50 Shades of Ignorance" in the Black Church. How does a person go from Evangelist "So-and-so," to suddenly, Dr. "So-and-so?"

Dr. Matthew L. Stevenson, III said it best in his mention that if he had to base his ideas of God around His spokespeople, he would think that God was illiterate, unlearned, and unable to speak on current events because their solution to everything is just "praise Him." Why? We do not have an intelligent strategy on how to diagnose the wiles of society. It is literally embarrassing to see how some of them ridiculously post on Facebook with misspelled words and run-on sentences.

Yet, they are too proud and vain to allow you to be transparent with them. That's not a good look, saints; it's just unbecoming on all levels. While these people are posting on Facebook, 24/7, they need to use their time wisely and take some online English classes. "Real talk." They have no more business posting on Facebook than a 2nd grader has trying to teach statistics. I know we that are strong ought to bear the infirmities of the weak, but some relationships you simply outgrow (because of **their** attitude, not yours). "Sometimes you have to 'unfollow' people in real life." #bossbabe

One assertion is that the extent of training in the Black church is most often Sunday School, and the way most of our preachers are trained is by giving them the microphone. Because church is extracurricular for most Christians and has no academic prerequisites, they get offended if you assume pass or fail on something. I pre-warned you on the Back Cover that this book was intended to help my people. And now I understand why Moses became so weary with the Children of Israel. They were Black! Nobody else in the world acts like them, but us.

Jesus told His disciples that He was going to give them a word, a mouth, and wisdom, which means anointed speech. Paul debated everyday for three months because he was intelligent. It was not just as a result of school; it was from an encounter. Stevenson (2016) said that some of us couldn't defend our beliefs for 30 minutes. A real encounter from God changes your comprehension, and it changes how you preach and teach. Bottom line: you cannot represent somebody that you hadn't seen before, and you can't preach what He said and not know how to say what He said.

I'm trying to remember what interrupted my flow, this time. It's okay; I'm anointed to pause and cover any given topic at any given point, and jump right back into my flow. So here we go. As a humble mouthpiece, reservoir, dissertation researcher, "penJprophetess," I absolutely enjoy quoting God's voice through others; it's in both my spiritual and academic DNA. Reference Lists were created because our personal opinions don't always count. Readers want to know whether experts on the topic contradict or correspond with how you feel. Without a selfish bone in my body, I always find myself exactly where I need to be to hear what God wants to say. Who cares if God said it to me, to you, to us, or to them? Because I listen to learn, and learn to share, He strategically leads me to the resources that He wants to use to become a part of my research.

When my friend, Damaras (Renee), asked me to listen to Dr. Stevenson's recent and powerful series, *Empty: I Never Knew You*, I told her that I was being forced to tune out everything and everybody for the duration of this project (particularly, Dr. Stevenson). I couldn't resist; it was totally "off the chain" and later served as a divine reference to a corresponding chapter. Although Dr. Stevenson is unequivocally, my most captivating mouthpiece of all times, the magnitude to which God was speaking directly to and through me for this book has been unprecedented and equally intriguing for me. Often, even as I have had to "take the edge off" sometimes, the Anointing was so heavy that I could almost feel the words jumping off the pages. Nevertheless, I differ from a lot of people in this regard: it does not matter to me who gets the credit, as long as God gets the glory.

Great orators like some of you can hear God speak as you talk; the reverse is true for me. I hear Him loud and clear while I am still and quiet. If I'm asked to speak spontaneously, I'm liable to shut down and go silent on you. I need serious prayer in that area of my inadequacies. NO one man has it all; only Jesus was given the Spirit without measure (John 3:34). I may not be able to present verbally, as strong as most speakers, but when we stay in our lanes and focus on our flow, the happy median is that our gifts compensates for our deficiencies.

God has a way of incorporating them for His personal glory, so just be you and do God. Whether by inspiration or revelation, or whether you speak it or write it, all that matters is who said it. The driving force behind my extensive research is to facilitate a comprehensive learning experience by which all of us can become lifelong learners. Now that I have taken this time and space to tell you why I am often compelled to draw on the knowledge base of other writers and/or theologians, I hope that you will allow Prophet Floyd Barber to inform my judgment about the intriguing topic before I was interrupted.

Behold, I will show you another mystery. From his school of thought, he believes that God was **NOT** always omniscient. Wait, hold on! Otherwise, why would an omniscient Being regret the decision He made to ever create the human race (Gen. 6:6)? If God knew ahead of time that man was going to sin against Him, then, why would He make a decision that He clearly, by His FOREKNOWLEDGE, had the ability to avoid??? Arising from Prophet Barber's "big bang theory" and his gathering of evidence from various passages of Scripture, he has added yet another lens through which we can explore. Watch this...

Here is where my awareness was truly stretched! He believes that God expanded His personal cognizance and **evolved** in His abilities until He **became** unlimited – much the same way that a boy evolves in his abilities to become a man. After all, the church has taught us that we were spirit beings, which I will revisit a little later. I am sure that this teaching is not without controversy; however, the veracity of this theory is that if God **always** knew everything, why would He have created a heavenly being (Satan), who later, along with 1/3 of the angelic populace would plot an insurrection against Him?

Now, you and I as human beings are smart enough to know that it is totally impossible to defeat an omniscient God, right? Then, Lucifer and his angels who were created far more intelligent should have known that God would be able to anticipate their **every** calculation in advance and circumvent their plot. Disseminating light on the subject and giving equal weight to this notion, Prophet Barber contributes to the controversy by claiming that Lucifer and the angels were quite aware that God possessed vast cognizance at that time. At the same time, they were conscious of the notion that He was **not** ALL cognizant.

This particular notion is best captured in Genesis 18:20-21. If He automatically knew **every**thing (as we have been taught), why did the LORD need to leave His throne in Heaven to come down to the earth to see for Himself, whether or not Sodom was as sinful as the angels had alleged? In the context of the previous notions, the Holy Bible is the most credible Book of the ages that Christians have accepted as truth. To date, it is the most read and distributed Book that has ever been written in the history of humans. And it happens to be the Book that serves as the compass for all of my assignments.

Accordingly, Prophet Barber's observation suggests that God **now** knows all things, but back during the Luciferian revolt and up until the time of the destruction of Sodom and Gomorrah, God did **not** know everything. He was **very knowing** but had not yet evolved to the place where He was ALL-KNOWING. Since this is not universally accepted or substantiated by other research that I am aware of, my only conclusion to this revelation is that even if God had not anticipated Satan's revolt, He was still wise and knowing enough to instigate a "bail-out plan" that would outwit him **after** the revolt.

I felt that! Whatever the conclusion, I am mutually supportive of the fact that we must rethink God in the light of Scripture and not in terms of popular, unsubstantiated opinion. In principle, the Prophet makes this point: "When points of view cannot be substantiated by any clear exegesis of Scripture, they are mere speculation. Never speculate, always exegete – because the testimony of Scripture is absolute!" Rather than being 100% Word, can we at least agree with him that most of our beliefs are part Word, part tradition, part cultural, and part opinion?

Since our human interpretations are filled with paradoxes, contradictions, and ambiguities, prayer for insight and humility to hear new truths based on the Word is the key to continuous growth. Although we sometimes take the Word of God out of context to support our opinions, the interpretation of God's infallible Word is often debatable, but the Word itself is never disputable. Why? *"All Scripture is given by inspiration of God"...* (2 Tim. 3:16a). Furthermore, Proverbs 21:30 contends: *"There is no wisdom nor understanding nor counsel against the LORD."* As a minimum, the variations of interpretations in much of this book will definitely make a great Bible Study.

Well then, based upon my limited knowledge and comprehension at this point, I yet marvel in astonishment as to why an all-knowing God would even put such a tree in the garden, **if** He already knew that the day they ate, their eyes would come open, and they would be as gods, knowing both good and evil. On the other hand, **if** He had wanted Adam and Eve to be like the angels, He would **not** have given the ability to fall or a free will to commit sin. Since God created them **with** a free will, what were His true intentions? Allow me to offer a simple response that may be to the extent of your comfort level. After family, the first thing that comes to my mind is GRACE. Consider this Scripture in the light of this consensus: *"Moreover the law entered, that the offence might abound. But where sin abounded, grace did much more abound"* (Rom. 5:20).

I treasure the idea that God creates or arranges situations that are conducive to us sinning. "Yikes," I may have hit another "brick wall" with that one. Maybe you would have been more comfortable if I had said that He allows such situations. But did not the **Spirit lead** Jesus into the wilderness to be tempted of by the devil (Mt. 4:1)? ... ***"But was in all points tempted like as we are, yet without sin"*** (Heb. 4:15b). While Satan is responsible for turning up the pressure that is permitted upon our flesh by God, He really wants to see if we will find a way to obey Him and rekindle the flame that we had with Him before our spirits ever left Him. Obedience is the quickest way to holiness.

Even though He already **knows** how committed we are to demonstrating our loyalty and expressing our love for Him, it is reassuring at the end of a trial to imagine God saying, "Now, I **see**." In order for us to learn how to **conform** to the image of His Son (Rom. 8:28-29), God gives us the spiritual ability to understand His nature. As a result of life's experiences and the process of building godly character, He **intends** for us to make quality decisions in the midst of our desire to make corrupt choices. Why Satan, a perfect creature, was able to become a rebel and instigate an insurrection against God is that God had placed in him what He later placed in man – the ability to make decisions. To see why God had to cut him down, read Isaiah 14:12-15. Since the very premise of committing sin is based in our decisions, holiness really has nothing to do with desire; it has everything to do with the power to resist, even while pressure is being applied to the flesh.

Your airbag in your car does not give you a reason to run into a brick wall. You are not going to set your house on fire, just because you have been given a fire extinguisher. And just because you have access to band aids, it should not inspire you to deliberately cut yourself. Here is the clincher: The grace factor should **not** make you **want** to sin or even compromise in order to sin; it should make you want to obey God and live HOLY! Salvation is a means to an end; you cannot be saved and refused to be delivered! As you consciously balance self-control with spiritual awareness, eventually, you are no longer sin cognizant. You practice righteousness until it becomes natural or a part of your nature. What you believe should translate into what you do (not just a confession). Thus, it is your love **for** God that gives you the desire to live a victorious life through His Son.

Whereas sin is error or an illusion that exists in the mind and manifests in our behavior, God does not deal with us according to our sins (Psa. 103:10). Please ask me why. He knows that we came into the world with the prenatal proclivity **to** sin. Profoundly, His **pleasure** is gained through our maturity to <u>endure</u> temptation. Once we are tempted, rather than judging us based on our poor decisions, He makes a way for our escape. I believe that He then judges us based on our refusal to come correct.

"For if after they have escaped the pollutions of the world through the knowledge of the Lord and Saviour Jesus Christ, they are again entangled therein, and overcome, the latter end is worse with them than the beginning" (2 Pet. 2:20). If you are interested in this topic at length, please refer to Trilogy-Part Two (Chapter Two) for a continuation of: *Where Is God In My Mess?* In order for truth to fully penetrate, you can expect some redundancy throughout my projects; it is intentionally augmented to accentuate emphasis where needed!

The word escaped in the previous Scripture is very critical here. Although Adam and Eve initially knew no sin, **they** were the **first man** that was created with a soul or with the ability to make right or wrong choices. Since Jesus is the ultimate way of escape, would it be a fallacy to say that God purposely gave Him a reason to die and redeem man back to Himself? *"That as sin hath reigned unto death, even so might grace reign through righteousness unto eternal life by Jesus Christ our Lord"* (Rom. 5:21).

One other thing that we may be able to agree on is that in Spirit we were already with God from the beginning, were we not? Since it is very difficult to live outside of Heaven and **not** act out of character, He must have known that once He gave us bodies and free wills, we would lose our everlasting minds. While processing this premise, Pastor Shannon and I brooded over the idea of whether or not God just wanted a reason to restore, redeem, recover, revive, remake and regenerate. At the very least, He could get much glory out of renewing our minds and revolutionizing a rebellious society! As this is the kind of renaissance that turns into real revival, when God revolutionizes a rebellious people, He definitely challenges old, negative beliefs by creating new ones that will give power to purpose.

Pastor Shannon and I even flirted with the idea of what will happen once man becomes immortal again and is redeemed back to Christ. Does God's vivid imagination go beyond the Book of Revelation? "For now, we can only see through a glass, darkly, and we only know in part" (1 Cor. 13:12). God could never reveal all of His thoughts and feelings and plans in one, single book. He is too immeasurable to be deduced and confined to human limitations, or contained in earthly documentations. However, the more intimate you become with Him (or with any writer), the more insight he or she will reveal. Along these lines, information becomes yoke-destroying, traditional-breaking, denominational-shaking, religious-demon-exposing, church-shattering revelation.

Here is another thought-provoking question that "brows" my curiosity. Since the Creator has the propensity to test His invention/creation, could it be that God knew what Eve would do, was going to be based on Him demonstrating for the sake of the second Adam what the first Adam would do as a result of what she did? I know that sounded a bit confusing because each time that I revise this book, I always end up reading that sentence more than once, myself. In Black folks' terms, could God have permitted Eve to hook up with Satan, to compel Adam to man-up and demonstrate to His Son, the sacrifice of becoming man in order to redeem man?

While waiting to get past the content evaluation of this book, my brother, Bishop Brandon Porter said so profoundly: "Faith reveals new opportunities previously promised." Before God could refer to Abraham as the father of faith, He selected to test his faith and obedience. If God had **not** already known that Abraham would allow Isaac to be the sacrificial offering, there would have been no reason for the ram. It was **after** Abraham stretched forth his hand to slay his son that the angel of the LORD called unto him out of Heaven, saying: ***"Here I am… For now I know that thou fearest God, seeing thou hast not withheld thy son"*** (Gen. 22:11-12). I feel like God was saying, "**Now** I see." In other words, "He was there all the time!"

57

Karen D. Reid (Ph.D. Candidate)

What was already in His mind to accomplish was in harmony with what He intended to establish. Furthermore, He wanted Abraham to pass the test based on the "bombshell" evidence of things not seen (faith) and his relationship with God (love), which gave him the ability to endure the test. We will forego attention to the complexity of the Adamic sin to concentrate on the reoccurring themes here. No, God was not delighted by the evil of mankind. Yet, because He foreknew the conclusion, He gave man the ability to fall and a free will to commit sin. This happened so that the plan of salvation could be instigated and His Word could be manifested through His Son. The probing concern for me is: "Are we there yet?" Back to Eden, that is.

CHAPTER FOUR

LET'S GET BACK TO EDEN

Why Adam would demonstrate perfect love and give up immortality for the woman God gave him is really the focus of my investigation. Meanwhile, why Jesus would give up immortality and leave the Father to die on an old rugged cross for the love of the Church is a large part of the conclusion. Although the implication is very profound, this revelation is really simple. Let's take into account what Paul emphasized in Ephesians 5:31-32: *"For this cause shall a man leave his father and mother, and shall be joined unto his wife, and they two shall be one flesh. This is a great mystery: but I speak concerning Christ and the church."*

As we have always based the Church as being the Bride of Christ around the explanation of Ephesians 5:23-25, the New Jerusalem is actually the Bride or the Lamb's wife. Ask me how. It contains the bride and takes on her character. John saw the Bride adorned for her husband because the time for the consummation had arrived. Can I validate that for you? Yes I can. *"And I John saw the holy city, New Jerusalem, coming down from God out of Heaven, prepared as a bride adorned for her husband. … Come hither, I will shew thee the Bride, the Lamb's wife. And he carried me away in the spirit to a great and high mountain, and shewed me that great city, the Holy Jerusalem"*... (Rev. 21:2, 9b, 10a).

Oh, by the way, if God is our Father and we are His children, the family is not complete unless there is a Mother. Right? Just as our physical life was given to us through our physical mother, our spiritual life would be given to us through our spiritual Mother. So would our heavenly Mother have a name? Allow me to go on a quick "rabbit trail" to show you another mystery. Galatians 4:26 says of our Mother: *"But Jerusalem which is above is free, which is the Mother of us all."* Nobody had ever taught me that Jerusalem is called the Bride and the Mother.

Because of divine order, there has to be a reciprocal or opposite to every law. The idea behind bringing awareness to this revelation is that our casual approach to the Word of God causes us to casually meander down the Scriptures that only make sense to where we are today. Therefore, we have no real historic context or handling on the logic of God for what He is doing and has been doing before the created order. My point was: the **concept** of the Bride includes not only the Church. But we will be united to God and the Lamb and live forever in that eternal city with all the rest of the redeemed from all the ages.

Yet, for the purpose of this chapter, I will go ahead and base my submission around the fact that marriage is the example that **Paul** used to mirror Jesus and the Church. *"For no man ever yet hateth His own flesh; but nourisheth and cherisheth it, even as the Lord the Church: For we are members of His body, of His flesh, and of His bones"* (Eph. 5:29-30). Undeniably, is this not what Adam indicated about Eve, in Genesis 2:23? A focus on the spiritual would be productive in identifying with the natural. If we continue to trivialize what Adam did for Eve, we would never be able to even fathom the genuine love that Jesus has for the Church.

Some things God prearranged that had absolutely nothing to do with us, but there are those other things that He irrefutably predestined that had everything to do with us. **If** it were predestined that Eve's seed would bruise the enemy's head, would it be safe to say that God was totally prepared to tolerate evil, in order to produce good? *"I form the light, and create darkness: I make peace, and create evil; I the LORD do all these things"* (Isa. 45:7). Again, **if** Adam and Eve had remained immortal like the angels, there would have been no need for Jesus to die and demonstrate God's immeasurable love for us.

Speaking of angels, they were spoken into existence. However, as God's desire was to reproduce of Himself, man was formed in His image and shaped in the outward form of Himself (Gen. 1:26-27). Strategically, He breathed His Spirit into man and gave him material bodies to enjoy His creation. Since the angels were commanded to worship, I have no doubt that God gets excited when they call Him, "Holy Holy." Because of our **free will**, He takes it personal when we call Him, "Abba Father." Oh, how the angels wish that they had our testimonies and were able to sing the songs we sing, especially the one about being redeemed. Why? Everything Satan did, God re-did it!

For example, Satan deemed that man should die; Jesus **re**deemed us back to Himself that we might live. Come on now; that was an easy place to shout amen! Wow, I just had an epiphany. Satan, getting kicked out of Heaven to operate in the earth realm is really the premise behind this whole controversy in the garden. ... *"I beheld Satan as lightening fall from heaven"* (Lk. 10:18b). Before Adam was created for the garden, Satan was already there as a prisoner. So when God formed Adam, it was not just the miracle of man. I recently learned that what God was doing was punishing Satan, by allowing him to observe a greater being than him.

As the dethroned angel who was not allowed to remain in Heaven, he was now on the sideline observing God play with dirt. So when God formed man from the dust of the ground and told him that it was not good for him to be alone, basically, He was conveying to Satan, the most beautiful creature that He had ever created that even though you got banished from Heaven, I'm going to also beat you with dirt on your own, new turf. And this dirt is going to be the beginning of man and the end of you. Because Satan observed woman being taken out of the man who had been walking with the voice of God in the cool of the day, he decided to take advantage of the woman who was most distant from God.

Too afraid to confront Adam with his plot, he approached the weaker vessel to make sure that he had a gateway to deception. Initially, had Satan gone to the man, Adam would not have responded to Satan's voice; God's voice was the only voice that He hearkened to. On the contrary, Eve was most familiar with Adam's voice. Thus, Satan had to confront the one who was less familiar with the voice of God. That's how he was able to tempt the weaker vessel to influence the man to give up what he already had. But as a result of the prophecy that Eve's seed would bruise the enemy's head, not only was Satan defeated in Heaven, our warring, radical and relentless God has been defeating him on his own turf ever since the eviction! Isn't that characteristic of a God that does not mind participating in inconceivable events to illustrate His incredible evidence?

Since the "fall-ball" did not start rolling until **Adam** was persuaded to eat the fruit, did he love the creature so much so that he chose to lay down a charge (Gen. 2:17) that came directly from the Creator? Better yet, should he have disregarded God's charge to avoid this tree, in order to please Eve? Or, should he have disregarded Eve's whim in order to please God? "Hmmm"... that's deep. In other words, should Adam have chosen to obey a living God versus submitting to a spiritually dead woman? *"Nevertheless death reigned from Adam to Moses, even over them that had not sinned after the similitude of Adam's transgression, who is the figure of Him that was to come"* (Rom. 5:14). Well now, since the coming of the second Adam was inevitable, was God counting on the first Adam being willing to die and go to hell for Eve, all in the name of an unconditional love?

When a wife gets out of the perfect will of God and commits sin, it stands to reason that a loving husband should immediately lead her back to God with repentance and reconciliation. Under normal circumstances, that is absolutely the case! Because of the **predestination** element here, did Adam really have a choice? Maybe, the mystery of the marriage correlation between Adam and Eve, and Christ and the Church is the chain of command that was in effect. Let's go deeper my brother or sister.

One of the first commandments given to man after the fall was to leave his father and his mother and cleave unto his wife and be one flesh. In the likely event that God knew that Eve would eventually become more than a help meet, it was not a question of whether Adam loved God more than he loved Eve. Neither was it a question of whether he had a choice to disobey God in his effort to cover Eve. Here is the key mystery that I wish to convey; are you ready for this?

Adam became sin (as a result of his own free will), in order to leave his Father and love his wife the way God must have intended for Christ to leave His Father, freely become sin, and love the Church. *"For He hath made Him to be sin for us, who knew no sin; that we might be made the righteousness of God in Him"* (2 Cor. 5:21).

Another thought-probing question is this: Did Adam exacerbate the situation by committing the sin with her? Or, would it be asinine to say that God was pleased that he covered her (by taking on her sin), in spite of what the charges were? What curse did God pronounce upon the snake? Before the serpent was a snake, he was actually a large lizard. If you notice in Genesis 3:14-17, the serpent was cursed to crawl on his belly and eat dust all the days of its life. That is an indication that before he started crawling as a serpent, he had the hands and legs of a lizard and was able to walk. The last thing God said to the serpent was that the seed of the woman would bruise his head. Every since He put more authority in the woman's uterus that He put in Satan, there has been a war between the seed and Satan from the beginning of time.

Physically, the curse came upon Eve when God multiplied her sorrow and conception. Although Adam's **ground** was cursed, causing him to labor for his provision (Gen. 3:19); God never **physically** cursed him for covering Eve in her sin. "In God's cursing the earth, He spared the soul. Had He cursed man, none of His posterity could have been redeemed. He would have been banished from God for all eternity. Even in God's punishment for Cain in cursing him **from** the earth (Gen. 4:11a), we see a type of eternal banishment. Yet, the door of redemption is left ajar through the blessing of Eve" (Thomas, 2017).

In other words, God judged Adam and allowed what had gone out of course to aid in their salvation. What does that say to you? It speaks volumes about Adam discovering his destiny and fulfilling his purpose to cover the woman whose seed was destined to bruise Satan's head. Adam must have discerned that God was in the process of giving the Church the responsibility to bear seed. And since Eve was the picture of the first church, he had to protect her seed to stop Satan from killing the church. Destiny is determined more around discernment than it is based on decision. In other words, when you are in relationship with God, the Holy Spirit will teach you discernment so that you can make decisions based on destiny. I felt that!

In fact, reader, when it comes to destiny, "The destiny that's for you is greater than the dirt that's on you! Deliverance comes when you realize that the dirt is designing you – not destroying you!" posted Pastor Manwell Faison. Despite her life-altering transgression, she still ended up becoming the mother of **all** the living. Hence, this is a likely basis for which he named his "wife," Eve. Only a help meet at first, she is now Adam's wife and the mother of the human race. Would that not validate the prerequisite for becoming a wife before you become a mother? Inevitably, you enhance your chances of becoming a better mother when you have advanced from being a godly wife. Now, let's return to some guiding principles in the course of getting back to Eden.

NEWSFLASH: God is not traumatized by our sins because no sin can change God's mind about who He ultimately predestined us to be. Just as Adam and Eve became discontent with God's original provision and perfect will, they could not abort His divine plan because they refused to **remain** in defeat. That's why I believe that God has both a perfect will and a permissive will. Because our past, present, and future sins were nailed to the cross, we were made perfect and blameless at Calvary, as long as we are willing to accept Christ as the **only** way back to the Father. Freed from the condemnation of sin, we are now free to live in perpetual victory. Therefore, what concerns God more is **how** we handle our sins in our righteousness (please read 2 Cor. 6:1-18).

When the husband is unable to avert the wife **from** sin, he has a responsibility to purify her **in** the sin. While we were yet sinners, did Christ not do this for us when He became sin to save us? As God could not stand to look upon sin (without judging it or atoning for it), He hid His face while His Son became sin and gave His life for the Church. *"That He might sanctify and cleanse it with the washing of water by the Word. That He might present it to Himself a glorious Church"*... (Eph. 5:26-27a).

Even though Adam dropped the "ball," the key mystery is that the love he had for Eve was symbolic of the love that Christ would have for the Church. And in order to put this mystery into our "history" book (the Bible), Jesus, being the last Adam had to come along and do for the Church what the first Adam did for Eve. Because God intended for the Church to be styled **as** a bride for His Son, I support the position that Jesus needed to learn complete obedience through Adam's classic example of a perfect marriage. Again, "Adam:" "where you at?"

I don't know about you, but this revelation, or parable, or whatever you "wanna" call it is blessing me. Every single time that I have revisited this information and made additional changes that were so necessary for its perfection, it made the sacrifices and the challenges so worth enduring and embracing. I totally agree with Moustakas (1994) in that: ... "We can never exhaust completely our experience of things no matter how many times we reconsider them or view them. A new horizon arises each time that one recedes. It is a never-ending process and, though we may reach a stopping point and discontinue our perception of something, the possibility for discovery is unlimited. The horizontal makes of conscious experience a continuing mystery, one that opens regions of laughter and hope or pain and anguish as these enter our conscious life" (p. 95).

I often wonder why God has allowed me to work on the same projects without success and publish so many rewrites without any rewards, when He could have saved me a lot of time, effort, money **and** stress, by saying everything in the first edition. Likely seeing that I would become weary with my "basement" experience or "underground movement," the Creator needed to test my obedience. Elisha's Anointing was such a priority that he was willing to live on locusts and honey and wild stuff. In essence I have gotten to that point. Yet, as a minor character with a major assignment, every test that I have had to endure in the process has everything to do with my purpose.

To be honest, I would not have chosen this journey, but at this point, I wouldn't trade it for the world. When you are elected and selected, "pain that brings success never regrets the PROCESS! Pain is that process that separates complainers from winners," posted Bishop Jerald Bailey. Because the race is not to the swift, nor the battle to the strong, I have not necessarily passed every test with "flying colors."

"Nevertheless-although-even so," each round has taken me higher and higher. By the end of my **final** rewrites, I hope to hear Him say, "**Now** I see."

Even at the time of this rewrite (Oct. 2016) and now in a season of necessary validation, I was in need of something bigger than me to help facilitate the shift. While trying to figure out by myself how to use what's on my life, my cousin, Carolyn Wright (the house prophetess), said the only thing that she could hear when she went before God on my behalf, was 1 Corinthians 15:58: *"Therefore, my beloved brethren, be ye steadfast, unmoveable, always abounding in the work of the Lord, forasmuch as ye know that your labour is not in vain in the Lord."*

Due to the work that was behind me and now in front of me, this Scripture was most appropriate as I was in a unique transition **and** under pressure to complete my doctoral dissertation. If she had not given me that Word a couple of months before I volunteered to spend my time, money, and effort producing a book for someone else who declined the project in its completion, rejection and discouragement would have shut me down completely. What I volunteered to do for free would have cost a real client, $3,650 for a finished product. Because of 1 Corinthians 15:58, here I am back at it again. UPDATE: Since sowing that seed, God blessed me with an editing project at $1,000 every month until completion, at only a few hours per week. It looks like rejection brought revival! At the end of the day, I'm having a "Tamar Braxton moment!" #WON'THEDOIT

Enough about me! "Let's get back to Eden." As I pointed out earlier, Adam was not in another part of the garden when Eve was tempted. As they were **together** when she gave also unto her husband to eat (Gen. 3:6), did he pause even for a moment to consider the repercussion of her influence, or the consequence of his own disobedience? I think not! I want you to ask me why. A man protects the woman that he respects! In line with 1 John 4:18 (with emphasis added): *"There is no fear* [apprehension or confusion] *in love; but perfect love casteth out fear: because fear hath torment. He that feareth is not made perfect in love."* Because there was **perfect** love between this male and female, they had NO fear.

This is why we should **not** allow the institution of marriage to be redefined. According to the principles of the Creator, same sex marriage is **NOT** perfect love. It is a phenomenon that goes against the very nature of God – who He is and what He created. Thus, we must not permit man's laws to change God's commandments! Laws can change; commandments do not. And anytime you change God's Word, you change the possibilities of all of His promises. Adam and Eve is my "larger-than-life" example.

WHOSE REPORT WILL YOU BELIEVE?

To support same sex marriage is like telling the Almighty God who is perfect and flawless in all of His ways that you would rather agree with man who was shapen in iniquity and conceived in sin. To say the least, it was appalling to me to read online, a statement that was made by a well-renowned, former Pentecostal bishop who had recently been dubbed as compromising his convictions for the controversial gospel of inclusion. He made the riveting observation that one can**not** be delivered from homosexuality, no more than heterosexuality or human-sexuality. "Are you serious?" Absolutely nothing can be farther away from the truth!

"And they that went in, went in male and female of all flesh, as God had commanded him: and the LORD shut him in" (Gen. 7:16). When God commanded Noah to bring every creature/species that was upon the earth into the ark, of every kind he brought **both** male and female, so that they could have the ability to preserve mankind and repopulate the earth. God was standing at the door, and everything that went into the ark had to be matched to his companion, or God would not have allowed them to enter.

He NEVER, EVER intended for homosexuality to exist. Yet, the beast of the field, every creeping thing, and the fowl of the air (everything except mankind) has sense enough to decline an abomination that America has accepted. Animals may smell each others' butt, but they would NEVER in a million years, "screw" each other in the butt. Can I just "keep it 100?" It's no shame in your abomination, so it's certainly none in my actuality. Animals can't even speak the term (homosexuality), conceive the act, or perceive the consequences. But somehow they know that's not natural. My question is: How much more does God expect of a man that was made in His own image and after His very likeness? You need to read or reread: Leviticus 18:22-29; Romans 1:27; 1 Corinthians 6:9; and, Revelations 22:15.

Again, your methods may change, but God's principles will **never** change! So you may as well turn right and keep straight and allow the Word to change you, rather than you trying to change the Word. It is hard for me to accept the assertion that a perfect God would allow someone to be **born** confused about their sexuality. It is an insinuation that God Himself is confused and double-minded in all of His ways. Not only is his statement ludicrous, it is a bunch of "foolery and befoonery." He is manifesting a belief system that has resulted in the spirit of error, which in the Greek (plane) means to wander or roam into a type of deception that leads to sin or sinfulness.

The reason why homosexuality has become such a stronghold in the Body of Christ is that the people of God failed to deal with the other, hidden sins of perversion that were much easier to conceal. So, to exploit his agenda that is now spiraling out of control, the enemy created a more observable offense that is rapidly becoming as normal in the church as it is in the world. The problem with this spirit of error is: deliverance was not a mandate because the folks who should have been deliverers were getting just as much tail as the toilet seat. In a time-sensitive era and a defenseless generation, they did not set the foundation for the futuristic! All things being equal, how in the world can deliverance take place among little boys who were being sexually assaulted and molested by the folks who should have been their deliverers?

Here is another characteristic example of the spirit of error. A close associate whom had been raised up on the fundamentals of Christ (His deity, virgin birth, blood atonement, resurrection, and His return), was now taught to a theory that He married Mary Magdalene and fathered two children with her. *"O foolish Galatians, who hath bewitched you?"...* (Gal. 3:1a). I discovered during my research that central to this claim is that Joseph was actually Jesus and that

Aseneth (his wife) was actually Mary Magdalene. This union that was supposedly officiated by Pharaoh of Egypt is said to have led to the birth of Manasseh and Ephraim (Mount, 2014).

Whoever supports this myth has been "bamboozled, hoodwinked and led astray!" Why do you think that any of these scandalous assertions are referred to as the LOST gospel or hidden messages that need decoding? This particular theory is based on the encrypted story of a group of persecuted Christians that disappeared from public view around 325 AD (Mount, 2014). While people go out of their way to discount the Bible, we don't question or dispute the textbooks that the White educators mandate your children to learn from. Prior to this foolishness, she had also shown me a handout of information where she was basically being taught that Jesus was not the Christ. "Unbelievable!" ... *"And this is that spirit of antichrist, whereof ye have heard that it should could; and even now already is in the world"* (1 John 4:3).

"Neither is there salvation in any other: for there is none other name under Heaven given among men, whereby we must be saved" (Acts 4:12). So whose report are you going to believe: the spirit of error that has overcome your teacher, the lost gospel of Jacobovici & Wilson, or Dan Brown's Davinci Code (a best-selling "thriller" that you find only in the pages of fiction)? Or, are you going to believe the report of the LORD (the Holy Bible that was, at minimum, **inspired** by a Holy God)? If God had intended to **inspire** a fifth Gospel, can we at least agree that He would have remembered to **include** a fifth Gospel? If He's omnipotent and omniscient, He can NOT be a God with Alzheimer and dementia!

Whatever He said in the first 66 Books, can you not see the signs of the time that He is standing over His Word to perform it. According to a survey by the Bible Society, it was concluded that around 2.5 billion copies of the Bible were printed between 1815 and 1975. Most recent estimates put the number at more than five **billion** (guinnessworldrecords, 2017). Why are people trying to decode lost books and other hidden foolishness, when, if they submitted to the world's best-selling and most widely distributed Book of all times, they would discover that it is enough to sustain and suffice. Besides, why worry about if and who Jesus was married to, when we need to be focus on end-time prophecy that is being fulfilled before our very eyes? As they said while we were growing up: "The Bible is right; somebody is wrong."

Man even has the audacity to make extensive plans to explore a universe and approach a Supreme Being that they deny as being the God of the Bible. Did not the Bible say: *"For the time will come when they will not endure sound doctrine; but after their own lusts shall they heap to themselves teachers, having itching ears; And they shall turn away their ears from the truth, and shall be turned unto fables"* (2 Tim. 4:3-4). *"Now the Spirit speaketh expressly, that in the latter times some shall depart from the faith, giving heed to seducing spirit, and doctrines of devils"* (1 Tim. 4:1). Yet again I ask: whose report will you believe?

Sadly, rather than reinforcing faith, purity and holiness like they have faithfully done so in the past, many of today's five-fold ministry gifts are driving on a "suspended license," and teaching as though they have earned a G.E.D. from the school of Satan (Generic Education for the Demon-possessed). Those were just classic illustrations of what happens when men become too clever for their own good. They remind me of the Black folks who called themselves building the tower of Babel. Allow me to say this in my best Ebonics: "How 'you-gone' invade the personal space of the Creator who gave you the whole earth?" In this case, how can you dispute the Word of the One who spoke you into existence with mere words?

Leaders: don't become educated fools in this hour, or Christian atheists who talk and live like there is no God, or like the Word has been misinterpreted. *"Knowing this first, that no prophecy of the Scripture is of any private interpretation. For the prophecy came not in old time by the will of man: but holy men of God spake as they were moved by the Holy Ghost"* (2 Pet. 1:20-21). Also, for further amplification, read 1 Corinthians 2:12-13. Followers: please be careful and not allow your **distorted** reception to alter your perception. As a consequence, when you allow these people to shift your perception, the deception that comes from the misconception can be toxic to your acceleration.

BREAKING NEWS: I don't care who was involved in carrying out the Word of God, whether it was Moses and the prophets or Jesus and the apostles, these "holy men of God spake as they were moved by the Holy Ghost" (2 Pet. 1:21). "Nevertheless-although-even so," whether King James or Constantine, Balaam's ass, your ass or my ass was involved, the truth of the whole matter is Proverbs 19:21: ***"Many plans are in the human heart, but the advice of the LORD will endure"*** (God's Word translation). Can you please admit the only book that has endured over centuries, millenniums, and many generations? Go ahead and say it slowly so that it will sink in firmly: the HOLY BIBLE!

It does not matter to God if you have a liberation theology, a "Jesus only" doctrine, or an "anything-goes" type of religion. The common denominator is still Leviticus 11:44: ***"For I am the Lord your God: ye shall therefore sanctify yourselves, and ye shall be holy: for I am holy"*** ... It has been said that omnipotence is His arm; omniscience is His eye. But holiness is His beauty. Out of all of God's attributes, He wants to be recognized for His holiness. The whole problem with many of us Black folks is that we are looking for an excuse to fulfill the lust of the flesh. If you don't want to live holy anymore, then, go to hell at your own expense. Don't look for rationalizations to denounce Jesus and lead other folks to hell with you.

In the New Testament, 1 Peter 1:16 says: ***"Because it is written, Be ye holy; for I am holy." "For God did not call us to be impure, but to live a holy life"*** (1 Thes. 4:7 NIV). God did not backslide, and neither did He change His mind about HOLINESS! In the KJV, holy is mentioned over 600 times, with 21 verses that include the word, holi**ness**. Whether you say you are a Christian, or you're just "spiritual," the big question is: Are you living HOLY? He instructed us, "children of Israel," to put difference between holy and unholy, and between unclean and clean (Lev. 10:10). "Israelites," "please don't hang up on me now." In the next chapter, I'm about to reveal to you who you really are, with your smart **"ass**-et". That's the real truth that's been hidden from you!

The point of the matter is this: Satan's attempt is to discredit present truths through leaders who have the ability to influence God's agenda. Whose report are you going to believe? Due to unconfronted error, Dr. Matthew Stevenson markedly contributes to the next section that was incorporated due to the urgency of the current season. After emphasizing that many of our leaders are not marked by spiritual fruit but by "nuts and flakes," "hear ye," the Word of the LORD.

THE SPIRIT OF ERROR

Since I am not as theologically astute as I would like to be, here is Dr. Stevenson's biblical support on this topic. Matthew 22:29 teaches us that when you don't know the Scriptures and/or the power of God, you "err" and open your life, your church, and your family up to the spirit of error. You either know more about the Word of God than the power of God. Or, you know more about the power of God than you know about the Word of God. If you are disjointed and you have more biblical information than supernatural power, you are going to open up to the spirit of error. If you are somebody who has more of the operation of the Spirit and demonstration (the power of God), and you don't have an equal marriage of the Spirit **and** the Word, the fire **and** the water, the blood **and** the wine, you are also going to open up your life to the spirit of error.

Unfortunately, in many streams around the world, most people are known for one and have no clue about the other. The bi-product is that their entire ministry model and/or philosophy have the spirit of error running through it. Deception drips into you like an IV from a hospital; it comes little by little. That's how deception works; it comes in measures, in frequencies, and in portions. It is never enough to be immediately seen by the discerning eye, but it is always just enough to come in and find areas of compromise in what you believe. The Word cautions us to be careful of the leaven of the Pharisees (Mt. 16:6).

Generally speaking, the vast majority of the Body of Christ has very inconsistent beliefs. We know everything about blessings but very little about curses. We know everything about angels but very little about demons. We know everything about Jesus but very little about the Holy Spirit. Because of our disjointed and out-of-balanced theologies that govern the whole of our churches and the whole of our Christian experiences, what you find in operation is the spirit of error.

In 1 Kings 22:22, the kings were seeking clarity about a certain war issue and wanted to evade the prophet whom God wanted them to consult. As a result, a lying spirit stood before the LORD, and said that he would go forth and be a lying spirit in the mouths of all of His prophets. In 2 Chronicles 18:21, this lying spirit that came out from the presence of God was enticing and prevailed in causing calamity and confusion. Because the lying spirit created the same fruit as the spirit of error, they could be related. If you are going to perpetrate such an error that people are born gay and that there is no deliverance for them, you should at least, blame it on the devil or the sin that tainted this world because of Adam's disobedience.

Since I am addressing this particular spokesperson, may I also add that "all roads do NOT lead to Heaven!" Jesus, who is the visible reality of an invisible God, says in John 14:6 that He is **the** way and the truth and the life, and the only way to the Father is through Him. The God of the Holy Bible is more of a complex Creature than your logical mind could ever give Him credit for. God, in all of His essence is too major for His minor creation [us]. How do you even have the nerve to defy the truth that's responsible for being the very foundation of your existence? And how can you even challenge the very nature of a God that's everywhere at the same time? He has no geographical boundaries. You can't even go to Him because He's already there! He doesn't have a future because He is simply, "I am."

When a people challenge what we know as the Word of God, it is a reflection of their defiance, but it also confirms that only sinful people defend sin. Do not allow what's between your legs to defile your logic. As a matter of fact, LUST HAS NO LOGIC! Just because your manhood has been breached and broken, do not attempt to reduce God down to your standards, or develop a mentality that's built around the trenches of your condition. Even if homosexuality is not your issue, but you are promoting this kind of image, I agree with whoever voiced the following sentiments: "Don't you dare shrink yourself for someone else's comfort. Do not become small for people who refuse to grow."

The most genius strategy of Satan is to make sure that there is a communication variant and a communication breech between Heaven and Earth. God was not the only one with a purpose for your life. Spiritual identity theft is when Satan keeps you from seeing, finding, or fulfilling your God-given purpose. He knows that if he is going to advance his agenda, he has to use deception to distort your purpose. The secret weapon that Satan uses to foster his strategy is to make sure that the "head" is in a "tailspin."

"There is a reason why he chose to act as a serpent to use in his act of deception. This particular beast of the field reminded him of himself. *Subtle* in the Hebrew spoke volumes of his outstanding characteristics: cunning, crafty, prudent, smoothness, and the ability to charm. The serpent, on behalf of Satan, gave no formal introduction. After he begins his conversation as if they already knew each other, he immediately started to accuse God of being selfish. He has not changed; he is just as subtle today" (Thomas, 2017). "Hey 'Adam,' 'where you at'? Do NOT fall for the 'okie-doke!' Take a stand and be the man!"

"So God created man in His own image, in the image of God created he Him; male and female created He them" (Gen. 1:27). Procreation was distorted by sin; that's why it becomes necessary to become born again. Then, after you're born again, my brother, Bishop Brandon B. Porter says you still need to grow up. *"But grow in grace, and in the knowledge of our Lord and Saviour Jesus Christ"…* (2 Pet. 3:18a). *"Therefore leaving the principles of the doctrine of Christ, let us go on to perfection"…* (Heb. 6:1). Grow up saints! Come out of churches that will not put pressure on you to change. Pastor, if you are still submitting to your genitals, or whatever your cravings are, you are not truly God's priest. So you shouldn't be representing Him before a crowd that's trying to get to know Him. You should never try to convince the public to try something that's not working for you. The proof of an effective Gospel is a changed life!

Per Dr. Stevenson, it was never God's intention for you to get a dumb license and a religious collar and bring your humanity into your mandate. Well, since it was alleged that he was a homosexual, someone asked how could King James properly interpret the Holy Bible? My first question is: Was he a king, or was he a priest? Furthermore, if he was worried about exposure and protecting his reputation, why would he have interpreted Leviticus 20:12 to say what it said? ***"If a man also lie with mankind, as he lieth with a woman, both of them have committed an abomination."*** If he was as desensitized to sin as we are today, don't you think that he would have reduced the Word of God to cheap grace messages that flaunt sexual sins in an effort to defend his own personal lifestyle, just as leaders do today? I feel that in his God-inspired wisdom, he conveyed the message that "sin is sin; no matter who it's in."

Thus, King James gives rise to my idea that if God could use Balaam's dumb jackass to save him from premature death (Num. 22:21-35), surely he could use a "smart-ass" to save us from eternal damnation! In Numbers 23, He even put a Word in the mouth of a sorcerer. Even so, in confronting "the elephant in the room," I apologize if my freedom of speech is ever offensive, but for me to tolerate you, you must tolerate me! If you have the freedom to change God's Word, surely, I have the freedom to defend His Word. Besides, how can teaching the fear of the LORD offend His people? I'm trying to protect your integrity! As I was born for the time when I am needed the most, I came on the scene to tell you that truth is never defamation! Never!

To the person who claims that one sin is no bigger than the other, 1 John 5:17 provide a better explanation. ***"All unrighteousness is sin: and there is a sin not unto death."*** Not to dismiss anyone's arguments, but here is my hermeneutic analysis of this text so that one can derive a correct understanding. Indeed, ALL unrighteousness is sin, but not all sins are equal. In the natural, just as you have felonies and misdemeanors, you may not suffer the same consequences for the misdemeanor. Yet, you are still liable to find yourself in the same cell with the one who committed the felony. "Hello Zion!" Either way, you will still have a record! But before we can deal with Adam and Steve, we must first deal with Adam and Eve. "Hey 'Adam,' 'where you at?' I'm 'gonna' need you to take a stand and be the man!"

Have you ever wondered why people are apprehensive of coming out of the "closet?" Let me go ahead and "put the shoe on the right foot." It is due to abomination and abhorrence, conflict and confusion, defiance and disobedience, rebelliousness and reproach, and nonconformity and noncompliance to the Word of God. Of course, all of this definitely brings about condemnation! When people are intimidated by contradiction, they will be apprehensive to be in opposition. But now that man's law has made an attempt to change God's Word, the restrictions have been removed. What does that say for America and for the Church?

For the Church, it says that you cannot judge America for what you have no authority over in the church. The Body of Christ has no authority to help change laws on homosexual matters when she has flaming homosexuals on the worship team and leading the youth department. What you don't have authority over in the House, you won't have authority over outside the House. What is says for America is that she is in SERIOUS trouble, especially with the recent election that has everyone in an all-out uproar.

Believe it or not, God has a way of ultimately showing us who is still in command. We may not have any cards left, but God is about to play His hand and show us that He is still God of the game. According to Stevenson (2017), He has saved His best move for 2017: the year of divine justice in America. The court system of Heaven is at attention, and we are about to see God as Judge (read Isa. 28:17 New American Standard Version). This is going to be a "Joseph" year whereas God is about to equalize the affairs of the earth and take back His rainbow. After the recent "no-holes-barred" effort to legalize same-sex marriage, watch how He demonstrates a righteous hatred that is connected to His holiness.

Rather than marching and protesting, you had better find yourself turning up your prayer life, particularly since this generation is determined to "turn up." The truth of the matter is: you will never find peace until you find the Prince of Peace. He did not say that He was one of the ways; He said: "I am THE way!" (John 14:6). In order to be convicted that sin is wrong, you must first be convinced that the Word of God is right! Here is the realization in the central concept of this qualitative inquiry. When God took the rib out of man, He took ALL of the woman OUT of him! "Did you hear what I had just said?" He placed that rib into a separate body and made the distinction between male and female.

Even when people feel that they were born "gay," perhaps, they were. I will go ahead and give them that. Besides, you have the right to be wrong. Yet, to a significant degree, we were all born with proclivities and propensities, and tendencies toward certain sins because even David confessed to being shapen in iniquity (Psa. 51:5). However, it champions the reason why Jesus went to the cross. He went to become the curse for us (Gal. 3:13), in order that we could become born AGAIN. You no longer have to deal with the curse of having been shapen in iniquity and conceived in sin. Go ahead and ask me why. *"Therefore if any man be in Christ, he is a new creature: old things are passed away; behold, all things are become new"* (2 Cor. 5:17).

I don't mean to "ruffle your feathers" or put a damper on your spirit. But I'm sorry, "Boo-Boo," the divine plan of God was to give the man of God a MANDATE – not a man **to** date. The mandate is found in Ephesians 5:28: *"So ought men to love their wives as their own bodies, He that loveth his wife loveth himself."* The last time I checked, the wife was a "WO-man," a man with a womb. In principle, if you do not have a womb, you cannot be a "WO-man" or a wife. According to Stevenson (2016), "The plumbing prophesies the purpose. If you don't know what you're supposed to be, look at your private. God gave you the hardware that you needed for your purpose!" You don't need a divine revelation to figure out what your purpose is. The doctor called you what you were, based on what he saw! If the devil didn't create you, he sure can't reinvent you.

Therefore, you do not have the right to be upset with God; He is not the culprit here. So how can you call good evil and evil good? Yes, Paul was given a thorn, but he did not ask God the question that many of us ask: "Why did you make me like this?" He asked God to remove the thorn, but God declined by virtue of the fact that His grace was sufficient. As also indicated by Stevenson (2016), homosexuality is not a thorn anyway. It's a thing that you love more than God. It's an obsession that you love spending time with more than Him. It has become like a roommate who's been in your life so long that you don't know life without it. If you ask God to remove it, what He's going to do is give you the grace to remove it yourself. The reason that He does not remove homosexuality is that He did not give it to you. Thus, you must do the work yourself; however, the longer you ignore the chance to repent, the harder it gets to turn.

When God told Paul, "My grace is sufficient for you," He was basically saying, "I have given you grace. I don't take thorns out. I didn't take a thorn off My Son, so what makes you think that I'm going to take a thorn off you?" It's your job to repent and change your number. It's your job to come out of that church that's making victims out of people who are going to make more victims out of other people. God's grace is sufficient for you, but it's your job to leave that choir that's a contributing factor to your behavior. Grace is NOT TIME to PROLONG your REPENTANCE! It's the supernatural ability that God gives to a human to do what a normal human could not do otherwise. It is by that supernatural power that you achieve the right to get rid of what the DEVIL has afflicted you with (Stevenson, 2016). That's why God specifically instructed me to listen to, *Empty.* Otherwise, we would have missed that "raw footage!"

Hey "ADAM," let me go ahead and sound like I'm trying to better myself, for once; where are you now, my dear sir? Even as we are often products of our environments, we must not change our identity based on our current condition. And even if we did, we have the power to change our environments in order to become new creatures. Whatever odor the enemy has left on you, or whatever scent that man has picked up on you, the blood of Jesus has the power to wash it off and clean you up as though it was never there. Then, you can go along with me; "Yes I did it, but the blood covered it!" When God made coats of skin to cover Adam and Eve's nakedness, it indicates that as a result of the Lamb that was slain from the world's foundation, their sins would not only be covered. Their sins would also be blotted out, taken away, and canceled (Gen. 3:21).

It's kind of like going to a hotel and sleeping on sheets that may have been infested with bedbugs, or contaminated with germs, or even infectious diseases. You don't know what kind of unclean spirits have slept on those sheets or under those comforters. Because you trust the procedure that the linen has been properly and carefully washed and sanitized, you tend to block the negative thoughts out of your consciousness. Spiritually so, when your sins have been washed, covered, and blotted out by the blood, God blocks them out of His mind and remembers them no more. In Isaiah 43:25, He says, *"I even I, am He that blotteth out thy transgressions for Mine own sake, and will not remember your sins."* Also read Psalm 103:12 & Micah &:19.

I am not sure how you ended up where you are, and I most definitely can empathize with your violation, situation, or your devastation because I was once tainted myself. In actual fact, I can personally witness to pain that has not been confronted. It leads to lust and/or addiction; and, as in so many cases, it's probably not even your fault. IF your sexual orientation is an issue for you, it may likely be a learned behavior. Whatever the case, do not allow recidivism to pollute today's "appetite" with yesterday's "leftovers." Moreover, do not allow the perpetrator to hold you captive to the abuse that has been inflicted upon you against your will. Whatever people did to you, you have the power to avoid doing it to yourself or someone else. What you do from here is now your responsibility, "by not giving your power of transformation to the perpetrator" (Jakes, 2016).

2 Corinthians 6:17 may be helpful in demystifying this process: *"Wherefore come out from among them, and be ye separate, saith the Lord, and touch not the unclean thing; and I will receive you."* Even as my God (the same God that had purpose for Adam and Eve after the fall) is both a divine Healer and a strong Deliverer, change does not come to half-hearted individuals. You must make a conscious decision to change whatever you are doing that still has you where you are. You may even have to make some choices between opposing solutions that leave you feeling like you will never be able to reconcile your own mind, let alone the situation itself.

Someone proposed that the 3 C's of life are choices, chances, and changes; you must make a choice to take a chance, or your life will never change. This proposal may not seem like much confirmation to support moving ahead, but do not listen to your feelings. Your feelings do not know your future. Yes, there is a lot of confusion on the details, but here is the anecdote to your woes, fears, and challenges: *"Stand fast therefore in the liberty wherewith Christ hath made us free, and be not entangled again with the yoke of bondage"* (Gal. 5:1).

"He whom the Son sets free is free indeed!" (John 8:36). Replace the lie with the truth and rehearse it until it becomes your reality.

Taking into account the politically-loaded challenges of sexual orientation in our culture today, I would never intentionally impose my values on anyone in a demeaning or dehumanizing way. While the church needs to learn the difference between evangelizing and antagonizing, it is out of character for us to insult the people that we hope to inspire. However, since Christianity and/or religion are viewed as significant factors in human functioning, I am simply upholding the moral and ethical guidelines of the Holy Bible and the principles and standards that it has instructed us to live by. Even though the Bible is no longer the nation's foundation for the moral fabric of our society, still, the moral grandeur of the real Christians is the factor that keeps God's hand of protection on us as a whole. When our nation embraces sin as a whole, we will ultimately lose the protection of God all together. When we don't invite Him in, He stays out.

There is a much bigger picture than what you see at the outset. Now that we have tipped over from a God-dominated mindset to an ungodly one, there will definitely be attacks on our freedom of religion and on our free will to fight for the cause of Christ. As one law opens the door for the next, don't be surprised at what's "coming down the pike." The clock is ticking for the countdown of the Lord's return. At any rate, I pray that the future impact of this project will serve to instill such a profound sense of masculine identity and commitment to womanhood that it provides the momentum necessary for you to THINK LIKE GOD AND ACT LIKE A MAN! In my southern colloquial, "come on 'y'all,' let's get back to Eden, and live on top of the world" (Donald Lawrence).

You may have ended up in some negative situations; it's okay. Because you were made in God's image, you are being developed and must not accept defeat. When God brings you out of the "darkroom," you will see exactly what He IMAGINED when He created you. In your process of ultimately becoming the finished product, the question is: Who are you? Just in case you may be experiencing some image issues, allow me to expand this chapter by adding a last minute, sneak preview of a coming attraction.

CHAPTER FIVE

HEY BLACK MAN, "WHITE-IT-OUT!" TAKE YOUR PLACE AND RESTORE YOUR RACE

THE SNEAK PEAK

Allow me to preface this "coming attraction" by informing you that due to timing and space restraints and new revelations, this chapter is intended to be the Introduction for Part Two of this book. After reviewing a number of additional ideas, I want to begin by sharing with you a moving example of what Yahspeople.com has to say about Esau and Jacob. We often quote, "God, the Father of Abraham, Isaac, and Jacob (Acts 3:13) because we agree that God made a covenant with them, and from them came the 12 Tribes, right? But have you ever considered why Esau was not included? After all, he was the twin brother to Jacob; were they not **both** the sons of the same Isaac? "Hmm..." We may be on to something here; let's go ahead and set the tone for yet, another mystery.

"And the LORD God formed man of the dust of the ground" (Gen. 2:7a). Cure (n.d.) of Yahspeople.com said that the last they looked, the ground is different shades of brown. Would this be an indication that God formed Adam of a particular hue? Hue is where we get the word, "human" – meaning man of hue or color. Dictionary. com defines the word human as being dark or dark brown. While many of us are of the opinion that America is one big melting pot of

no color lines, the Most High had somewhat of a different impression of people who lack hue or pigmentation or melanin. If you are familiar with the struggle between Esau and Jacob, maybe you will be able to relate to what I am about to present. If you think that we have already treaded through some "deep waters," you may need some new "boots" for this one.

When Rebekah inquired of the LORD, she wanted to know that if He had blessed her, why was there so much trouble or disorder in her pregnancy. *"And the children struggled together within her"... And the LORD said unto her, Two nations are in thy womb, and two manner of people shall be separated from thy bowels* [these two sons would be the progenitors of two separate nations/two manner of people]*; and the one people* [Israel] *shall be stronger than the other people* [Edomites]*; and the elder* [Esau] *shall serve the younger* [Israel; the elder serving the younger will happen again in history as a promise of the Most High to the Israelites]. *And the first came out red, all over like an hairy garment; and they called his name Esau"* (Gen. 25:22a, 23&25 with emphasis added).

There is no universal consensus here, but does that not sound like the first White man to you? As I am holding on to what stands out as core and eliminating details that will present some interesting theories here, I never set out to "color" this book with racism. So no offense; my only intention here is to expose my people to their real Black history and their true identity – who they are and who they are not. Really, I had no clue that this book would even evolve into this particular chapter. Even with coming up with the book title itself, it was just something in me that wanted to avoid sounding both politically and grammatically correct. And here we are now, after six years of explicit efforts that this book has developed into a whole, new paradigm.

It happens to be at a time when God is definitely exposing superiority and hegemony amongst our White Christian leaders through the 2016 Presidential election between Donald Trump and Hilary Clinton. How can Christian Evangelicals "publicly" support someone for the oval office who mocks and insults minorities? As this election campaign has been one, big "side show," the obvious motivation is that this successful businessman represents their "die-hard" Republican values that do not support or promote the Negro "Jews." Keep reading, and I'll show you.

"Enthusiasm for a candidate like Trump gives our neighbors ample reason to doubt that we believe Jesus is Lord," Christianity Today Editorial Director, Andy Crouch (2016) wrote. "They see that some of us are so self-interested and so self-protective, that we will alley ourselves with someone who violates all that is sacred to us." In my opinion, "ESAU" is still determined to come out "head-first," and "by any means necessary." It's no wonder that Matthew 20:16a says: ***"So the last shall be first, and the first last"*** ... Come on "Jacob;" it's your turn, and it's your time! "Take a stand and be the man!"

In another recent article, *It's Embarrassing to Be an Evangelical This Election. The So-Called "Evangelical" Vote Has Some Explaining to Do,* Wallis (2016) claims: "Any Gospel that is not good news to the poor is simply not the Gospel of Jesus Christ. The mission statement of Jesus in Luke 4 has almost nothing to do with the voting practices of White Evangelicals in this [2016] election year." Yet, society expects Black folks (with their gullible selves) to swallow anything that they are fed by the White man. Generally, the only thing most White, mega ministries want from us is our financial support. Look at their board members and the leaders that run their churches. The fruit is in their root. God gave Obadiah a vision concerning Edom (the proposed White race), which I feel is taking place even now, particularly as it relates to Donald Trump. Due to the political implications here, it is imperative that you read Obadiah 1:2-6.

Anytime your theology or your doctrine is not sound and does not match the Word of God, it takes you into an illusion. Nevertheless, the only folks that are nervous are those who are not submitted to the protocols of the Kingdom. When my sister, "Shannon," tried to convince me to leave Dallas early to go home and vote (in an effort to help keep Trump out), my response was: "My trust is not in Trump," or even in my already-insufficient, disability check. Then, when I was channel surfing one night, I paused at Bishop Joseph Walker's telecast (for the first time), just in time to hear him say: "Don't confuse your strategy with His sovereignty. Just when you think you got me labeled, God will adjust the results." That was for me!

This is what the Word has to say about Trump's kind: ***"Go to now, ye rich men, weep and howl for your miseries that shall come upon you. Your riches are corrupted and your garments are moth-eaten. Your gold and silver is cankered; and the rust of them shall be a witness against you, and shall eat your flesh as it were fire. Ye have heaped treasure together for the last days"*** (James 1:1-3). Therefore, I'm not worried about who's in office in 2017; it's the year that my breakthrough is on **God's** calendar. For starters, my birthday falls on the 17th day of January. Oh, did I neglect to inform you that 17 is the biblical number for victory?

IF God's grace allows me to continue to press forward, 2017 should be my year to graduate with my last degree. And ironically, this is the year that I will regard 17 years as a self-published author, who has unfortunately spent over $30,000, writing and rewriting projects that never left the ground. I'm not sure who coined this phrase, but it stands to reason: "Faith that has not been tested cannot be trusted." If everything was quick and easy, there would be no need for faith. Before God gave Abraham a son to enjoy for a lifetime, he used faith to put a knife to his dream.

Even if the seed came from a dead womb, the Word is still alive. And even if the seed dies, the promise is still good. Likewise, God has made me some promises that He must make good. As mentioned in Trilogy-Part Three: "The significant point is: whenever God sends a Word or a promise, He is not afraid to put it into a dead womb. God's Word is so powerful that the infertility of the womb will not negate the intensity of His Word" (Reid, 2010). Thus, as a sign of my due season, I am going to "rebirth" and "remix" this "baby" until my victory goes viral.

I know that we have believed for years that each New Year was "THE YEAR;" while most years, I cried the old one out and the new one in. Nonetheless, it is a matter of faith and warring for what you believe. God has to teach us how to use what's on us in order to get out of us what He has invested in us. "Faith is taking the first step even when you don't see the whole staircase" (Martin Luther King, Jr.) Hence, as I publish this book by faith and not by sight, you will soon see that this is my year, my season, my time, and my turn. "You heard me?" "Faith doesn't make things easy; it makes things possible" (Bible Studies). Just by the mere fact that you purchased the book is a good sign. "Thank you for that!"

I feel like the man of God who answered Amaziah, in 2 Chronicles 25:9 (with emphasis added): ***"The Lord is able to give thee much more than this."*** [according to Eph. 3:20, God is not into fixed incomes]! SOMETIMES, HE HAS TO RAISE UP "PHARAOH" JUST TO SHOW HIS POWER! ***"For the Scripture saith unto Pharaoh, Even for this same purpose have I raised thee up, that I might shew My power in thee, and that My name might be declared throughout all the earth"*** (Rom. 9:17). Here is what happened to the Pharaoh of that day and what will happen to the Pharaoh/Presidents of our day: ***"Pride goeth before destruction, and an haughty spirit before a fall,"*** thus saith Proverbs 16:18. "Put that in your pipe and smoke it."

I know somebody that is much more powerful than the President, and who can destroy both soul and body, so continue with caution. The immutable reality is found in Ephesians 6:12: ***"For we wrestle not against flesh and blood, but against principalities, against powers, against the rulers of the darkness of this world, against spiritual wickedness in high places."*** "Nevertheless-although-even so," ***"I will lift up mine eyes unto the hills, from whence cometh my help. My help cometh from the LORD, which made Heaven and Earth"*** (Psa. 121:1-2). For those of us who are true believers, the oval office is not our higher power. While my focus remains Esau and Jacob, rather than Trump and Clinton, it is important here that in correcting our prejudices and setting them aside, we must have an ear to hear what the Spirit is saying.

Genesis 25:22-25 seems to speak volumes about why the White man has aggressively and consistently fought to be first. A reasonable assumption is that since the birth of Esau and Jacob (if it could be proven that Esau was truly the first White man), the struggle has never ended. A major issue to consider is that the White nation is seen as conspirators who attempt to persecute the Black people and hide their true identity as Israelites. Yet, I cannot wrap my mind around why they would want our big boobs, big butts, big lips, and dark skin.

Although I have never considered myself to be prejudice, there are certain feelings that are just uniform across populations. We have failed adequately to consider the excerpt that follows: "For years, through religious doctrines, renaissance art and pictures that depict White people in scenes from the Bible, the world has been led to believe that the people of the Bible were White. In the face of biblical evidence to prove the contrary and with the truth finally beginning to emerge, there are still those amongst Black people who continue to remain in spiritual bondage and cling to this lie" (Real Israelites, 2006). "White-it-out," Black man! Take your place and restore your race!

Have you ever noticed that Jacob's color was never mentioned in the previous passage of Scripture? Was that on purpose, or was Esau's red color explicitly mentioned for some distinctive reasoning? As influenced by my research, I also get the vague sense that maybe it could be that Jacob's color most resembled his father and mother and all of the other people on the earth since the time of Adam? Yet again, did Genesis 2:7 not point out that man was formed from the dust of the ground, which suggests that the Most High shaped man with hue or color in mind. Since He designed man to have pigment, it is not ironic that Black people uniquely come in all shades of brown. That could be why they <u>enviously</u> named us "Colored" people.

God even arranged for the Black man to make his own Vitamin D when his body is directly exposed to the sun. Ask me why. He created and formed melanin to synthesize the sun's rays to help the man of color to flourish. On the contrary, since very few foods naturally contain Vitamin D, the proposed White man (Esau) has to have foods that are fortified with Vitamin D. Fortified means that vitamins have been added to food to supply the Vitamin D daily needs. In other words, people of color or with melanin get their Vitamin D by the sun through the skin. Since the red man is lacking in Vitamin D and cannot process the sun properly, too much sun on his skin produces skin cancer (Cure, nd).

While every nationality and tribe of the earth has color except the Caucasian, one logical assumption that most people can agree with is that they must tan to look like everyone else. So why was "Esau" created? Why was he born different? What is his purpose? In

Genesis 25:26-27, Jacob was a plain man who dwelled in tents; Esau was a **cunning** hunter. As a red man and the eldest son of Isaac, his descendents (the Edomites or the red nations) were created to be an enemy to the Children of Israel. God gave these Europeans and Caucasians the strength and power to rule the world, but in the end they will be destroyed.

God loved Jacob but hated Esau (read Mal. 1:1-4); so, was He being biased or prejudiced toward the red, hairy man who lacked melanin in his skin? No, I can be a bit more diplomatic than that. Maybe God "preferred" Jacob or chose one over the other for some purpose or another. Later, the Edomites must have taken offence to God making a difference between Esau and Jacob. Even dogs can sense when they are not loved. To oppose what God chose and to hate what God loves could possibly be the conspiracy that ultimately led to slavery? Wow, I received that revelation coming out of Dollar Tree. Imagine if I were coming out of Macys. L☺L

Otherwise, how could one nation depict such hatred and envy and jealous over another nation, just because of the color of their skin? Eventually leading to what we know today as the Ku Klux Klan, this one White supremacy group focused on opposing the Civil Rights movement, and even called for the "purification" of American society. Something to ponder; right? "The reason why the Klans wear hoods is that when they are done, they go back to being your doctors, your lawyers, your governors, your police officers, your senators, your teachers, your judges, your co-workers, etc." (origin unknown). Because of God's plan for the people He preferred, my question is: Was the struggle between Esau and Jacob, more over power because we had purpose? Wow!

Unfortunately, the Black man is oblivious to his God-given purpose. Since the White man knows that we were fearfully and wonderfully made, they capitalize and become billionaires off of our ignorance. We are the salt of the earth, creative and full of zeal; that's why we are so hated. Just to refresh your memory, the following inventions were invented by Blacks: potato chips, the mailbox, the blood bank, refrigerated trucks, laser cataract surgery, traffic lights, closed circuit television, 3D special effects, air conditioning unit, auto cut-off switch, hair brush, guitar, gas mask, folding chair/bed, fire extinguisher, fire escape ladder, elevator, door stop/knob, clothes dryer, the Almanac, baby buggy, curtain rod/support, the touch-tone phone, including caller ID, not to even mention NASA's Black Female Scientists. "Now what!?!"

Until we learn to stop being ignorant to who we are, "the haves" will always have it because they will keep bleeding the "have-nots" to keep it. Not only do we lack knowledge, Black folks reject knowledge and are destroyed because of it (Hos. 4:6). Even when White folks hate each other, the one thing that they'll have in common is that they don't like you. What Black folks have in common is the "Napoleon complex" (the little guy syndrome). "If it 'ain't' White, it 'ain't' right."

Allow me to address the validity of this rebuke. We spark intimidation from the other nations because they realize that if we ever get over our identity crisis and have a unity revival, we will be a force to reckon with. The only thing that stopped those Black folks from building the tower of Babel was their inability to understand and communicate. They were so close to invading God's personal space that He had to come see for Himself (Gen. 11:5). Before He was forced to confuse their language, He probably wondered if He had created a monster.

We are just that powerful; yet, we can't get "turned on and turned up" in a productive way because we have given the White man the "remote control" to our lives who has turned us off to our purpose. Rather, he has our eye gate channel turned to Criminal Minds. He has our ear gate channel set to the kind of rap music that promotes "niggatism" instead of God's wisdom. He has our mouth gate channel turned to fast food restaurants to keep us eating "carbs" and sugary foods that contribute to early death, and at minimum, keeps us unhealthy and always overweight. Our bodies were not made for that!

That's why God put the first man in a garden, and he lived to be 930 years old, even after he had sinned. *"And God said, Behold, I have given you every herb bearing seed, which is upon the face of all the earth, and every tree, in the which is the fruit of a tree yielding seed; to you it shall be for meat"* (Gen. 1:29). Then, after the flood, the Lord said: ... *"Yet his days shall be an hundred and twenty years"* (Gen. 6:3). When our ancestors continued to live from the garden, they lived much longer and suffered fewer diseases than we do today. Ever since the White man started producing chemically-processed foods, they have been killing us off in record numbers. Rather than bringing our bodies under subjection, we rebuke cancer when we should have been binding that hog maw and chitterlings demon. Sometimes it's too late to bind "diabe-tes," after you have built up a tolerance for "Wen-dy's." And then we wonder why cancer has become such an epidemic. It's not the devil; it's what we are feeding our bodies.

The first time that I actually heard the level of wisdom that's being presented in this chapter, actually being taught in a church setting was while I was in the middle of concluding this chapter. Revelation knowledge is hidden from many of our ministers because they pervert the Gospel with their own act of **self-will**. Some require contracts and first class reservations and multiplied thousands of dollars before they will even think about keeping their commitment to serve God's people. "Really?" What about 1 Corinthians 9:18-19? *"What is my reward then? Verily that, when I preach the Gospel, I may make the Gospel of Christ without charge, that I abuse not my power in the Gospel. For though I be free from all men, yet have I made myself servant unto all, that I might gain the more."*

I am determined to complete this revision today, as of December 31, 2016, but I just woke up with one last assertion in my spirit. It irritates me when I see young, able-bodied, "novice" pastors with 10 members and a grandiose spirit, refuse to find a job and provide for their own family. Yet, they will get an attitude with the saints whom they likely owe money to, for not supporting them, and offended at God for not "raining" miracle money down from Heaven to support their "lazy" habit of doing nothing that counts for something.

Then, if they happen to die without life insurance, which is one of the main reasons why they should have taken their lazy behinds to work, the widow has to depend on family and church folks to scramble up money, just to send them back to the dirt, while it looks like they're laying peacefully in the casket saying, "Thanks 'y'all' for 'footing' my six-foot bill." That "ain't" God; He does things decently and in order (1 Cor. 14:40). I don't care how well you can preach, if your gift does not afford you health or life insurance, you need to go out and find a JOB.

While I was waiting for my publishing consultant to finalize my contract, Dr. Stevenson validated my contention at his 2017 Fire Conference. He said that the problem is: our preachers don't want to strive for mastery (1 Cor. 9:25). Rather, they want to experiment on God's people; so, they quit their full-time jobs and hurry up and go full-time ministry, when they have not perfected their "preach." Instead of working a part-time job until they have a full-time "preach," they make you pay for their cell phone bills and take care of their kids. "P☺W!" While you're too lazy to strive for mastery, the point is: you must become a master before you deserve to be paid!

Whenever you master something, you're able to do it on demand, and you're able to do it perfectly in non-conducive environments, and in every season and for every reason. The LORD has not called you to something that He has not intended you to master. Otherwise, you abuse your power in the Gospel when you allow the ministry to become your personal industry, or your franchise, or your family dynasty. "WE ARE NOT HERE TO MAKE UP FOR YOUR MANHOOD because you believe that the Anointing on your life is bigger than a 9 to 5!" (Stevenson, 2017). "Now what?" Okay, it is now January 17, and it's my birthday! Finally, I just received an email that my contract was finalized (on my birthday). So that means that I won't be listening to any more of Dr. Stevenson's scopes before this book is sent to the "delivery room."

Here is where I left off before I was expediently interrupted by Dr. Stevenson, who is obviously one of my teachers in this season. If you are in ministry for somebody to take care of you, you are not even worthy to feed God's sheep. Get out of the ministry and hang up your mantra. Jesus asked His disciples: ... *"Lovest thou Me more than these?"* ... (John 21:16a). IF you were called, God called you to take care of the sheep; He never called sheep to take care of the shepherd. "Umph!" The sheep depend on you; you depend on EloHIM. And if HIM does not come through for you, it's not the them that you should be irritated with. Wait a minute; I know that I have gone off point again, but since you guys have not read my Trilogy, let me go back and borrow an excerpt that I wrote years ago, in Part Three. It's powerful. Watch this:

"Do you realize why the widow woman in 2 Kings 4:1, had nothing saved but a pot of oil? Yes, she **was** married to a prophet who had a vision for the people of God. Yet, he was unable to see the necessity of insuring his family, so that when he died, his wife would not be begging. The widow's husband, Obadiah, had a tremendous ministry, but he was considered as a minor prophet, probably because his legacy did not outlast his life. A real man will make it hard for the next man coming along. I may miss you after you're gone, but if you leave me with the right inheritance to remind me of your **diligence**, your legacy will help me to get over my sorrow. If you leave me with nothing, it gives me two reasons to mourn: you were sorry while you were alive, and now I'm broke because you were sorry. [WJW, that's deep]

Dead or alive, man of God – make sure that your name spells, 'VICTORY.' It is twice as hard on the family when they have to go through the grief of losing their 'priest.' Then, to be forced to raise money to bury their provider that did not care enough about his family to invest in their well-being is just awful. No insurance policy, no retirement plan, no annuities, no investment account, no mutual funds, not even your own house – nothing left but your clothes and some children for somebody else to take care of. Because nine times out of ten, if you were too lazy to work, your wife was too" (Reid, 2010). If any part of this book ever irritates you, just remember I'm on a mission; then, take Communion, and you should be fine.

While temporarily living in Dallas, I took a "stab in the dark" from a last minute internet search and chose to attend Greater Gospel Kingdom C.O.G.I.C. in Ft. Worth, Texas. The divine connection and monumental Word by Elder Jakari Bryant Edmunds was proof positive that my steps had been ordered to the right place at the right time. He discussed intriguing implications and outcomes emerging from my previous analysis. Consequently, the information was so confounding that the "stone-faced" look on one of the Elder's face and his lack of support, made him look like he was "stupidfied" and "STUCK on stupid."

Sorry to say, while most church folks are used to "sipping and sopping up spiritual soup," they freeze and frown on real "meat." Dr. R. A. Vernon said that "y'all" shout on ignorance and sit on substance. Even as the Elder was well-dressed and "kind of" distinctive looking, his demeanor made me feel like slapping him back into reality. Under an extremely, heavy Anointing, God must have sent me there to be the speaker's "cheerleader." On the same, exact page as I was in this chapter, one of the things that really moved me was his elucidation of Genesis 18:17-18: *"And the LORD said, Shall I hide from Abraham that thing which I do; Seeing that Abraham shall surely become a great and mighty nation, and all the nations of the earth shall be blessed in him?"*

In accordance with this Scripture, can you guess who's blessed off Black folks? As per Elder Jakari, the Chinese people are blessed off us because they make money off our wigs and weaves. The Arabs are blessed off us because they make money off our gas purchases. White folks are blessed off us by taking advantage of us socially, communally, economically, politically, and in any other way they can. Everybody is blessed off of us except us. Since the government actually recognizes how unique we are, they deliberately reduce us to living off of EBT, government cheese, welfare, and disability. The government does not expect us to prosper. So why should its officials change the policies when the majority of the nation's profits come from Black people?

As indicated by Elder Jakari, former President Bill Clinton locked up more Black men than any other president in the history of this country. And Hilary Clinton admitted that she likes the works of Margaret Sanger who started the abortion clinics to exterminate the Negro population because "they grow like weeds." It is the height of stupidity to think that we need to kill the babies to protect them from gun violence. Whereas the President (the one with no political or military background is saying, "Let's make America great again," did he really mean, "Let's make America White again?"

America has NEVER been great to our kind. For 300 years America terrorized and enslaved Black people. For 100 more years, America denied basic civil rights to Black people (Jim Crow and oppression). Today, America fills jails with Black people, while police officers keep shooting them. Then, America gets angry if Black people don't celebrate this history. The violence is not new; it's the cameras that are new. Furthermore, how can he change America when some of his own companies are bankrupt?

Enough about Mr. Trump; what about the nude photos of the First Lady that circulated before they ever get in office? "The fact that so-called Evangelicals support an immoral 'thug' like Trump proves that Christianity has nothing to do with their belief system. It's just a cover for right wing politics. If Jesus returned today and looked at His Church as practiced by these folks, He wouldn't recognize it," said Bob Robinson. Bill Cosby gets accused of multiple women of sexual assault, and he loses his endorsement deals, television shows, re-runs, residual payments, and his reputation. He gets sued and is ruined. Donald Trump gets accused by multiple women of sexual assault and millions of Americans vote him to be the President of the United States. I coincide with whoever coined this statement: "You can't fix the system through the same system that created the system."

In other words, slavery was never abolished; it was redesigned. Old slaves were in chains; new slaves are in denial (origin unknown). And now that we have a new President and legalized marijuana, you mean to tell me that you are content with profiting off of people who are serving time for something that has been legalized? "What in the 'hood' is this?" Again, why should they change a system that's against the Black man and making more money off this one race than any other race in this country?

Elder Jakari also upheld sources in his position regarding proof that the European Jews who are currently in Israel right now are the ones who funded the slave trade. They are the ones who beat us and raped us of our identity, and then called themselves Jewish because they knew who the real Jews were. Even the Historian, Herodian said that the Egyptians were Black people. Along the lines of Elder Jakari's research, the Arabs started the slave trade and told the White man where we were (in Africa and West Africa). Israel is a part of Africa, not the Middle East. The White man changed it to the Middle East.

Consistent with Mark 13:8, these are the beginning of sorrows. Nevertheless, God is going to defeat the nations who have scattered His people to the four corners of the earth through slavery (read Lk. 21:2124 & Psa. 83). Even the United Nations' Working Group of Experts on people of African descent justifies reparations for a history of racial terrorism (The Washington Post, 2016). Slavery reparations could cost trillions of dollars. Not only does the government know who we are, they realize what's been done to us. ***"For thus saith the Lord of hosts; After the glory hath He sent me unto the nations which spoiled you: for he that toucheth you toucheth the apple of His eye"*** (Zech. 2:8). Also read Isaiah 43.

God has set us apart, not because we are so special or great, but out of all the nations of the earth, He CHOSE us to be His people. Moreover, He had already made us in His image and after His likeness. The way they came against God's chosen people was through slavery. When the slave masters taught them the Bible, they dehumanized them and would not allow them to read Genesis and Exodus. Why? Not only did they not want to teach them their history. They realized that there would come a time when God was going to deliver His people again out of the next "Egypt" (America). When Matthew 20:16 says: ***"So the last shall be first, and the first last: for many be called, but few chosen;"*** Jesus was speaking of the Jews and the Gentiles! "Hello Zion!"

Even though most Whites tend to deliberately view Scripture with a Western European mindset of White supremacy, they realize that the opposite position is true. And that is: the ancient biblical Hebrew Israelites were a Black skinned people. Pharaoh and the Egyptians took the Hebrew Israelites into slavery and refused to let them go. Where did you ever hear of White folks being slaves and sold on slave ships? Then, how can they deny that the Israelites were any other race than Black?

In Psalm 83, I admonish you to read how they conspired to completely wipe those Israelites off the face of the earth. It's a no-brainer! If you stop tweeting and start reading, you will learn that when God said, "Let My people go," He was talking about the real Hebrews that are still in the earth today. Those nations wanted to wipe us out, and until this day, they continue to try and wipe us out. *"What shall we then say to these things? If God be for us, who can be against us?"* (Rom. 8:31).

"For the Son of man is come to seek and to save that which was lost" (Lk. 19:10). I know that just because you accepted Jesus Christ as Lord, you don't think you are lost anymore. But if you are still poor, broke, bound, or sick, you are still lost. That's why God took Ezekiel to the valley of dry bones and asked: "Can these dry bones live?" (read Eze. 37). I know that they have the worst blood pressure and cholesterol problems and all other manner of diseases. And I know that everybody is against them, but can these dry bones live? Was God really asking Ezekiel if it was possible for His Black people to live in the worst of conditions?

Even Jesus Christ lived in the "projects" of Nazareth; that's why Nathanael asked: *"Can there any good thing come out of Nazareth"* (John 1:46). The unbelieving Jews and the Jewish people are unwavering in their belief that the Messiah has not come yet. I wonder why. They really don't know who He is because they couldn't receive Him, just as they refuse to receive us today. *"I am come in my Father's name, and ye receive Me not: if another shall come in his own name, him ye will receive"* (John 5:43). The truth of the matter is: they can't relate because they never had a real relationship with the Christ whom we know. *"And if children, then heirs; heirs of God, and joint-heirs with Christ; if so be that we suffer with Him, that we may be also glorified together"* (Rom. 8:17).

To the real, believing Jews, something better than good has already come out of Nazareth. His name means power; in fact, His name has the power to tread upon demons. He came to conquer nations. *"The government shall be upon His shoulder: and His name shall be called Wonderful, Counsellor, The mighty God, The everlasting Father, The Prince of Peace"* (Isa. 9:6). You won't find what you are looking for in *Black Lives Matter*. You will find it in this Gospel; thus, THE GOSPEL MATTERS! It has the power unto salvation to deliver you from your sins, sickness, and poverty. The Anointing has the power to destroy yokes and break curses.

Oh, but no, God's chosen people are ashamed of the Gospel of Christ but proud of their sins. That's why they can sit up and watch *Love & Hip Hop.* That's why they can listen to songs that glorify sin: "I smoke, I drink; I'm supposed to stop, but I can't." That's why they can listen to songs about sex that sounds like this: "Ain't nothing wrong with a little bump and grind." That's why they can sit on their phone and go to sleep with demonic music in their ears. But when they are asked to pray or read the Bible and quote a Scripture, they don't have a clue. Yet, they can quote ungodly music because they are unchanged in their minds. Do you not realize that the devil owns the media; his agenda is to make you glorify sin (Edmunds, 2016).

Wow!!!!! What a powerful eye-opener. I'm not easily moved, but that Sunday, "I went in." You could just feel that this young man had been in God's face and spent some time in the secret place. It takes an encounter to receive revelation knowledge and preach under that kind of an Anointing. If people are coming to you for tweets instead of truths, you may need an encounter. Everything about Elder Jakari's message was confirmation that I had embraced the perfect chapter for this book and incorporated it for such a time as this. He was even led to pray over me and speak into my life. Can you see how God has continued to order my steps to develop this end-time project for a people that He promised to redeem? Anyway, you can support and glean from Elder Jakari's wisdom and *The Gospel Matters* Movement by visiting the website at jbbeministries.org.

Meanwhile, God is causing everything to fail that we have put our trust in because He wants His Black people to return to Him. Sometimes I ask God: Why are we some of the most oppressed people upon the earth? Why is it so hard for us to get our prayers answered? According to Jeremiah 5:25: ***"Your iniquities have turned away these things, and your sins have withholden good things from you." "Mortify therefore your members which are upon the earth; fornication, uncleanness, inordinate affection, evil concupiscence, and covetousness, which is idolatry: For which things' sake the wrath of God cometh on the children of disobedience"*** (Col. 3:5-6). O.M.G. Please take the time to also read Jeremiah 3:3-15. Everybody can't preach prosperity; somebody has to carry out the spirit of Isaiah and Jeremiah.

After waiting almost two months to push my book through Content Evaluation, God revealed another reason why we fail to see immediate manifestation. While many of our relationships have spiraled out of control, there are Christians who literally cannot stand one another. *"For he that eateth and drinketh unworthily, eateth and drinketh damnation to himself, not discerning the Lord's body"* (1 Cor. 11:29). We should all remember this the next time we take communion: When we don't love another Christian, it's a part of Christ's body that we are refusing to accept, recognize, or "discern." If you have unresolved "beef" or an unforgiven or unaddressed "ought" with your brother, you should not take or issue Holy Communion until you have fulfilled Matthew 5:24-25: *"Therefore if thou bring thy gift to the altar, and there rememberest that thy brother, hath ought against thee; Leave there thy gift before the altar, and go thy way; first be reconciled to thy brother, and then come and offer thy gift.".*

Furthermore, how can we speak to God in an unknown tongue and not speak to one another in plain English? *"By this shall all men know that ye are My disciples, IF ye have LOVE one to another"* (John 13:35 with emphasis added). Don't speak in another language until you first learn how to love in the one you speak. We are not known by our tongues; we are known by our fruit! *"Though I speak with the tongues of men and of angels, and have not charity, I am become as sounding brass, or a tinkling cymbal. And though I have the gift of prophecy, and understand all mysteries, and all knowledge; and though I have all faith, so that I could remove mountains, and have not charity, I am nothing"* (1 Cor. 13:1-2).

If you don't have the love of God in your heart, there is no love of God in your love language; it's just learned behavior. We are fighting in the Spirit like cats and dogs! Then, we often end up in poverty or with cancer because we're literally eating and drinking damnation to our souls. Repent to each other, and see won't your status change. When man repents, God restores! Indeed, we make choices and decisions that impact the way we live, but as children of disobedience, Black people are a cursed people who suffer the wrath of God. Also read the 27th and 28th chapters of Deuteronomy. You may not want to admit it, but as descendents of the Tribe of Judah, He was talking to us in Deuteronomy 28:45, when He said: *"Moreover all theses curses shall come upon thee, and shall pursue thee, and overtake thee, til thou be destroyed; because thou hearkenedst not unto the voice of the LORD thy God, to keep His commandments and His statues which He commanded thee."*

Thus, in 2 Chronicles 7:12-13, when God appeared to Solomon by night (the same man who stated: "I am black, but comely"), God was specifically speaking to the people whom He had chosen unto Himself: *"If My people, which are called by My name, shall humble themselves, and pray, and seek My face, and turn from their wicked ways; then will I hear from Heaven, and will forgive their sin, and will heal their land"* (vs. 14). The curse has not come without a cause (Prov. 26:2). BLACK PEOPLE, WE ARE HIS CHOSEN PEOPLE, and that's our personal "recipe" for success and prosperity! Yet, we tend to do everything but humble, pray, seek, and turn. *"For thou art an holy people unto the Lord thy God, and the Lord hath chosen thee to be a peculiar people unto Himself, ABOVE all the nations that are upon the earth"* (Deu. 14:2 with emphasis added).

It's no wonder that they give us a Black History month. In my opinion, they know our real BLACK history; that's why we are the only ones they acknowledge for a month, every year, so they don't have to admit to it every day, for a lifetime. One of the "50 shades of Black" is that as long as we don't recognize who we are, the longer they can keep us local and not make us global. The irony is that they don't recognize another race of people in this way because in some strange, subtle way, they realize that we are God's chosen people. Of course, they will never come out and tell us that because they want to "white-wash" us and keep us with slave mentalities that continue to poison us, and in environments that deny us.

Many of my own issues are systemic. For instance, when I was hired at a predominantly Caucasian establishment, it was the most professional and highest paying job of my life. Yet, I quit because my manager "assumed" that I did not want to be promoted. She "assumed" that I was just satisfied to be the "token Black." As a result of her assumptions, she promoted a White lady over me who came in after me. Even if I would have declined the position, give me the opportunity to make that decision. Don't just count me out because I'm Black. Devastated because I felt devalued, I had just walked away from an environment that made me feel like a slave among my own people. I did not go through that to come here and go through this! So against my better judgment, I said, I'm OUT!

After making the shift to come to this place where I felt so much better about myself, unfortunately, I still had not found an environment of opportunities, or a stream of "you can do it people." To avoid staying in an environment that treated me lesser than what I deserved at this point, I chose a downward spiral that led to additional bankruptcies and severe depression. Even with the skills that God had gifted me with, I eventually became afraid of success and intimidated by Fortune 500 companies.

Here are some notes that I came across at the last minute; could it be that God wanted me to tell you that intimidation is an assault on your destiny? Intimidation is a comparison issue, not just a matter of what you believe, or refuse to believe about yourself. God has to deal with the way you **see** yourself. When you see yourself in the right light, it doesn't matter what is before you. It's not about what you are up against; it's about what you believe about what God has invested in you. A series of decisions are before you that cannot be postponed. There are things that God had invested and implanted in your future that are demanding your decisions and demanding your movement and your courage. The devil is afraid that if you ever get courage enough to have an anointed try, or to make an anointed decision to move forward, eventually you will become endowed and equipped enough to handle the thing that is bigger than you.

Ultimately, because of my own intimidation issues, I needed a serious self-esteem "transplant." I had been torn down for so many years by those who had authority over me, that despite my skill-set and my anointing, I was too intimidated to try anything new, or anything that I considered bigger than me. Good seed in bad soil, we wither and die because our circumstances have yielded very little fruit. Because we have fallen among "thistles" and been defined by people whose "thorns" have" choked us out," we simply do not realize how big we are. Thus, we see them as giants and are grasshoppers in our own eyes. "And so we are in their sight" (Num. 13:33). It's not only time to hope again; we must desire the things of God. *"Hope deferred maketh the heart sick: but when the desire cometh, it is a tree of life"* (Prov. 13:12).

Obviously, Malachi would not rest until he wrote Malachi to Israel, the last book in the Old Testament. Cure (n.d.) carried forth the perspective that he had to write this book because the prophecy was important to the understanding of Israel's relationship and promise. In Malachi 1:4, the Edomites would be called the border of wickedness. In this regard as viewed by Cure (n.d.), every where the White man sets his foot, he conquers it and brings his wickedness with him. He appears loving, but by the sword, he obtains lands and forces the so-called savages of that land to accept his image of God and the Messiah to help make them civilized.

This is the same theme as it pertains to Esau in Romans 9:8-23. God's purpose in raising up the White European nations and giving them the superior role is that He wants His chosen people to know that He is the only power that will deliver them out of captivity, just like Egypt could only be brought down by Him alone. The Edomites or so-called White race hates Israel because the Most High God hardened their hearts toward the Israelites. Pharaoh could not resist the power of God in hating the Israelites. According to Cure (n.d.), the White man's purpose in life is to be the wrath of the Most High to the Israelites and to the world for a **season**. Then, He will destroy them as He did the Egyptians. If Black folks had known their history, the 2016 election results would not have devastated them. It would have been more like "shock therapy" to them.

"Shall the thing formed say to Him that formed it, Why hast Thou made me thus? Hath not the potter power over the clay, of the same lump to make one vessel unto honour, and another unto dishonour?" (Rom. 9:20b-21). Does the Most High have the power to do what He wants to do? YES! *"What if God, willing to shew His wrath* [Edomites], *and to make His power known, endured with much longsuffering the vessels of wrath fitted to destruction: and that He might make known the riches of His glory on the vessels of*

mercy [Israelites], *which He had afore prepared unto glory"* (Rom. 9:22-23 with emphasis added). We are not honorary Israelites; we are the true descendents! So, "White-it-out," Black man! Take your place and restore your race!

According to the ancient artifacts and the Egyptian Hieroglyphics, the real Hebrews was all shades of the earth, ranging from dark skinned to light skinned, but with color, and they wore braids and beards or afros and beards, according to their law. "Historically, Egypt was a civilization of dark-skinned African (Hametic) people, which can be confirmed by looking at any artwork from Ancient Egypt" (Will, 2009).

In Acts 21:37-38, Paul was "assumed" to be an Egyptian, and so were Joseph and Moses. If there was an assumption, it gives me reason to believe that they were men of color. Moreover, we should all be familiar with how Revelations 1:14-15 describe the Son of Man. It is certain that pictures of Jesus that many Western people are familiar with are just a fantasy of mainly nineteenth-century evangelism. Jesus was, we are told, a native of Nazareth and His mother and father were Jews. It is almost certain, therefore, that His skin color was what is described as olive and that His hair was dark, as in general in the Semitic people of that area.

A politically correct response would be that Hollywood is very much controlled by the traditions of the past and simply provides its audience with what that audience finds acceptable. Since that audience is mainly western and used to the (mainly) nineteenth-century representations of Jesus and His contemporaries (and possibly because most actors are Caucasian), that is what they show. The White man highlights the reduced emphasis on this aspect with intellectual achievement. However, Hollywood is not, and never has been, concerned with ethnic accuracy. To this extent, I must agree with the Real Israelites (2006) that we cannot evade the issue that color does make a difference; it is the difference between the truth and a lie.

Although color is a subject avoided in today's politically correct society, the Bible contains detailed narratives on physical appearance. Because the history of Black people has been erased, we, more than any other nation struggle with the misconceptions about our self image. This is not only because our history has been overlooked, but the denial of our contribution to history was based on maintaining the myth that Black people are inferior in order to make slavery justifiable. This is good place to "White-it-out!" Since I believe that God considers this topic worthy of attention, I have the obligation to indicate in Scripture what stands out as primary themes. To summarize the core facets of this investigation, pay close attention to my research from the Real Israelites (2006).

JOSEPH

"When Joseph's 10 brothers came into Egypt in Africa to buy corn, they could not recognize him as their brother. They did not recognize him because Joseph had dwelled amongst the Egyptians from a child. His brothers could not distinguish him from the Black Egyptians because Joseph himself was Black. If he were White, he would have stood out and raised the curiosity of his brothers straight away."

MOSES

"When the new Pharaoh of Egypt promulgated an edict of genocide to cast all the Hebrew male babies into the Nile River, Miriam and her mother hid the baby, Moses, in the bulrushes. When Pharaoh's daughter came down to the Nile to wash herself, she saw the basket and the baby. She knew the baby was a Hebrew, and she adopted him. Moses was then raised in the house of Pharaoh as his grandson. If Moses had been a White child, he would have stood out like a sore thumb. It would have been impossible to conceal him because the Egyptians are a dark-skinned nation.

If we turn our attention to Exodus 4:6 and the miracle God showed Moses, we are *told: 'And the LORD said furthermore unto him, Put now thine hand into thy bosom. And he put his hand into his bosom: and when he took it out, behold, his hand was leprous as snow.'* Leprosy is a disease that turns the skin white. The miracle was to turn Moses' hand white. He was then told to put his hand back into his bosom again and as the Bible says: ... *'Behold, it was turned again as his other flesh'* (vs. 7b). Common sense tells us that if Moses had already been a White person, this miracle would have been impossible to perform. Once the skin had been turned leprous and white, it returned to its original flesh. If the miracle was to turn it white, then the original flesh would have had to been black.

Continuing with the story of Moses, after he had slain an Egyptian for smiting a Hebrew, he fled to the land of Midian. While he was there, the Bible tells us a story of how he helped the daughters of Jethro to water their flocks. Upon her return, when she was asked by her father why she returned early, she replied: ... *'An Egyptian delivered us out of the hand of the shepherds'* (Exo. 2:19). Moses was described as an Egyptian [he was dark-skinned]. The Egyptians are Hamites." [Keep reading; I will explain the difference in the Hamites and the Semites].

MIRIAM

"To prove this point further, we need to turn to the story of Miriam. Miriam, Moses' sister was cursed because she grumbled against Moses having an Ethiopian wife. In Numbers 12:9-10, it says: *'And the anger of the LORD was kindled against them; and He departed. And the cloud departed from off the tabernacle; and, behold, Miriam became leprous, white as snow'...* This Scripture proves two things. For Miriam to have been turned white, she would have had to have been black to begin with. And to repeat the point I made earlier, to have white skin according to the Bible is to have the curse of leprosy! This refutes the spurious claims made by White Christian fundamentalist groups who have taught for hundreds of years that to be Black is a result of a curse!!! It is the contrary. These laws of leprosy were given to the nation of Israel, and they could not apply to White people."

KING DAVID

"Next we turn to the story of David when the prophet, Samuel, was secretly sent by God to anoint him King in Bethlehem. In 1 Samuel 16:12, the Bible describes the future king of Israel by these words: *'Now he was ruddy, and withal of a beautiful countenance'...* In his book, Ancient and Modern Britons, David Macritchie refers to the word, ruddy. Again, it was noticed that the adjective, ruadh, or as we pronounce it in English, ruddy and red signifies both black and tawny, and red, or ruddy."

SOLOMON

"Now if his father, David was Black, his son, Solomon would have had to be Black. Just as the Bible describes David in the verse above as ruddy (black) and beautiful; Solomon describes himself in the same way. In the Song of Solomon 1:5 (with emphasis), Solomon says: *'I am black, but comely* [beautiful], *O ye daughters of Jerusalem, as the tents of Kedar'...* In the Dictionary of the Bible, by Dr. William Smith, volume 2, 1888; pg. 1526: Qadar/Ke'dar means 'Black-skinned man.'

The Bible compares the Israelites and the Ethiopians together. In Amos 9:7a, the Bible says: *'Are ye not as children of the Ethiopians unto Me, O children of Israel?'...* The Roman historian, Tacticus, wrote that many of his time believed that the 'Jews were a race of Ethiopian origin.' Keep in mind that in Tacticus' time, there was no country called Africa. The whole of Africa was called, Ethiopia. In other words, the Israelites were of the Black race."

CHRIST

"Moving to the New Testament, we turn our attention to the descendent of David and Solomon, Christ. In Matthew 2:13-14, we read that when Christ was a child, Herod made a decree that all Hebrew males be killed. Fleeing for the safety of their child, we are told that Joseph and Mary ran into Egypt to hide among the Egyptians. As mentioned earlier with the example of Joseph, the Egyptians and the Israelites are similar in appearance. Being in Africa, a land of Black people, Christ and his family could disguise themselves among the Egyptians.

When we turn to the Book of Revelations, John, the revelator, gives a detailed description of Christ; he writes: **'His head** [the hair on His head] **and his hairs** [His beard] **were white like wool, as white as snow** [fully grey]**; and His eyes were as a flames of fire; And His feet like unto fine brass, as if they burned in a furnace'...** (Rev. 1:14-15a with emphasis added). Now there are two things to gather from these verses. The first is the texture of Christ's hair, and the second is His skin color. When you read the beginning of the verse, His texture of hair is described as being like wool. Wooly hair is black hair.

Next, it describes the skin color of Christ's feet. Keep in mind that your feet are the same color as the rest of your body. John describes it as being like brass. Now brass is a derivative of brown. It is a copper color. Now if you take brown copper and burn it in a furnace (oven), it will turn jet black. As a matter of fact, if you take anything and burn it in an oven, it will turn black! Josephus, a Jewish historian of the first-century said that 'Christ was a man of simple appearance, mature age and dark skin'."

THE WORD, CHRIST

"Due to the Greek influence on the language we speak today, the Savior is called 'Christ' rather than 'Mashiyach,' which is Hebrew equivalent. A quick inspection into the New Webster's Dictionary reveals another interesting point about the name, 'Christ.' The etymology of the word, Christ, as given in the said dictionary is: [ME & OE. Crist.LL Christus, GR Christos, the Anointed, spread over, smear, grime]. Grime is defined as dirt, especially sooty dirt, rubbed into or covering a surface, as of skin" (Real Israelites, 2006).

Now back to "lil-ole" me, the "pen☺prophet"-researcher. One of the "50 shades of ignorance" is that we, as a race of people does not realize and accept the fact that the Old Testament is the Black folks' history book. Now when I read the Old Testament, it's like I'm looking at a reflection of "the man in the mirror." Consequently, I have a whole, new perspective. The New Testament is God's covenant to the Gentiles (everybody else). This is the kind of information that the White man seeks to hide from us. No, I'm countering that excuse for you Black folks. They're not even trying to hide it anymore because it's all over the internet. Because we refuse to READ and conduct our own research, we are "ignant" and destroyed for a lack of knowledge. We would rather Google everything but what we need to know and learn.

We forget to incorporate the last part of this Scripture that says: ... ***"Seeing thou hast forgotten the law of thy God, I will also forget thy children"*** (Hos. 4:6). Of all the nations in the world, whose children are the worst off and the less blessed? Need I prove to you any further who we are? "White-it-out," already! The Old Testament Scriptures contain the history, culture, and genealogy of the Black Israelites. We must embrace the truth that God's chosen people [Black folks] are destroyed for not being taught and/or knowing (having knowledge of) who we are, where we came from, and why we are still here. If you "white-it-out," you may be able to take your place and restore your race.

As you may know, Juneteenth is a holiday that commemorates the June 19, 1865 announcement of the abolition of slavery in Texas, and more generally, the emancipation of African American slaves throughout the Confederate South. "Right?" Wait; allow me to digress for a moment. How could Columbus have discovered America when the Indians were already here? #randomthought In any case, a parable was told to me recently that when the slaves were notified by their masters that they were free, they all cheered. They were happy, dancing and singing until 5:00 p.m. When supper- time came, they wanted to know: "What 'we-gone' eat?" Someone answered: "'Y'all' can go to McDonalds if you want to. You FREE!" The moral of the story is that we as a people don't even know what to do with our freedom. L "White that out!"

Almost every nationality that comes to the United States seems to make it over night; primarily, we are the ones who are still left struggling. We are yet sounding like those Black folks who were following Moses. Always complaining, murmuring and grumbling, they wanted to turn their backs on God and return to Egypt. If we simply had knowledge, we wouldn't need faith. It was recently disclosed to me that faith was needed by the Gentiles, which is why the New Testament was written. All God needed the Israelites to learn in the Old Testament was obedience. *"Now therefore, if ye will obey My voice indeed, and keep My covenant, then ye shall be a peculiar treasure unto Me above all people"...* (Exo. 19:5).

Still today, we find it hard to simply be obedient, and that's the major reason why we are still struggling and can't get ahead. That's why our Black men are becoming extinct while they die in the streets as a consequence of police brutality. Do you realize police brutality among our Black sons is literal prophecy coming to past? *"Thy sons have fainted, they lie at the head of all the streets, as a wild bull in a net: they are full of the fury of the Lord, the rebuke of our God"* (Isa. 51:20). Jeremiah prophesied it too: *"Therefore her young men shall fall in her streets, and all of the men of war shall be cut off in that day, saith the Lord of hosts"* (Jer. 49:26).

In Part Two of this book that Melody Trent is going to assist me in writing, we are going to compare many of the characteristics of the Israelites with us as being Black in today's society. Murmuring and complaining and being disobedient are not the only traits that we have in common; you are going to be amazed. Every time I went to her salon, it turned out to be some of the most informative Bible Studies that I have ever encountered in life. Whereas I am no longer chasing after "flesh," my hunger and thirst for wisdom and knowledge is like my spiritual compass that pulls me away from tradition.

After all, "deep calleth unto deep." Can you imagine; getting pampered and learning biblical history at the same time? I absolutely loved it! Responsible for starting me on this life-changing journey, this W.O.W. woman (woman of wisdom) who has no claim to either of the five-fold ministry gifts, blew my world wide open with her insight of Old Testament Scriptures. Meanwhile, to illustrate the implications of data driven from my research, I have selected some additional, Old Testament Scriptures to strengthen the theory that the original Hebrews were dark-skinned Blacks.

"Our skin was black like an oven because of the terrible famine" (Lam. 5:10). *"Their visage is blacker than a coal; they are not known in the streets"...* (Lam. 4:8a). *"For the hurt of the daughter of my people am I hurt; I am black; astonishment hath taken hold on me"* (Jer. 8:21). *"My skin is black upon me, and my bones are burned with heat"* (Job 30:30). ... *"His locks are bushy, and black as raven"* (Sol. 5:11b).

In the New Testament, Acts 13:1 says: *"Now there were in the church that was at Antioch certain prophets and teachers; as Barnabas, and Simeon that was called Niger"...* Watch this: *"Art not thou that Egyptian, which before these days madest an uproar"... But Paul said, I am a man which am a Jew of Tarsus"...* (Acts 21:38a- 39a). To say the least, nearly all of the kings and prophets of the Old Testament were Jews from the Tribe of Judah. Here is the key to understanding the world conspiracy and what I have attempted to convey to you in this chapter, beginning with Esau and Jacob. "Christ was born out of the Tribe of Judah, i.e. the descendents of Judah. Judah was Jacob's (Israel's) fourth son. The term Jew, derived from the name, Judah, denoting a family lineage, an ethnicity, a race, not a religion. Christ was not Jewish; He was a Jew by blood" (Will, 2009). *"For it is evident that our Lord sprang out of Juda; of which tribe Moses spake nothing concerning priesthood"* (Heb. 7:14). "P☺W!"

Upon further investigation, Will (2009) claims: "The modern-day Jew**ish** people are Jew**ish** by religion; Jew-**ish** means that they are Jew-like. Their race is Caucasian; there is no Jewish race as they claim. Today, those calling themselves Jews and/or God's chosen people do not demonstrate the customs, culture, or values of the biblical Jews, nor do they uphold the Laws of Moses as they are written. They do not match the physical description of the Jews, nor does their history match the prophecies of the Jews in the Old Testament." I'm having a Jonathan Nelson's, "Oh Jesus" moment, right about now. This is like, "burning my eyebrows off'!"

"It is well-publicized that the **Caucasian** Jew**ish** people today, including the current occupiers of the land of Israel, are actually descendents of the Khazar Empire in Eastern Europe. The Thirteenth Tribe, by A. Koestler; The Synagogue of Satan, by A. Carrington; and

The Hidden Tyranny: Harold Rosenthal's Confession, all support this fact and are available in PDF online. Today's Jews practice Cabbala and Talmudism, rooted in satanic witchcraft and immorality. The usury-based financial reserve banking system is dominated by 'Jews,' although the Torah forbids the practice of lending money at interest. The slave trade was heavily financed by 'Jews;' now we see why.

Many of the poor people in the world today are the true Israelites/ Jews. Christ proclaims in Revelation that there would be false Jews in the last days, while the real Jews suffer in poverty. He said: *'I know thy works, and tribulation, and poverty, (but thou art rich) and I know the blasphemy of them which say they are Jews, and are not, but are the synagogue of Satan'* (Rev. 2:9). The Jewish state of Israel is responsible for soldiers and civilians dying every day in Palestine, Afghanistan, and Iraq. If the American people were informed of the true identity of the Israelites, they would no longer send their tax dollars to Israel; neither would they send their soldiers to die in proxy wars for Israel" (Will, 2009 with emphasis added). Why is this not being taught in our churches? This is definite a good place to "white-it-out!"

After the earth was destroyed by the flood and replenished by the generations of Noah's sons, Shem, Ham, and Japeth, emphasis is placed on Ham, the father of Canaan, in Genesis 9:18. According to Thomas (2017), these are the people who have been ostracized and used by his brothers. But it seems that the Holy Ghost is sending a message in this text that Ham will be used by God to help overspread the earth. The Zondervan Bible Dictionary defines Ham as the progenitor of the dark races (i.e. Africans). Is not Africa the largest Continent on the earth? "Come on somebody!" "I'm working up in here!" Ham's descendents were referred to as Egyptian nigers. The name, Ham, means niger, noise, black, heat. Isaiah 17:12-14 will give you a distinct description of the Africans and their culture.

They inhabited the southern parts of the world and did not embrace the righteousness of Noel. As a result, it is said that Nimrod, one of Ham's descendents via Cush, introduced the worship of the sun (idol worship). Even though God established His covenant with all of man through the sons of Noah (Gen. 9:9), what the White man fails to acknowledge is that all of the patriarchs descended from Shem, the righteous seed. They included Abraham, Isaac and Jacob, and even our Lord Jesus Christ. *"Israel also came INTO Egypt; and Jacob* [Israel] *sojourned in the land of Ham"* (Ps. 105:23 with emphasis added). "These 'Negroes'[the patriarchs] are **NOT** African; they are Semites [who came into the land of Ham].

They are the Jews who inhabited Israel until being chased **INTO** Africa by the Romans after the destruction of Jerusalem in 70 A.D. The Jews fleeing into Africa is prophesied by Christ in Matthew 24, Mark 13, and Luke 21. The REAL **Jews** of the Old Testament broke the Laws of Moses. For this, they were punished and cursed (read Deu. 28:15-68 for a list of curses prophesied by Moses). The curses include being scattered throughout the earth, being enslaved by the enemies, and being forced to forget their true heritage" (Will, 2009 with emphasis added).

"And the LORD shall bring thee into Egypt [bondage] *again with ships, by the way whereof I spake unto thee, Thou shalt see it no more again: and there ye shall be sold unto your enemies for bondmen and bondwomen, and no man shall buy* [redeem] *you"* (Deu. 28:68 with emphasis added). *"The children also of Judah and the children of Jerusalem have ye sold unto the Grecians, that ye might remove them far from their border"* (Job 3:6). *"You only have I known of all the families of the earth: therefore I will punish you for all your iniquities"* (Amos 3:2). "Only one family of people has ever been brought into slavery with ships. 'Black History,' as it is understood today, is summarized in the above passages of Scripture. The Jews were slaves once in ancient Egypt and again in America" (Will, 2009).

"Our history is often defined by slavery. We are taught that our forefathers were captured on the African continent and shipped all over the Western hemisphere, to be sold as human property. There were we raped and robbed of our heritage and a foreign culture was imposed upon us by our captors. Our entire identity was reconstructed. But is there more to our past than appears on the surface? Only through looking beyond the surface do you get a deeper meaning. Then and only then can you come to a truer understanding.

A people without a history are a people that are lost. Although most Black people have knowledge of slavery, we still fail in our attempts to discover who we were prior to this time. What is fed to us about our past has been obscured to conceal the atrocities that were committed against us. The result has been the descendents of slavery who continue to stumble in darkness and who have not discovered themselves. This solemn demise has caused us to become victims of amnesia, the marks of a lost race" (Real Israelites, 2006).

Christ spoke of the miraculous rebirth of this dead and scattered nation. He referred to them in Matthew 10:6 as the lost sheep of the house of Israel. *"These twelve Jesus sent forth, and commanded them, saying, Go not into the way of the Gentiles, and into any city of the Samaritans enter ye not"* (Mt. 10:5). In other words, Christ sent His apostles only to the scattered Israelites (the real Jews, not the Jew**ish** people). *"Therefore let all the house of Israel know assuredly that God hath made that same Jesus, whom ye have crucified, both Lord and Christ. For the promise is unto you, and to your children, and to all that are afar off, even as many as the Lord our God shall call"* (Acts 2:36, 39).

Because of this discussion, I'm certain to have harvested some additional enemies. "Good. That means [I've] stood up for something, sometime in [my] life" (Winston Churchill). All the same, the main thrust of the Gospel is the work among the descendents of Israel [particularly, the Tribe of Judah], not the Gentiles! In Romans 9:11, Paul clearly explains why Christ sent him to preach among Gentiles. His own nation, the Jews [as well as the other tribes of Israel] rejected Jesus as their Savior. Thus, salvation came to the Gentiles.

Romans 11:17-26 shows that God broke Israelite branches off the Abrahamic family tree because they did not believe Him. In their place, He grafted in believing Gentiles, making them children of Abraham (see Gal. 3:29). In the future, God will graft back in the broken-off Israelites (Rom. 11:23). The time of Israel's regrafting begins when God adds the "fullness of the Gentiles" to the Church (Bibletools, 2016). See Romans 11:12, 25. Did I not tell you that the New Testament was written for the Gentiles, and the Old Testament was the real Jews' (Black man's) history book?

In my final analysis, hear this "laser-vision" disclosure. The so-called "Blacks/Negroes" are the real Jews, the lost TRIBE OF JUDAH. Are you interested in knowing the remaining, 11 lost tribes of Israel? 2) **Benjamin**: West Indians; 3) **Levi**: Hatians; 4) **Simeon**: Dominicans Indians; 5) **Zebulon**: Guatemala, Panama, Equador (Maya); 6) **Ephraim**: Puerto Ricans (Tahinos); 7) **Manesseh**: Cubans; 8) **Gad**: North American Indians; 9) **Reuben**: Seminole Indians (Florida Everglades); 10) **Napthali**: Argentina and Chile Indians; 11) **Asher**: Brazil, Columbia, Uruguay Indians (Inca); 12) **Issachar** (Aztecs). "Those whose fathers are of so-called Negroid and Indian descent throughout North, Central and South America make up the 12 Lost Tribes of Israel" (Real Israelites, 2006).

We were all scattered abroad and gathered all over the world and brought to America (read Deu. 28:64). *"And the Lord shall bring thee into Egypt again with ships"...* (Deu. 28:68a). You don't have to take a ship to get into Egypt; the spiritual Egypt is America! He was talking about us who came over from the Atlantic slave trades. Jesus said in Revelation 2:9: *"I know thy works, and tribulation, and poverty, (but thou art rich) and I know the blasphemy of them which say they are Jews, and are not, but are the synagogue of Satan."* This is the Gospel truth that needs to be decoded! Billions of us have died, not even knowing who we are.

The people who claimed to be Jews in Israel are European Jews. Moving forward to Part Two, we will show you the connection between the biblical Hebrew Israelites and the Trans Atlantic Slave Trade and how the Israelites escaped the invading Roman armies in Jerusalem and fled into the interiors of Africa. Taken from Africa, Europe, and the Middle East, they were captured and sold on cargo slave ships. Henceforth, the population reduction is targeted toward destroying a particular people in the earth – people of color (Will, 2009).

Now I see. As a matter of fact, we all should have a much clearer understanding of Psalm 122:6; which says: *"Pray for the peace of Jerusalem; they shall prosper that love thee."* But do your own research and come to your own conclusion. After careful deliberations, I am convinced that we are the Lost Tribe of Judah. *"Judah mourneth, and the gates thereof languish; they are black unto the ground;*

and the cry of Jerusalem is gone up" (Jer. 14:2). *"Thus saith the Lord GOD, Because that Edom hath dealt against the house of Judah by taking vengeance, and hath greatly offended, and revenged himself upon them"* (Eze. 25:12). Continue reading this passage to see how God has pronounced vengeance upon Edom because of His people, Israel.

On the other hand, here is GOD's decree to His people, in Amos 9:13-15 (MSG): *"Yes, indeed, it won't be long now. God's Decree. Things are going to happen so fast your head will swim, one thing fast on the heels of the other. You won't be able to keep up. Everything will be happening at once – and everywhere you look, blessings! Blessings like wine pouring off the mountains and hills. I'll make everything right again for My people Israel: They'll rebuild their ruined cities. They'll plant vineyards and drink good wine. They'll work their gardens and eat fresh vegetables. And I'll plant them, plant them on their own land. They'll never again be uprooted from the land I've given them. GOD, your GOD says so."* I have always known that my fabulous dreams were not just fantasies. You go figure, and take those final passages of Scripture for what it's worth.

Even in the beginning of sorrows, I'm anticipating "better days ahead!" If you don't look for them, you won't see them, even if they came. Hitherto, since Jesus never lived on disability or in the projects on Section 8, why should you? As for me, *"I had fainted, unless I had believed to see the goodness of the Lord in the land of the living"* (Psa. 27:13). Here is to all of my White brothers and sisters: *"But glory, honour, and peace, to EVERY man that worketh good, to the Jew FIRST* [us], *and ALSO to the Gentiles* [you]: *For there is no respect of persons with God"* (Rom. 2:10-11 with emphasis added; read also Rom. 3:29; and, Acts 11:1, 18; 13:42, 46-48; 14:27; 15:7, 14). Did I not tell you earlier that salvation came to the Gentiles because of the unbelieving Jews?

"I say then, Have they stumbled that they should fall? God forbid: but rather through their fall salvation is come unto the Gentiles, for to provoke them to jealousy" (Rom. 11:11). Even as they also received the Word of God, and God granted them repentance,

it's no wonder that they act toward us the way they do. Just as Joseph was a light to lighten the Gentiles, and the glory of his people, Israel (Lk. 2:32), Esaias prophesied in Romans 15:12 that there would be a root of Jesse that would rise to reign over the Gentiles, and in him would the Gentiles trust. Was that former President Obama, or not? "I'm just saying;" it "ain't" over until the BLACK MAN SINGS! As it is written: ... *"Eye hath not seen, nor ear heard, neither have entered into the heart of man, the things which God hath prepared for them that love Him"* (1 Cor. 2:9). Well, as the preachers often say, "I'm out of time, but I'm not out of Word."

CHAPTER SIX

MAXIMIZING THE MANDATE THROUGH A MODERN-DAY MINDSET

As I was in my God-ordained transition for a few months, I attended a certain church in Dallas with my sister, as this was when I first learned of her alias. After filling out the visitor's card, I could not figure out why she stood up when they called out, "Shannon Brown." Anyway, the only thing that captivated us from the message was the speaker's opening statement. He said that he was taught to be brief, be specific, and sit down. Obviously, that has been quite challenging for me when writing. Consequently, there were so many details on the last chapter that I have had to add even another chapter to include what would have been the rest of that chapter. It is going to be a tough act to follow, but I am determined to pour into you until I'm all poured out.

However, I have finagled these changes in several chapters to avoid giving you "TMI." I would hate for an information overload to prohibit you from proceeding to the final chapter. As the previous chapter and the current chapter is my "drive-through" version of the forthcoming, Part Two edition, eventually, I will get back to my original plot. Besides, I don't expect you to read this book and absorb this information in a week. So, in order to get through it, think of it in textbook style. More than ever before, it is intended to be a teaching mechanism; however, I am working overtime to see that you don't have too many boring (-_-) moments.

THE BIG IDENTITY CRISIS

Before we can proceed to the next chapter and get back to Eden, we must maximize the mandate through a modern-day mindset. Like I stated earlier, identification is a major issue for the Black man because he does not have a consciousness of who he really is. Indeed, we have tried to "turn-up" through religion, philosophy, educational systems, and self-made Black organizations. Even as our blood cries out for justice, it calls for salvation. The Real Israelites (2006), who have extensively examined the previous concepts from both a spiritual and philosophical perspective believe that until we repent and turn back to the heavenly Father through Christ's example, we will continue to remain separated, oppressed, suppressed, repressed, lost, confused, and destroyed as a nation of people.

Even though we are no longer slaves, we are still affected by that spirit and by that curse. How long will My people be oppressed? (read Isa. 3:5). The White man calls you a "nigga" and criticizes you for being lazy. He determines who you are and dictates how far you can go. He calls your children "thugs" and your women "who'es." The White man even believes you evolved from a monkey. *"He shall judge the poor of the people, He shall save the children of the needy, and shall break in pieces the oppressor"* (Psa. 72:4).

Meanwhile, where did you really come from? What is your real name? What is your position? The pivotal question is: What have you spoken over your own self? Are you another "illegitimate baby," looking for your real Father? Have you allowed others to name you? Have you assumed a pseudo identity that was placed upon you by the opinions of others? Or, have you suffered from an identity crisis because of the absence of, or the lack of love from your biological father?

Maybe you cannot comprehend the love of God because your father failed to lead you into the reality of a true godly relationship. Jesus said of His Father in John 17:23b, that God has loved us, just as God has loved Him. Can you imagine God loving you as much as He loves His only begotten Son? If you did not have an example of the love of the Father from your earthly father, you may not be experiencing a love relationship with Abba, our heavenly Father. Accordingly, "at the core of every sin are choices that take place of what is lacking," says Bishop A.R. Williams (2013). To cut down on any further misconceptions, let's "fast forward" and draw from some additional teaching by Bishop Williams. In my own words (of course), and now at the pinnacle of truly finalizing this project, this was a "must-share!"

Our young Black men [the Tribe of Judah] have turned to gang banging because the gang leaders have committed to being a father figure. Your Black son, your Black brother, your Black nephew, and even your Black uncle are likely looking to identify with somebody who will make them feel special. Ask me why. They have not experienced the love of a father. They will shoot and kill someone just to gain respect. Consequently, they are carrying an emptiness on the inside that only a father can fill, and trying to compensate for a void that can only be fulfilled by the abundance of God's love.

Looking for identity, not only will young, homosexual men go from man to man to satisfy their feminine desires for same-sex attraction. Heterosexual men will go from woman to woman to rationalize their masculine tendencies for opposite sex attention. In both scenarios, it is likely because they did not get validated by their father, and/or they have not been taught the validity of the love of the heavenly Father. Somebody has convinced the homosexual man that the best way to promote the homosexual agenda is by turning other men out. On the contrary, the heterosexual man has been convinced that to prove their manhood, they need to conquer as many women as possible by spreading their seed and producing more babies. Neither ploy is God's way of establishing right relationships.

Nowadays, lesbian relationships are almost as common and widespread as man with man. You know these young ladies were never exposed to Mother Teresa, so they harmonize with whatever society salutes. It is plausible that lesbians did not establish a proper relationship with their father and/or mother, or even, their spouse or boyfriend. Ultimately, they found their identity in another woman and made choices based on not having the unconditional love of a real man. Generally, when women do not get love from our natural fathers and/or if we have never realized it from a spiritual father, we need somebody to touch us, hold us, cover us, and caress us. As a consequence, we suffer an identity crisis and start looking for love in all the wrong places and in the arms of all the wrong people.

Young girls often turn from one guy to another. They have baby after baby or one abortion after another, when all they needed was a father to say, "I love you." "I got you." "I'm here for you." Overall, my position is this: at the end of the day, the father did not maximize his mandate because he was never taught the magnitude of his manhood. #powerful On balance, females most often commit suicide because somebody forgot to tell them how much they are loved. Men steal because they do not realize that God loves them enough to provide for them. Universally, what people do is often **not** who they are. Why is the love of a father so important? Since people naturally need affirmation and respect, a father gives us identity, and his love gives us value, security, and self-esteem. Without this initial validation from a father, a child is lost. When adults are not grounded in the love of a father figure, we become victims of mistaken identity.

That's why I have a problem with female pastors. In my opinion, they are in an identity crisis themselves. What can a woman **in** an identity crisis do for a man **with** an identity crisis? "Oh, my bad;" that was "yesterday's dinner." My niece just told me that "I was doing too much." Maybe, the person that I'm trying to be in her life has carried over into the purpose that I am trying to fulfill in this project. Created to look just like your Father, you are **not** a product of your abuse. You are neither, the outcome of one night of passion, or the result of a "Motel 6" episode. As an offspring of Adam who was made in the image and after the likeness of the Father, you also were fearfully and wonderfully made to become His son, or His daughter. As it is written: ***"But as many as received Him, to them gave He power to become the sons of God, even to them that believe on His name"*** (John 1:12).

Please allow me to stroke my Black brothers' egos while I ease you into a deeper revelation. In our intuitive processing to the search for meaning, can we at least agree that the reason man is so much like God is that he was made in His **image** and after His likeness? A new opportunity to modify old generalizations, then, could this be an indication that man physically looks like God to a great degree? Many have used the argument that God is all spirit, but consistent with the Word, He does have an **image** too! Let's activate our imagination here.

Since man is made in the image and likeness of God, does that make him <u>predominantly</u> spirit that has a soul that lives in a body? Here is my perception: now that man is human, he **was** a spirit (that which was in the Spirit or mind of God). That spirit that was in the will of God **became** a soul, which is the you that houses the Spirit that now lives in a body. Your spirit was able to live without your soul, but since your soul is who you **became**, your spirit is not who you **are**. Allow me to "rewind" and identify a few Scriptures that are worthy of attention.

As it is written in Genesis 2:7b: ... *"And man became a living soul."* Is that not what I just said? The breath of life was God's Spirit that was breathed into the man's nostrils. *"God is a Spirit: and they* [the souls] *that worship Him must worship Him in spirit and in truth"* (John 4:24 with emphasis added). Years ago, some people had an epiphany that we are spirit beings, and that "deep" revelation escalated all over the Body. I'm not even sure why this is important here, but just for argument sake, I beg to differ. Needless to say, I have had a different epiphany.

In fact, I just heard someone on television brag about being a spiritual being living in a human existence. It sounds good to people who don't know any better. However, this is not a spirit world, so how does that work? It doesn't. In order to be spirit beings, you must be celestial. The fact that God, angels, and demons **are** spirits makes a strong case that only spirit beings can exist in both a spirit and a human world. As human beings, we cannot exist in both places at the same time. That is the basis for my argument. Why can't human beings who are no longer spirit beings, live as spirit beings in a human existence?

Basically, as I said earlier, you **WERE** a spirit, but He took your spirit that was already in His **mind** and in His plan, blew life into it, and created a living soul. In other words, your spirit is God's breath, blown into your nostrils. He knew us in the Spirit because we were in

His Spirit to make us human. Now, that makes you a human that has God's Spirit or breath **in** you, which is the part of Him that goes back to Him. If you were still predominantly spirit, you would be in Heaven or in the mind of God, and not doing what humans predominantly do (sinning). Predominantly, unless we are walking **in the Spirit** and allowing His **mind/spirit** to be **in** us, which was also in Christ Jesus (Phil. 2:5), we are fulfilling the lust of the flesh (Gal. 5:16). ☹

You will not become a spirit again until it leaves your flesh and goes back to God. So how does the soul fit into the equation? The soul is the you that resulted from a spirit that now lives in a body. The body houses the God-man that's waiting for your soul to become the manifestation of the son of God. Luke 12:20 indicate that it was the fool's soul that was required of him (not his spirit). ... *"For they watch for your souls, as they must give account"* (Heb. 13:17b). They were not instructed to watch over our spirits. Ask me why not. If we get our souls right, we won't be a human being with **a** bad spirit.

If you are not a partaker of salvation, your spirit will leave you and go back from whence it came, but *"the soul that sinneth, it shall die"* (Eze. 18:4b). Wickedness cannot be expected to escape the Divine vengeance on account of His Father's piety. Typically, children who do not replicate their fathers' integrity give them a bad name. So what would the Father look like having a bunch of "out-of-control" human beings walking around claiming to be spirit beings? God is a Spirit that has more spiritual attributes than human attributes; yet, He cannot sin. We are humans that have more human attributes than spiritual attributes because we have souls that give us the freedom to live in sin.

When God released our spirits into an alien world, He gave us a soul to reveal the real us that we were created to be. Can't you see the word, real, in reveal? He already knew what He had in mind for us to be and ultimately, who we would become. We just didn't realize that we came here to become the sons of God. There the word, real is again in the word, realize. He wanted to create a **real** family **outside** of Himself. It gave the Father more glory to give His spirit beings that were accustomed to living in a spirit world, the **chance** to be born again, and a **choice** to become "little gods" (Psa. 82:6). Wow!

I'm "gonna" need to give my own self an offering. What gives a parent more pleasure than giving birth to a child who **chooses** to be obedient when they are giving a chance, and who chooses to be good when they have a choice to be bad?

If we were still those spirit beings before they were released, we wouldn't be acting like sinful, "outer-space invaders." He would not have had to ask: "Adam, where art thou?" In essence, He was asking Adam to reveal where his heart was. The **heart** refers to the **center** of man's being, which is his spirit. My whole case in point needs to be paralleled by Psalm 51:10: *"Create in me a clean heart, O God; and renew a right spirit within me"* To be precise, you have a heart, but you are not a heart. This emphasis underscores the actuality that you are a soul that lives in a body that has the Spirit of God within you.

I think that I'm having too much fun here as I have allowed my critical thinking skills to markedly analyze my position. I don't know why I'm going so deep with this, but stay with me; you'll eventually see where I'm going. What I'm trying to illuminate here is the fact that the Spirit is where God lives; your soul is where you live. Thus, the Spirit that is WITHIN you is the heart of the soul. While we are wearing our earthly "body suits," does that make us spirit beings (as those in Heaven)? Or, are we human beings (souls) that came here needing to be born again and baptized in the Holy Spirit? At some point, that would enable us to go back to God to live as spirit beings (again) and throughout eternity? I know the Word says that God is a Spirit, but can you go ahead and show me in the Bible where it says that man is a spirit?

Finally, for evidence most critical to the assertion of whether we are spirit or not, I want to challenge you to examine the following Scriptures. ... *"The first man Adam was made a living soul; the last Adam was made a quickening spirit"* (1Cor. 15:45). "Enough said." No, no, no; I just came across the key to this whole inquiry. It lies in 1 Corinthians 15:47-48 (with emphasis added): *"The first man is of the earth, earthy: the second man is the Lord from Heaven [Spirit]. As is the earthy, such are they also that are earthy [soulish]: and as is the heavenly, such are they also that are heavenly [spiritual]."*

In short, I just made my case! Why didn't I see that at first? I could have reduced the "blah, blah, blah." Since I don't have time to backtrack and "unkill" the overkill, simply, you are a man (a soul) **"in whom"** is the Spirit of God. Here is my last, little "post it" note: You are NOT a breath (spirit); you are a soul. Still not satisfied? Read Genesis 41:38, Numbers 27:18, Proverbs 17:27, John 3:6, and 1 Corinthians 2:11. **"But there is a spirit IN man"** ... (Job 32:8a with emphasis added). Stop teaching that we are spirit beings; you even have Hollywood repeating that error. Just keep it simple; we are human beings!

If you are still unconvinced, your poignant and pointed queries regarding spirit and soul would certainly make for interesting dialogue and intellectual stimulation in your next Bible class discussion. Consistent with having been professionally trained by a perfectionist, I know that sometimes it may seem like I am "beating a dead horse." Even so, my multiple revisions move me toward more accurate and complete layers of meaning. According to Kockelmans (1967) as cited in Moustakas (1994): "We penetrate deeper into things and learn to see the more profound 'layers' behind what we first thought to see" (p. 30).

Here is what was supposed to be my point before I went off on another "rabbit trail." In order for man to be "soooo" much like God, the plausible hypothesis is that God is a Spirit-man with unlimited attributes. As I said in an earlier chapter, some theologians even teach that He is a man who <u>evolved</u> into being the almighty God. It's no wonder that Psalms 82:6a confirms: ... **"Ye are gods; and all of you are children of the most High."** Intrinsically, our invisible spirit man gives residence or a home to God's Holy Spirit in order for us to have the ability to relate to Him in spirit and eventually evolve into having unlimited attributes.

Created in an image that resembles our Father and with a soul that enables us to think like Him and make the right choices, He expects His children to function like gods. In order to do that, we must submit to the Spirit that lives within us. What can come out of God but gods? Once He breathed into the man's nostrils, man became God individualized to operate as an independent soul. Now that's how you really maximize the mandate in a modern-day mindset.

The final challenge of keeping the key issues in focus, Prophet Barber's plausible hypothesis that really stretched my imagination was that God is Black. Even as I made a previous attempt to prove that the Israelites were Black, I cannot substantiate this claim as a fact. Would you at least allow me to present it as an utterance? If Adam was formed in God's image from African soil, would Adam not be a Black African who resembles the image of his Creator? Image can be described as the way something is imagined.

Since Moses was allowed to see God's hinder parts, Exodus 33:20-23 also indicate that He has a literal face and hands. *"And He said, Thou canst not see My face: for there shall no man see Me, and live"* (vs. 20). ... *"While my glory passeth by, that I will put thee in a clift of the rock, and will cover thee with My hand while I pass by"* (vs. 22). In other words, since no man can see God's face or His glory and live, Moses saw His goodness (God's hand which was the result of His glory).

Then, if God has a face and hands, He must have legs and feet: ... *"And there was under His feet as it were a paved work of a sapphire stone"...* (Exd. 24:10). In line with Ecclesiasticus 23:19, "The eyes of the LORD are ten thousand times brighter than the Sun." If these are facts, He is not just a Spirit or some figure of speech, or just a stretch of the imagination. God has an actual image that can be imagined in valid, humanistic terms. Thus, while we dwell mostly on Him being just Spirit with no literal features to behold, how could man be made only in His likeness when He said both image and likeness?

Even as no man was able to see His **face** and live, what is central to making this case is that since God only created one man, ever (from what I have read), could that not characterize God as being as Black as the first man that was ever created? To gain needed confirmation and increase credence in the interpretation, let's get back to Eden! As Jesus was also born in the middle of a desert where there were people of color, how could He have blonde hair and blue eyes? Perish the thought! To demonstrate commonality of my desert assertion, a kinky, curly hair and a darker skin tone would be more likely for that time period. Are you ready for the clincher? In Isaiah 19:25b, God said: ... *"Blessed be Egypt My people"...* Whose people? "Aight then."

FYI, Egypt is **not** in the Middle East; Egypt is in Africa, and Black Africans founded Egypt!

Maximize your mandate and know your history; it is a weapon! According to Malcolm X, "A race of people is like an individual man; until it uses its own talent, takes pride in its own history, expresses its own culture, affirms its selfhood, it can never fulfill itself" (Blackissue. com, n.d.). To further celebrate diversity in my notions and to offer additional wisdom to nurture your hermitic heritage, I recommend that you read the following books: *The Black Presence in the Bible & the Table of Nations; Black Genesis:* and *The Prehistoric Origins of Ancient Egypt;* and, *The Black West: A Documentary and Pictorial History of the African American.*

Despite myths to the contrary, Sibyl Pamela Brinkley's feedback is worthy of inclusion: "We sprung from the loins of exquisite strength, excellence, beauty and wisdom! I'm honored of my Black heritage! My legacy is the springboard of the greatest substance on Earth! 'Blacknificence'!" Isn't it disdainful that they forgot to tell us in our History classes about Black people who became rich during the California Gold Rush of 1848? This was an entire story, complete with photographs galore of Black cowboys and Black millionaires of the nineteenth-century, American frontier that was ironically omitted in our History books. "God, why didn't they **cover** us?"

Amongst the criticality of the previous assertions, clearly, this next assertion is a powerful and difficult aspect of the search for meaning which some of our White brothers would rather avoid. Following the position inaugurated by Prophet Barber: "Perhaps this would explain the universal envy of the Black man throughout the world. Instigated, of course, by the devil, could it be that he knew that the prototypical man – Adam – was a Black African man, being most like God in His original state? God must look like a Black man because the Black man looks like God. Maybe that was intuitive when they chose Morgan Freeman to play God in Bruce Almighty." "P☺W!"

Since Daniel describes the texture of **GOD'S hair** as pure wool (Dan. 7:9), and Jesus skin as bronze (Rev. 1:15, 2:18), I am convinced that the previous theories have great merit. Moreover, I was surprised to hear that Kenneth Copeland said in his book, *Honor: Walking in*

Honesty, Truth, and Integrity, that the devil has a personal vendetta against the Black man because he is the most powerful human being on the face of the earth. Meanwhile, Black man, you had better MAN-UP and "bring Black back," maximize your mandate, and act like the creative god that you were created to be!

Theoretically speaking, you look more like God than any other man on the planet, so stop allowing the enemy to "punk you out!" Being male brands you into the image of God, but becoming masculine develop you into His likeness. You must understand that although you took on the distorted image of Adam after the fall, yet, being imperfect, you were made and woven together while God's eyes were glued to your unformed body. Even your very substance was not hidden from Him (Psa. 139:14-16). Your Father not only knew what you were made of, He was already aware of what you were capable of doing before becoming who you were created to be. Life happens, but don't give up before you blow up!

Maybe you were only doing what was normal to your environment, and I embrace you for your survival skills. But you can come out of the "closet" now and not allow your past to dictate your future. He knows exactly where you are and who you are; it's not even about the sin you're in. It's all about the glory that comes out of the man that He expects to man-up and **cover** the Black woman that was created to be your Black, African queen! I hope that settled the image quandary! After all of the ridicule that envelops my projects, especially since I have been accused of male-bashing, I felt the need to "blow the cover" off my Black brothers. If truth be told, the White race has definitely not covered them. Now, before I refer back to my original conclusion, let me say this while I still have the "mic:" I'm back and happy to be Black!

In the event that some of "y'all done got it twisted" and is still confused, hear ye again, the Word of the LORD: ***"And the rib, which the LORD God had taken from man, made He a woman, and brought her unto the man. And Adam said, 'This is now bone of my bones, and flesh of my flesh: she shall be called Woman, because she was taken out of Man"*** (Gen. 2:22-23). Hey "Adam," "where you at?" I do not intend to be offensive, judgmental, or even condescending, but "it is what it is!" God made the man to do for the woman what she cannot do for herself. He made the woman to do for the man what he could not do for himself. Together, it is now God's intention for them to procreate and replenish the earth!

Rather than revising the Bible, we must repent for our behavior! Since the Bible is not subject to our lifestyle, sexual orientation or doctrinal persuasion, the Scriptures do not have to be rewritten; they need to be reread! God said what He meant and meant what He said! To sum it all up, I have chosen some interpretive expressions that will hopefully leave you comfortable with an alternative explanation. If you were not born with a womb, it is proof positive that you were **NOT** created to act like "Eve!" And if you were not born with a scrotum, you were **NOT** created to act like Adam, no ands, ifs, or buts about it! Be healed, delivered, and be set free, **NOW**, in the name of Jesus Christ!

I even sense that somebody will get free as a result of reading this chapter! Even if it was for one individual, it was worth everything that I have had to go through, just to get to you! God woke me up unusually early this morning, just to tell the **real** men in the house, "let's get back to Eden, and live on top of the world," and maximize the mandate but with a modern mindset. Given rise to the important implications of racism and other, important social implications, I hope that the previous, two integrated chapters provide unquestionable evidence and a useful summary that will be viable and useful for further research.

CHAPTER SEVEN

"AND I DID EAT" ...

Hey "Adam," "where you at?" Since he was the first earthly god and Jesus was the last human Adam, God had no other way to demonstrate to His Son, the love between a man and his bride. Adam, the first human example, was given the **man**date to expose unity and the duty of a bridegroom. Originally, both Adam and Jesus were immortal, but in order for either of them to die and save their brides from eternal damnation, they had to become sin and go to hell. And in order for us to be born again and become gods as in Psalms 82:6, they had to choose to pull off immortality and die as men. "You heard me?"

In the beginning, Adam and Eve were **as** gods, knowing both good (intimacy with God before the fall), and evil (an awareness of Satan after the fall). At present, Jesus refers to us **being** gods as the children of the Most High. Here is the divinely-revealed truth. We are saved today because Adam, who knew no sin, became the sinner and took Eve's place. And Jesus, who knew no sin, became sin and went to hell and took man's place. Bottom line: **without the sinner, there would be no need for the Son.** In my preacher's voice, "I can't get 'no' help up in here." Just as Eve was made for Adam, we were born for God's Son.

Even as God had to create a Judas to betray Jesus, somebody had to sin so that Jesus could become the Savior (read Rom. 3:25). What good is a Savior without sinners to repent? This is another good place to maximize the mandate. Here we go: if you are man enough to mess up, when humanity meets divinity, you will be god enough to MAN-UP! "Hello somebody!" Steeped in the notion of redemption (for all of the anti-Christ folks who refuse to accept Jesus as THE Savior of the world), we **MUST** go through the Christ in order to get to the Creator! Now that was a good place for the real **Christ**ians to take a stand and shout amen!

There is absolutely no exception, substitute, or ands, ifs, or buts about it. Move your "buts" out of the way and accept John 14:6. No, that's okay; you don't even have to be distracted to find your Bible. Since I am no longer trying to preserve space here, allow me to save the drama for the devil. *"Jesus saith unto him, I am the way, the truth, and the life: no man cometh unto the Father, BUT by Me."* "It's a wrap!" While most "butts" have cracks in them, that's the only "but" that needs no "reconstruction."

Even Satan recognizes Jesus as the Christ! Hold up; I need to "rewind" and grab something from Part Two of my Trilogy. "If the princes of this world had known what the cross would release to us, his 'folks' would not have crucified the Lord of glory (read 1 Cor. 2:7-9). His intent through Eve had been supported by a disobedient Adam who did not understand the purpose of God. The debt was an overpayment; it wasn't just a life for a life. It was God for man – innocent blood for a guilty Adam. Jesus' death is not considered a murder because their hands were manipulated by God to wipe out sin forever. Jesus declared that no man took His life. Yielding His Spirit, He laid it down as a ransom for many.

It is all about the blood of Jesus! Without the shedding of blood there would be no remission of sin. The cross was the appeasement for divine justice. The divine substitute was: I gave Christ my sin (rebellion), in exchange for God's righteousness, the same rights that He gave His Son. We both received something that neither of us deserved" (Reid, 2010). So **Christ**ianity is not a religion; it's a reality that recognizes Jesus as the Christ! Thus, sanctification is the process that makes righteousness a lifestyle. It is utterly devastating to actually witness so many "church folks" becoming **anit**-Christ, especially when their foundation and faith hinge on the premises of strict holiness. Faith is believing in something that you cannot see; still, you KNOW it's there.

The reason that many are being driven to become disbelievers is that the Bible must fulfill itself. If you noticed, I avoided saying, unbelievers. Can I suggest to you that an unbeliever is someone who does not believe at all. But a disbeliever is someone who is struggling to continue to believe what they thought they believed. Here is why I am devastated but not dazed at the disbelievers that were once identified as believers. "Many FALSE prophets shall rise and deceive MANY (Mt. 24:11), but Jesus had already forewarned us to "take heed that we be not deceived" (Lk. 21:8a).

Seeing us as the righteousness of His Son, not only must Satan surrender to the authority of Jesus. The Father must acknowledge the begotten Son when dealing with His adopted sons. To underline this parallel, once we recognize Jesus as the Son of God and accept Him as our Lord and Savior, the Christ in us cannot allow us to go to hell, as long as we **allow** the God in Christ to conform us into the image of Himself. Significantly so, if Adam had loved Eve more than Jesus was willing to love us, we should have been married to Adam; or, at least, he should have become our redeemer.

Inevitably, once man failed God, God looked everywhere for someone to redeem us from the hand of the enemy. He tried bullocks, heifers, goats, Abraham and Isaac. Then, when God could not find a lamb that was spotless, He looked under the altar. There He found a Lamb that was **already** slain from the foundation of the world (Rev. 13:8). O.M.G.! I am feeling the fire of the Holy Ghost right about now! In reality, He actually died before He was born. As Jesus transcended time and saw Himself fulfilling His purpose, He said to the Father: "If You would prepare Me a body, I will go down and redeem man back to Myself." Before Jesus could fulfill his providence, Adam and Eve had to fulfill their purpose. "And there you have it." "It was a SET-UP for a COME-BACK!" ... *"WHO IS THE FIGURE OF HIM THAT WAS TO COME"* (Rom. 5:14b with emphasis added).

That was so powerful that I have forgotten the title of this chapter. God took me somewhere; I am literally having to "reset" and find my way back to the subject matter. Hold on; I'll get there. I think I got it! Although Eve was beguiled by the serpent, Adam was too perfect to be beguiled. A man that is mature in his manhood knows how to maximize his mandate. Now that was some good "meat" right there too. "Nothing's left on that bone but some rub." That's why I love revisions; they help me to even, maximize my mandate. Could Adam's masculinity be a reason why the serpent totally ignored the man while he talked to the woman?

I just saw a life-lesson in that question? "Eve:" "where you at?" Woman of God, since the man is now your head, **never** allow your vulnerability to prevail over his masculinity. I am advocating that Adam was not oblivious to what took place with Eve; he was simply a representation of the Father. Since he was formed in His image and likeness, he thought like God because he was a god. And because God made him a god and put him in charge over the garden, Adam was so god that God wouldn't even allow Himself to name the animals. He even had dominion over the sun and was able to do what Joshua could not do. Joshua had to pray for the sun to stand still; Adam only needed to command the sun to stand still. I'm glad this chapter is short because I can't take much more of this!

If Adam had the ability within himself to **only** reproduce **perfection** as I described earlier, then, my consensus that Eve was made whole and with the same dominion has great merit. With the benefit of hindsight, I have already anticipated your next question. If Adam reproduced perfection, why was the "first lady" hoodwinked, bamboozled, and led astray? "Really?" Did you not get the "memo" that it was a set-up? Hey "Adam," where have you been? "My bad;" maybe you are a woman of God and the Eve in you has your attention elsewhere. Seriously, do you **still** not see what I see? If you're on Facebook, more than you are in Hisbook, you may be slow for real. "Nevertheless-although-even so," you might be slow, but you worth waiting on. I refuse to give up on you because I really need you to get this. Let me say this one more time: ... **"Who is the figure of Him that was to come"** (Rom. 5:14b).

Again, the question was: If Adam reproduced perfection, how did First Lady Eve "go south?" The one time that God specifically addressed Eve, He asked, **"What is this that thou hast done?"** (Gen. 3:13). I imagine that this pivotal question had everything to do with the enormous weight of her decision. Not blaming Adam, she replied,

"The serpent beguiled me, and I did eat." Okay, that was the title of this chapter: *"And I did eat."* "Look at your neighbor and say: 'She's back'." Oh, I was just reminded of a message that Bishop D. Dewayne Rudd preached some years ago, entitled, *Anointed but Weak.* The weaker vessel of a perfect union, if Eve was made for Adam, inevitably, God must have created the serpent for Eve. That's exactly why both the man and the woman were boldly compelled to confess: ... *"And I did eat"* (Gen. 3:12b, 13:13b).

Again, it wasn't that the woman was inferior; she just had a different purpose than the man. Had God's purpose not prevailed for positioning the serpent, I must continue to reemphasize that her seed could **not** have bruised the enemy's head. The only way to know that the seed is growing is when the weeds appear. Despite the weeds, "can't nothing stop a cycle like a seed!" While it takes more time to make something than to form it, I believe that Eve was built perfectly to fit in a precarious position to fulfill an overpowering purpose. Satan had a plot, but God had a plan. From that day forward, when man decides to interrupt a cycle in the life of the woman, he sows a seed. When Adam sowed the seed of unconditional love, it validated the plan and instigated a way of escape for the man that failed as a result of the plot.

At the efficient rate that Satan carried out the orders makes me wonder whether he was privy to the plan. At any rate, one thing that I do recognize is that he was not brilliant enough to know that eventually, the cross would be the appeasement for divine justice! Even as the enemy made headway in rendering null and void, the plan of salvation, **NOTHING could stop the cycle of the enemy like the seed of the woman!** P☺W! That was worth highlighting, right there. Yes, she was beguiled, and she did eat. "Nevertheless-although-even so," **the serpent breached security for a reason, but the woman left the garden on purpose.** "Talk to me somebody!"

Consistent with the prior viewpoint and in harmony with my next Scripture (1 Timothy 2:14-15 with emphasis added); Adam was NOT deceived. Whenever a man is maximizing his mandate and thinking like God, He **can't** be deceived! As Satan was unable to penetrate the plan of God, Adam was very conscious of his decision.

"And Adam was not deceived, but the woman being deceived was in the transgression [breach of command]. *Not withstanding she shall be saved in childbearing, if they continue in faith and charity and holiness with sobriety."* Carrying out God's plan to expand the COMMUNITY is what saved the day and gave the woman of God her "wake-up call!"

Hold on; the plot line thickens. After Adam was given a few moments to reflect on Eve's transgression, I feel that the reason that he **did eat on purpose** is that he chose to become mortal to avoid being separated from **himself**. He wanted to leave the garden with the woman that was bone of his bone and flesh of his flesh. "What a man; what a man; what a man!" To the same extent that nothing can separate us from the love of the Father, even sin could not separate Adam from the love that he had for his woman. This concept hinges on the premise that since God does not design anything for our ultimate destruction, they left the garden together.

As a matter of fact, they advocated Matthew 19:6b (with emphasis added): *"What therefore GOD hath joined together let not man* [nor Satan] *put asunder."* This is why I feel that God allows divorce. That statement sounded like an oxymoron, didn't it? No, what I mean is, you are not truly a "match made in Heaven" unless HE joined you together. So what He does not ordain, He is not obligated to sustain. To even think of ending up with the wrong person in multiple marriages is good enough reason for me to be alone than to be married wrong.

For now, can we at least come to the agreement that to forsake Eve, Adam would have equally forsaken himself? "Beloved," he could not do that because they were a "match made in heaven!" If he had forsaken himself, not only would he have forsaken Eve who was him. He would have forsaken the mandate for which he was created. If Adam had "dropped the ball" after Eve, the game of life would have been "O.V." (over)! What you are seeing here is a preview of a "movie" that had already been produced. To view the preview in detail, I admonish you to read Luke 21:25-28. If you are still looking at Adam's disobedience and Eve's transgression, you are on the wrong "channel."

God had already recorded the real story in His mind (you know, while Adam and Eve were still spirit beings). They just came along and played-out what He had planned to capture on the "big screen." The way you have seen things play out in the past will soon say: THE END! Get ready for the new release! It's called, THE SHOW-DOWN AT THE NEW JERUSALEM! In Bishop T.D. Jakes' voice, "Get ready, get ready, get ready!" Seriously, you had better keep watch for the Owner of your house (please read Mt. 24:36-39)! According to Acts 1:11: *"Which also said, Ye men of Galilee, why stand ye gazing up into Heaven? This same Jesus, which is taken up from you into Heaven, shall so come in like manner as ye have seen Him go into Heaven."* In anticipation of the "show-down" at the New Jerusalem, also read Acts 3:19:21.

What I started to reestablish before I was interrupted by the preview of a coming attraction is that, **their** name being Adam (Gen. 5:2) is an indication that **Eve was Adam!** I am particularly respectful of Prophet Floyd Barber's view in that, "Her name became Eve when she became the mother of all living, God called both the man and his wife 'Adam' because He intended a symbiotic relationship in which the woman, being absorbed into the man, ends up finding her true self – oxymoronically – by losing herself in her husband."

A replication of previous reflections is a crucial part of understanding this chapter. Since God first gave him dominion and placed him in charge of the garden, would it be decent and in order for God to put Eve out, without Adam's consent? After all, God is a God of order, right? Since Eve was absorbed into her man, could one even exist without the other? Nay verily, perish the thought! When we look at them in the seventh and eighth chapters of Genesis, their eyes were opened; they knew they were naked.

At first, the Adam's family was operating in the Spirit; Adam was even able to name the animals. But the day you eat of this fruit, you shall die a spiritual death where the spirit of man will no longer have Holy Communion with the Spirit of God. Flesh was given permission by man's will to block God's relationship in speaking from Spirit to spirit. The death that man experienced was the deafness of his spirit man to hear directly from God (without being born again). Together, when both sinned and the five senses evolved, the glory of God that once covered their bodies, lifted, and they realized: "Oh snap," I'm

133

naked; I need to put some clothes on." This is the moment that they shifted from the dispensation of innocence, to the dispensation of consciousness. When sin deafened the sensitivity of man's spirit where he could no longer hear, that's when they sewed fig leaves together, and they made themselves aprons.

Oh, by the way, since you came into the world naked and unashamed, who told you that you were naked? Who made you self-conscious and paranoid about the way I expected you to present yourself to Me? It was after they stopped walking in the Spirit and started viewing things from the natural eye that they were driven to walk after the flesh. Who snuck in the garden and changed the rules of My House and made you feel the need to take cover?

The House rule is that you come to Me just as you are (without one plea). That's the way I made you, and that's exactly how I see you (naked and unashamed). I can never be intimidated by what I made because if I made it, I understand it. And if it's broken, I can fix it. That's exactly why Hebrews 4:16 says: *"Let us therefore come boldly unto the throne of grace, that we may obtain mercy, and find grace to help in time of need."* When we repent **grace**fully and unashamedly, not only does God embrace us with grace and mercy. In addition, it fosters an attitude of repentance and honesty about our struggles so that sin has no place to HIDE.

It is obvious here that Adam and Eve introduced the "fig leaf" religion or a behavior that depicts a hidden agenda (i.e. to establish one's own righteousness). So now, when God speaks, the flesh tries to reason with what He said. What salvation does is causes you to become alive again to hear fresh from God. Salvation is the resurrection of your Spirit through your new nature. The significant point here is this: there is no disgrace to being transparent. The dishonor in not being transparent is that we conceal sins that the blood has the power to cover. As a way of foretelling his redemption, God reconciled man into right standing through the sacrificial blood of an animal. He made coats of skins and clothed them because of the blood in the skins.

Allow me to deviate here for a moment. In Genesis 4:1b, where Eve conceived Cain and said, "I have gotten a man from the LORD," she knew that she was supposed to birth something that would destroy the enemy because of the prophetic word that claimed her seed would bruise his head. Seeing that the woman does not have the type of seed that a man has, Eve thought that perhaps, her first son, Cain, might be the son that would rise up and bruise the enemy's head. Each time that she pushed the man's seed out of her body, she had the expectation that this might be the Messiah that was going to redeem man back to Himself. Nonetheless, the bleeding lamb that Abel offered up to God and the bleeding man (blood that was shed as a result of his murder) points to the fusion of the revelation of God that the Lamb was actually a man.

In concurrence with Bishop Donald Thomas (2017), God turned His anger from Adam and Eve, to the innocent animals (the sacrifice), and slayed them with the sword of His mouth. Once these animals had been killed, He proceeds to remove their skins with the sword with which they were slain. The same sword which saved them, also prepared their clothing. It was substitute clothing which was designed to cover their natural nakedness until the eternal clothing provided by the Lamb of God could be made manifest. That would come not only to cover our nakedness, but more importantly, to take away our sins.

When we look at the fact that God made Adam and Eve coats of skins, God was willing to kill as many animals as it took to properly clothe the first man. This act signifies that He would spare nothing for His children. It also spoke of the fact that He would kill and kill, until man would be redeemed, and that death would reign until God Himself would be satisfied. "Why was God so adamant here," I asked? It was important to Him that the breaking of His Commandment by Adam was fully paid. To say the least, that speaks volumes about the wonder-working power of the precious blood of the Lamb that can wash away our sins and cleanse us from ALL unrighteousness!

Isn't it ironic that the only thing that Jesus ever cursed was the fig tree? In a season when the tree should have been flourishing, it had leaves on it but no fruit. "Adam," you can never again try and cover up your sin with unfruitful actions that imply judgment and rejection. Accordingly, the appearance of religiosity is never enough to guarantee salvation. The fruit of genuine repentance must be evidenced to generate real change. To say it another way, transparency comes with accountability. To cover your nakedness takes away your innocence. If you are not willing to be transparent, it may be that you are still susceptible to the fall. Come on now; was that not some unadulterated substance, right there?

Before I get ahead of myself, allow me to stop and crack the "woman-code." The reason that Eve was not left to herself is that Adam loved her as much as he loved himself. O.M.G. – if I could for once, meet a man like Adam! In case you were wondering why I *didn't* get married and am still waiting on *purpose*, "ooops, there it is!" I keep dipping into my final chapter, but my point is: "Plenty of men will want to share a night with you, but the right man will want to spend his life with you" (origin unknown). Until then, I remain #successfullysingle. Like so, Eve was not looking for a lover; she waited for Adam to become her husband!

Again, whom did God address in the ninth verse, after they had hidden themselves from His presence? Not that He had lost sight of Adam, but for some strange reason, God asked the question, "Where art thou?" If God was Black and used Ebonics like the author here, He likely would have said, "Hey Adam, 'where you at'?" While Eve was still hiding behind Adam's covering, God did not speak to them. He spoke directly to him, and he **alone** had to face God. "Why, you don't say!"

When Adam went to "court," in Genesis 3:10, he was **not** pondering over a way to point the finger at Eve (his wife). I am convinced that he intended to establish a way to cover and protect her from the "Judge." He never told God, "**We** heard Your voice in the garden;" or, "**We** were afraid;" or, "**We** were naked, so **We** hid ourselves." "NO, men and women of the jury, I did eat; and yes, I am guilty! My wife is **not** on trial here! I am the one who has been subpoenaed by God! So 'jury,' 'don't get it twisted'!"

Especially typical in today's western culture of society, the man sins with the woman; and then, he allows her to fall **with** him. I'm so glad that woman was God's idea and not Adam's. That's why he put him to sleep, so that he wouldn't make stupid suggestions like the one I just mentioned. Stereotypically, before man will admit, "And I did eat," the woman is betrayed, denounced, and labeled as a "who'e." Frankly, man of God, that's not Bible; that's ugly! Just as Adam took upon himself Eve's transgression, Jesus took upon Himself the iniquities of us all because He was the last Adam. And, believe it or not, God expects you to do likewise. "Don't hang up on me now!" I'm still trying to get through to you! This chapter goes way beyond Adam and Eve. It actually hits home! Stay with me!

Man of God, your actual nature is revealed by how you treat your wife! You have to know her in order to dwell or deal with her. Signifying the commitment that Adam made, the answers to a man's prayers are determined by the way he dwells with his bride. Since I know that you are not going to stop and read, let me get it for you because I want you to see this: ***"Likewise, ye husbands, dwell with them according to knowledge, giving honour unto the wife, as unto the weaker vessel, and as being heirs together of the grace of life; that your prayers be not hindered"*** (1 Pet. 3:7).

Another central aspect of this chapter is that shepherds should protect their sheep in much the same way that a man protects his bride, whether the sheep fall by the wayside, or fall in sin with the shepherd. In biblical times, the priest covered you – no matter how you sinned, why you sinned, how many times you sinned, or with whom you sinned. Here is a simple analogy in the days of the Tabernacle. If a slayer committed a killing unawares and unwittingly, the pursuer that chased after him was forced to let him go, once he grabbed the horns of the altar. Hence the reason, it was called the "Sanctuary;" it was the place of refuge (read Jos. 20:3-6).

Pastors, fathers, husbands, and men in general – you are considered as the priest of your domain, and your responsibility is not only to execute order. You are to cover and protect those that are under the realm of your dominion. ***"No man can enter the strong man's house and plunder his property unless he first binds the strong man, and then he will spoil his house"*** (Mk. 3:27). As the strong man that has the power to bind and loose, nobody should ever be allowed to touch or harm anyone within your fold, without **first** coming through you (whether right or wrong, guilty or innocent).

Since God had initially told Adam not to eat of the tree before Eve was reproduced, God was not talking to Eve, or about Eve, when He asked Adam, "Who told thee that thou wast naked? Hast thou eaten of the tree, whereof I commanded thee that thou shouldest not eat?" (see Gen. 3:9-12). NO! He was talking precisely to the priest of the garden. "Did **you** (Adam) do what I told **you** not to do?" (see Gen. 3:9-14). Here is where God blamed and cursed the serpent for beguiling Eve. Then, He cursed the ground because Adam hearkened to the voice of his wife.

This is where I feel that our men really get it twisted and take the Scripture out of context: *"And the man said, "The woman whom Thou gavest to be with me, she gave me of the tree, and I did eat"* (Gen. 3:12). Contrary to popular belief, I do not see that he was looking for justification or making excuses for his disobedient behavior. It was because God gave Eve to Adam that he made the above claim. He must have realized that if he **refused** to eat, he could not remain with the woman that **God** had taken from his side to be his help meet.

Scripture proves that Eve was truly deceived, but if I were the devil's advocate, I would say that she hooked up with Satan just to see if she could get Adam's undivided attention. In my rationality (when he flaunted her before God in the previous Scripture), he must have been bragging on the God who was powerful enough to create for him, a woman who was not only created to cause the head of Satan to be bruised, but one who was cunning and crafty enough to provoke him to keep his vow and demonstrate perfect love.

Alternatively, when most men make the statement: "This woman You gave me," they are sarcastically complaining and trying to make God responsible for their mistake. One Man of God, who referred to his wife in this way, claimed that she was crazy, and in her defiance, she neglected to do anything he asked her to do. I overheard another Pastor wishing that he could trade his wife in for the woman that he should have married in the first place. First of all, God would not give thee a woman to demonize because "every good gift and every perfect gift is from above, and cometh down from the Father of lights, with whom is no variableness, neither shadow of turning" (James 1:17).

Furthermore, *"The blessing of the LORD, it maketh rich, and He addeth no sorrow with it"* (Prov. 10:22). So if you're feeling sorry, do not blame your bad relationship on God. Just be honest; either you, or the devil created that foolishness! You made your bed hard, but now you feel forced by your religious standards to sleep in it. A qualified conclusion is that if she was the woman **God** gave you, like Adam, you would be bragging and not complaining. Proverbs 18:22 still holds true: ***"Whoso findeth a wife findeth a good thing, and obtaineth favour of the Lord."***

Are you yet wondering why you don't get many favors? Man of God; at the risk of sounding "uncouth" and unsaved, allow me to conclude this chapter in my worst Ebonics. "You 'be-damned' because 'you done' married the wrong, 'damn' woman!" "Don't judge me!" I am really trying to communicate in a manner that is consistent with the professional expectations of those in the Human Services profession. However, you can find "be damned" in Mark 16:16. Now that may have deserved a disapproval face. Never mind; I couldn't figure out how to make that one. Let's go with the joking face: X-p. While I dare not underestimate my flawed, human tendencies, please take a breather here. The next extensive chapter is where it literally hits home for me, personally. Are you ready for this one?

CHAPTER EIGHT

THE 21ST-CENTURY ADAM "SIN-DROME:" AUTHOR'S "DRIVE-THRU" VERSION OF "P.M.S."

Before I break down the details of this chapter and "peel this onion back," allow me to bring clarity to my difference and my uniqueness. Some things I am required of GOD to write: *..."For unto whomsoever much is given, of him shall be much required"* ... (Lk. 12:48b). *"Wherefore, though I wrote unto you, I did it not for his cause that had done the wrong, nor for his* [her] *cause that suffered wrong, but that our care for you in the sight of God might appear unto you"* (2 Cor. 7:12 with emphasis added). Years ago, when I would sing along with Yolanda Adams: "The battle is not yours; it's the LORD'S... He only wants to use you;" I had no clue that the reality of this song was foreshadowing my destiny. When I was suicidal and fighting to survive "P.M.S.," (what I've coined as the Pastor's Mistress Stronghold); I did not realize that God was literally preparing me for the "necessity that is laid upon me" (1 Cor. 9:16).

"For I reckon that the sufferings of this present time are not worthy to be compared with the glory which shall be revealed in us. For the creature itself was made subject to vanity, not willingly, but by reason of Him who hath subjected the same in hope. Because the creature itself also shall be delivered from the bondage of corruption into the glorious liberty of the children of God. For we know that the whole creation groaneth and travailed in pain

together until now. And not only they, but ourselves also, which have the firstfruits of the Spirit, even we ourselves, waiteth for the adoption, to wit, the redemption of our body" (Rom. 8:18-23). Not only does the creation of the earth groans for us to come forth, "even we ourselves."

Thus, whether you've gotten over it, or not, Paul speaks my sentiments: *"For we would not, brethren, have you ignorant of our trouble... that we were pressed out of measure, above strength, insomuch that we despaired even of life"* (2 Cor. 1:8). As a precursor, allow me to lay a brief foundation for those of you who may not know my real story. First, to offer a neutral perspective and to maintain a balanced posture here, there certainly are areas of lack that make us susceptible to the inherit power that is associated with leadership. As a result, there are cases of women who intentionally seduce the man of God for the simple fact that she is enticed by his power. Then, many of them scream "victim," once the relationship goes "sour." Even as physical attractions are a normal process of human relations, the line is crossed when relations move beyond sensory to sensual and graduate to sexual.

In the case of a teenager who became one of the mistresses to the most trusted man in her life, this is how men in positions of power use their influence to sculpt and groom young girls to become who they become. Particularly, when that trusted man is at least, 20 years older, it adds a different dynamic to the situation. Ask me how. When you have a "vet" in your corner, over your life, and in your ear calling you his daughter for 15 years, you develop a set of skills and a series of sensitivities that allow you to go undetected. All the same, research supports that "a man in this power of trust and authority becomes unavoidably a parent figure and is charged with the ethical responsibility of the parenting role. Violations of these boundaries are, psychologically speaking, not only rapes but also acts of incest" (Rutter, 1977).

Since the clergy's position incorporates both spiritual and moral authority in an environment or "forbidden zone" that is expected to be safe, any relationship that violates this professional boundary is considered abuse and not an affair because this is an ethical violation that is not considered consensual. Why not, one may ask? Any sexual contact by a man in power that occurs within professional relationships is inherently exploitive of a woman's trust. (Rutter, 1977). Even though sex is often interpreted as consensual on the part of the victim, the relationship is more detrimental than a relationship between two adults with an even power balance (Parnitzke & Freyd, 2013).

The question was asked by a clergyman: "When it comes to sexual misconduct or abuse, does the clergy's spiritual position or authority realistically distinguish them from doctors, coaches, teachers, counselors, mentors, CEOs, etc.? Absolutely! Because of the power imbalance, distinctively, the clergy has the propensity to exploit the congregant because he or she may be emotionally dependent on his or her professional character as <u>spiritual</u> advisor. Therefore, betrayal by an authority figure that is held to a **much higher standard of conduct** can significantly, disrupt or distort the spiritual and emotional well-being of the individual.

Evidence suggests that those who seek redress from the religious institution where the abuse took place are often perceived as enemies of the church as well as the perpetrator. This perception can leave the victims further unsupported and suffering the consequences of entrapment, secrecy, justification, denial, concealment, and the fear of rejection. Unless the cycle is broken by someone who is stronger than the victim, the woman gets mad at God and the church. Or, she remains in church environments in silence. Hopefully, that answered the clergy's inquiry. #.)

In short, one may ask: What starts such a "bleeding cycle" as the one detailed in my Trilogy-Part One? As an 11 year-old whose family was neglected because the authority figure in the home had extramarital affairs and children outside of the home, what happens after he returns later to establish a storefront ministry? Because he did not have the respect and the support that he felt entitled to, the hated daughter became the victim of naked beatings with razor straps and extension cords. Leaving home as a **virgin** with unembellished "female problems;" can you see that she was honestly looking for "Daddy," and not "Dick?" The monstrous reality is that the teenager would not remain 17 years old, and eventually, truth would prevail.

As I was going to say before I was compelled to insert the precursor, an irreconcilable, 21st-century "Adam" would probably reverse the "script" from the previous chapter. He might say something to this effect: "The woman whom Thou gavest to be help, or my sheep, or my goddaughter, or my secretary, or my assistant is the same woman that caused me to lose my reputation, hundreds of members, and thousands of dollars." That's my perception of the 21st-century Adam "**SIN**-drome" as it relates to P.M.S., or a Pastor's Mistress Stronghold.

A generally accepted retort might be, "I must sew **my** 'fig leaves' and cover my own 'ass-et,' especially since the woman You sent me left the fold without my blessing and against my better judgment." Supporting this reaction is contradictory because his blessing is really considered a curse, and his better judgment was from the devil! This is the the type of man that Bishop T. D. Jakes says is too proud to get better because he's so busy protecting his image that he refuses to bring anybody into his reality. While I aim to grasp the full nature of CPSA (clergy-sexual perpetrated abuse) in my continuing doctoral research, I suggest that you read Part One of my Trilogy, *From Mistress to Ministry*. Or, you may be oblivious to the part of my story that sent ripples throughout my Pentecostal denomination. I can only hope that your view of the remaining scenario is not equally consistent with those who have colored my writings with their habits of thinking, feelings, opinions, etc.

My goal is to bring understanding about the phenomenon of clergy misconduct and on the degree to which the following details help to clarify my Trilogy and/or differentiate between conflicting meanings. The question is whether or not you want the truth. Well, here it is anyway. When a relationship is set in motion because a teenager who is young and dumb is summoned to a hotel for a *private counseling session*; the reality is: she did not fall intentionally; she was pushed. Not expecting the reality that was "brewing," everything that happened for the next 15 years was dictated by this one, 21st-century Adam premeditated invitation. In any event, never judge another person's story because they sin differently than you, or because they got caught and you got away, or because they chose to declare what you choose to deny.

Looking back in retrospect, he would have been covering and protecting the teenager properly, had he **NOT** influenced his spiritual daughter to become a partaker of his adulterous affairs for the next 15 years. Now, can I submit for your consideration, the real "nuts and bolts" of this case? To be overtaken in a fault is one thing, but "a mistake repeated more than once is a decision" (Paulo Coelho). Nevertheless, that is perception after the fact. Like Eve, the teenager was beguiled by the enemy to give Pastor of her "fruit." The intrinsic reality is that "Adam" "did eat," but he did not protect the female from the enemy whose plan was to destroy a "cycle destroying seed." "Hey 'Adam,' where you at?"

"CAN WE TALK?"

In my own defense, the way to cover me would have been to accept the responsibility (like Adam) and then, **completely** acknowledge that **he** failed God. Given all the knowledge that he knew about morals and righteous living, together with the facts that he had about the unique demands of my personal background, what would have been the most selfless, compassionate, and loving act possible? "To take a stand and be the man." Bottom line – point blank! Often, people love hard but hurt loud.

The both of us should have healed as long as we could keep it private. *"When I kept silence, my bones waxed old through my roaring all the day long"* (Psa. 32:2-3). Consequently, when I could no longer keep silent, I gave him fair warning that a book was forthcoming. Yet, he took no actions to dissuade me. The right steps could have corrected what had taken place; and/or, they could have prevented what was about to take place. Since he refused to take heed to the warning, the time to own and embrace the struggle and be hyper vigilant was after the "**sin**-drome" was explored and publicly exposed (read Psa. 32:5). "Can we talk?"

"When pride cometh, then cometh shame: but with the lowly is wisdom" (Prov. 11:2). Along these lines, once it did go public, not only did he refuse to use wisdom; neither did his leaders use wisdom. Sorry to say, that's C.O.G.I.C. news! Do you ever wonder who's going

to get the worse judgment; those that did it, or those that knew about it and did nothing to stop it? "Hmmm…" That's a powerful question. That's why I am so appreciative of the "good-humored" Bishop, Craig Baymon, who has left an indelible mark on my heart. It didn't take a rocket science to figure it out, but being the seer Bishop is; God opened his big☺eyes to this situation the very first time I visited his church, just as I was around the age of 20. Because he was "independent," he had nothing to lose.

At the appointed time (after counseling me for years), he literally SNATCHED me up out of that foolishness! "I cannot make this up;" you see I have witnesses. For years, he continued to give me "wake-up calls" and "check-out times," but this time, he gave me a "24-hour eviction notice." In his tone of voice, all I could hear was: "I 'double-dog-dare' you to stay!" I could almost see those great big eyes, "mean-mugging" me through the phone. I guess, in God's mind, I had stayed long enough to bring back some "jaw-dropping" footage that would accomplish my purpose. At this point, He must have said, "Enough is enough!"

The next day, I got the "hell-out-of-dodge;" so fast that I barely had time to say I QUIT! For the sake of space, I must restrict these specific details to Trilogy-Part Two. The Bishop had put the fear of God in me and literally, **scared** the hell out of me. I'm still grateful today! He may be a mutual friend of all of the people involved, but he is not intimidated by friendship to speak the truth. Why? Because the Holy Ghost does not lie! "Truth is one bell you can't 'unring'." Even my godbrother, Bishop Brandon B. Porter, said if he had known what was going on before it ended, he would have come and snatched me out of that mess way before it did. When I was much younger, he was good for "crashing my parties." Like an angel, he would just appear out of nowhere. Believe it or not, God kept my secret hidden for such a time as this.

Did He not say: ***"In EVERY thing give thanks: for this is the will of God in Christ Jesus concerning you"*** (1 Thes. 518 with emphasis added). He did not say give thanks in only the things that make sense. When you submit to the process, everything means all things; the same "all things" that Romans 8:28 said would work together for good.

This is how I wrote it in Trilogy-Part One: "For every David, there is a Saul. Now as I look back in retrospect, I am convinced that there was no 'Payless-pump-wearing' competition that could walk in my shoes! What I mean is: I was precut, predestined, prescheduled, prearranged, and preapproved to fit in a particular place in history that nobody else could fit but me. I was GRACED for this, I tell 'ya! At the crux of this scandal is the mere fact that I am the one that qualified for the 'script;' yes, the job that you see me doing right now! I had to go through that, in order to write this!" (Reid, 2014). Not only have I been elevated *From Mistress to Ministry*; I am in the process of being upgraded from a church secretary to a best-selling author. wink-wink,-),-).

At any rate, when the prey has been enticed and manipulated beyond their ability to say no, he or she is only able to experience true reconciliation in the **absence of** personal humiliation. Accordingly, the circumstances that fostered my hostility in this dehumanizing and demonizing situation were the mere fact that he painted me as the villain, and I became victimized twice (once by the perpetrator and then by his supporters). The plot thickens. Under the cloak of repentance and as a result of the 21st-century Adam "**Sin**-drome," he eventually stood in his pulpit to offer an exceptionally, elusive apology for committing what he referred to as an indiscretion to the people who failed to hold him accountable. I'm confused; no, maybe it was an indiscretion "on steroids!"

It is much easier to ignore that thing that you always suspected was not right. Yet, we would rather put a religious mask on sin than "call a spade a spade." Fostering meaningless generalities, that's exactly how, in the church, we basically train people for acting. Since you cannot fix a lie, and "talk your way out of what you've behaved yourself into," informs Stephen Covey, you may as well own up to the truth. Besides, "God wants genuine repentance and not a scripted apology," posted Pastor Manwell Faison. Why? Anything covered up does NOT get healed!

Stay away from people who can't take responsibility for their "**sin**-drome" but make you feel guilty for being angry at them for the sin they committed against you. The Paternity Court Judge, Lauren

Lake, asked the defendant: "How can you be offended when you have been offensive?" "Can we talk?" Despite the consequences, I admitted that I made a conscious decision to participate in this affair. When the Trilogy became my God-given assignment, he wasn't the only one exposed; I exposed myself. As I was fighting for my life rather than my pride, I suffered unfathomable consequences behind this assignment as well. I have had to deal with guilt or the internal remorse of doing wrong, and shame (the external regret that I am wrong).

Not to even mention the painful emotions of rejection and not even getting invited back to celebrations such as "Homecoming Day" at the church that I helped to establish and build. After leaving "home" over 22 years ago, you mean to tell me that I'm still barred from the "family reunions" and we're supposed to have the same Father and be the Bride of the same Christ? "Really?" But you expect us all to show up at the same "Show Down" at the New Jerusalem, and act like nothing ever happened. Or, is it that you expect to make it, and hope I don't show up? "The devil is a 'damned' liar!" Literally; I had to give my Father a "thumbs up" on that one.

You cannot treat me like a step child when we're supposed to have the same spiritual DNA. If I am your sister in Christ, you're supposed to treat me like you treat the rest of your Father's children, not avoid me like I'm the public plague. I'm just about to get my doctorate too, but let me say this the way I learned to talk back in the projects of north Memphis. That may be Black, but it "sho-ain't" Bible! It may be ghetto, but it "sho-ain't" godly! To say the least, church folks can act like the biggest "hood-rats" in the world. Like I told one brother recently; "You may be able to divorce your wife, but you can't divorce a 'sistah.' So don't die without speaking to me." You may make it to your destination, but you may not make it to the destiny of your expectation.

I realize that I touched on the topic of love in an earlier chapter, but here is a recap. *"If a man say, I love God, and hatheh his brother, he is a liar: for he that loveth not his brother whom he hath seen, how can he love God whom he hath not seen?"* (1 John 4:20). Please stop and read the entire chapter. You will see that love has to be our "ID badge." You cannot call yourself a man of God and see me in the airport, and avoid and ignore me like you never knew me. Maybe we have been trying to win the world, the wrong way. It's not that they don't want God; it could just be that they don't recognize Him. According to John 13:35: we are recognized as Christ's disciples by the way we love one another: ***"By this shall all men know that ye are My disciples, if ye have love one to another."***

Let me go ahead and "take the edge off" and get back into the Spirit. Whenever I'm writing about CPSA in the dissertation courseroom, my mentor has to constantly tell me to watch my tone and learn to be objective. Since I'm so passionate in my convictions, sometimes I have to slow down and say: "WH☹☹SA." Now feeling like the "unsung hero" of my former ministry, I absolutely loved my job as Executive Secretary-Treasurer/Trustee. When I prepared for meetings, we didn't just meet to figure out when we would meet again. Have you seen my Leadership Manual? The one thing that I took away from the ministry **and** the leader (who was an EXCELLENT administrator with the gift of leadership), is the know-how to orchestrate real ministry. No worries; it's definitely paying off for me. But that's when church for me was more of an experience than an event. Since resigning though, I have never been able to feel that "home-court advantage" again. Rather, I have always felt like an "outsider looking in."

The ONLY thing we owe each other is to love one another (read Rom. 13:8). How can you be estranged on Earth and expect to dwell together in Heaven forever? Again, it's not congruent to speak to God in super-sonic tongues, and not communicate with your brother/sister in plain English. These same people can have such a false humility; yet, the way they speak in tongues, you almost need to "press 1 for English." I gave a compliment to one of my Father's children over a year ago; if she said, "Thank you," your dead uncle did. I was dumbfounded because I had a much higher expectation of her than that – at least give a "sistah" some professional courtesy. How hard is it to type, "Thank you?" If you took the minute to read a compliment, why not take another minute to respond to it?

I reach out to people in "perspicacious" ways, just to ask, "Can we just all get along?" I do not-NOT talk to certain people because I refuse to talk to them; it's that they refuse to talk to me. When

American soldiers are **accidentally** shot down by another American soldier, the U.S. Army calls that friendly fire. In other words, we expect to be shot at by our enemies, but we do not expect to be shot at by the person who's in the foxhole with us. Consequently, the church, the sanctuary, the House of God that is supposed to be a cease-fire zone has become a shooting range. But guess what; I am an "unerasable" element of world history. Even as I have tried to run away from the place that I call home, God has summoned me to go back and LIVE in the same place I DIED. Some people were hoping that I would surrender quietly and walk away silently. Better yet, God has promised to resurrect me at the "burial site."

"I therefore the prisoner of the Lord, beseech you that ye walk worthy of the vocation wherewith ye are called, With all lowliness and meekness, with longsuffering, forbearing one another in love; Endeavoring to keep the unity of the Spirit in the bond of peace" (Eph. 4:1-3). Let me ask you one more time, "Can we talk?" But "watch me what I say." There will be a few people who will totally ignore all of the other 13 chapters in this book, but this is the chapter that I am bound to get attacked for. "Whatever." "It is what it is." It's not that they don't know any better, but most people are defensive because they are in denial and don't want others to hear the truth. The way to break the power of an epic fall is by responding to truth appropriately.

In any event, "Kindness is in our power, even when fondness is not" (Samuel Johnson). Now, that should have put **you** back in the Spirit. This particular co-pastor was one of the member/leader/family members, who in the end, came to my DEFENSE by the leading of the Holy Spirit, and tried to usher me out of this mess. The husband, who also took part in the exit strategy, later asked a mutual friend, "How is that 'heifer' doing?" "What?" To keep it simple, saints, allow me to ask the same question that Paul asked the Galatians: *"Am I therefore become your enemy, because I tell you the truth?"* (Gal. 4:16). In other words, you've built your whole church off of lies. You've built your whole vision off of deception. You've built your whole program off of secrecy, and now you "wanna" demonize me because I'm a bonafide truth teller?

In Paul's Epistle, he told the Galatians that he was tempted to leave them along because of their **immaturity**. In so many words, he said, "I'm tempted to ignore you, but I realize that if I be me and stay true to what God has called me to do, you can't hurt me. I can't be injured by you." It's in your Bible (Gal. 4:1-19). He decided to keep doing what he was doing because his commitment had given him a realm of security (my sentiments exactly). But here it is 22 years later and they are still "feeling some kind of way" because I spoke out and embraced my truth! Basically, you have made me your enemy because God has made me somebody's deliverer.

Bishop Joseph Walker posted on Facebook: "Before you can raise the dead, you must forgive the living." In my own words, before you can save the lost, you need to learn how to love the ones in the house. And, before you open the doors of the church, you need to tear down the walls that lead to your own heart. I never questioned their obedience when they disclosed their personal testimony. Wow; I just opened my phone/email to a couple of inspiring quotes from Thoughtful Mind. One was: "Humility has such power. Apologies can disarm arguments. Contrition [remorse] can defuse rage. Olive branches do more good than battle axes ever will" (Max Lucado with emphasis added). And the other one was this: "There is no exercise better for the heart than reaching down and lifting people up" (John Holmes).

I'm not trying to be the victim here either; please hear my heart on this. I'm ready for an amicable relationship on this side, with the people that I'm supposed to meet up with on the other side, and spend the rest of eternity with because we're on God's side. To say it another way, I just want all of us who call ourselves saved, to stop being so deep and rather, be a reflection of the WORD and not your world! Grow up saints! This last-minute "footage" came about after I was awakened at 3:33 in the morning, two days before Christmas (2016), and decided to do some final tweaking here. I hope that it blessed you as much as it blessed me.

At first, after brushing my teeth and going downstairs for my morning cappuccino, I was "kinda-like," sitting on the side of the bed with my housecoat half-way on. Then, I said out loud: "I may as well get comfortable here because I'm feeling the Anointing." I'm seeing clearly why God woke me up so early. After spending the last, two days on the editing project for Bishop Thomas, my mission for this holiday weekend is to "make this do what it do." And yes; I'm exhausted, but I "gotta" keep pushing in pain until purpose comes out of my past.

One day, as I was driving along, during this recent, writing "sabbatical/transition/sta-cation," I literally started thanking God for my baby, "Baby." Isn't it crazy when you can feel more love from a dog, than the people in the church? She stays in my room most times, and when she wants to get my undivided attention, she stares me down until I make eye contact. Then, she jumps around and leads me to her treats that I have hidden in my closet. When I told someone that I had fallen in love with a dog, guess what they said. "Another one?" This was the right one, "Baby!" She kept me content in my environment and from ripping and running, "to and fro, seeking where I may 'stayeth'." I could discern when my time to move out was getting closer. God allowed "Baby" to pull away from me, so that the transition wouldn't be so hard on me. Here, I just needed to digress for a moment to show you what it feels like to have a dog for a best friend.

"PUPPY LOVE" – "Til Death do us Part"

If truth be told, when another person's deliverance is taken **personal**, it will not be taken **serious**. Did you get that? To say the least, I could not have produced this book, or even my Trilogy, except by the inspiration of the Holy Ghost. My writings may not be perfect, but you had better recognized that it's purposed. Just as it pained me today to hear someone tell me to let it go; that was like telling me to give up my baby for adoption. #sigh# You want to detox me of my experience and my expressions because you are not open to the encore of my exposure.

"For it is a shame even to speak of those things which are done of them in secret. BUT ALL things that are reproved are made manifest by the light: for whatsoever doth make manifest is light" (Eph. 5:12-13 with emphasis added). Never allow the where you were to hinder you from becoming who you really are. Even as I have allowed it to rehab me, writing was never my dream pursuit. Now as a tested voice, I will always "be the leading lady in my own story" (Robin Roberts).

Jesus **needed** to go through Samaria because that was the quickest way to Galilee. "Nevertheless-although-**even** so" there cometh a woman of Samaria to draw water, and the rest is history (read John 4:3-42). I needed to go through Raleigh in Memphis, TN because it was the quickest way to my destiny. There cometh some bleeding women (the "other" woman with the issue of blood) and some religious leaders in iniquity, who needed to read my story. By the time Jesus finally made it to Galilee and the Galileans received Him, He told the nobleman whose son was sick: *"Except ye see signs and wonders, ye will not believe"* (John 4:48). I refuse to be refused; by the time you finish my latest projects, I would have made a believer out of you, via signs and wonders!

When I reflected upon my purpose and intuitively arrived at its essence, I discovered the reality that was rooted in my experience. "All things are working for my good," but the noteworthy part of Travis Greene's lyrics that has become my new anthem is that "He's intentional." In the midst of it all, 1 Samuel 15:22 offers a welcome reprieve, and that is "to obey is better than sacrifice." Further down (1 Sam. 17:48), while everyone else ran from the battle, David ran **to** the battle. In order to function synergistically with these references, I'm satisfied to highlight the reality that Jesus saw the best in me when others could only see my mistakes.

As it turned out, rather than *humbly* owning up to his moral failure as the cause of all the damage, the leader's behavior led to the impression that he was the victim. As a result, I became the villain to members, family members, friends and associates. "When a toxic person can no longer control you, they will try to control how others see you. The misinformation will seem unfair, but stay above it, trusting that other people will eventually see the TRUTH, just like you did" (Bishop Dale Bronner).

"I never knew how strong I was until I had to forgive someone who was not sorry and accept an apology I never received" (Not Salmon.com/hateloss). Although I don't owe my past anything because "death" pays all debt, this is what happened the last time that I confronted him by phone for a mutual apology. He said that he could not understand how I could make such a ruckus (with my writings) out of a relationship that he considered himself to only be a best **friend,** a good shepherd, and a godfather. Oh, by the way, "We don't lose friends; we learn who our real ones are" (unknown). But this is what "sealed the deal" for me; he boldly stated that he had NO REGRETS. "Are you serious?" What was he really saying? He had no retention of a moment that he mishandled. "Alrighty-then."

If there could have been a mutual, godly sorrow in this regard, 2 Corinthians 7:11 would have been most applicable here: ***"For behold this selfsame thing, that ye sorrowed after a godly sort, what carefulness it wrought in you, yea, what vehement desire, yea, what zeal, yea, what revenge! In all things ye have approved yourselves to be clear in this matter."*** But clearly, he still had not gotten over himself. After he had already tried to curse me by telling me that my life would never come to any good because of my decision to walk away, is this the response I get after I have poured my heart out to express how this has affected me personally, spiritually, mentally, emotionally, and socially? Wow! Rather than apologizing for being wrong on all levels, he distantly apologized for maybe playing a part in my misinterpretation of the Scriptures and a situation that he had planned to keep me in indefinitely. Then he said, "I forgive you."

Not only did he continue to make me out to be the villain, he had gone out of his way to evoke sympathy from the church that he left confused and divided, from the supporters that he left angry, from the critics that he left thrilled, and from the family that he left devastated. Collateral damage not only hurts you; the 21st-century Adam "**Sin**-drome" hurts everything that is connected to you. Predictably, a leader loses credibility with his followers when he/she allows the evidence to become undeniable. At the end of the day, an initial public denial of wrong doing leads to an embarrassing confession when the evidence becomes too weighty (Stockhill, 2014).

Despite the consequences of developing a lifestyle of deception, the crux of the matter is that the Church marginalizes sin when they send out folks that the Holy Ghost has not commissioned; and, when they neglect to discern that some of these leaders are pedophiles and sexual abusers. When you have real discernment, you don't see men as "tress" (upside down, or as a baby coming into the world would see them); you see them as they are. Just because their daddy was a bishop does not qualify them to carry God's Word. Just because they have a good "hoop" (the shout that don't count), a great cliché, and a few "high-fives" from your neighbor does not meet the criteria of God to be a priest. They use David as an example to be carnal and to be human. Then, when they get caught in an indiscretion, or a fall, or a slip, being human becomes the justification that we have all fallen short of the glory of God.

Jesus is the best example to pattern our lifestyles, our habits and our behavior by. Yet, because most folks don't want a leader who gives them a level to live up to, they remain with the one who gives them permission to be unchanged. And since the preacher who relishes the limelight is the only Bible that most church folks read, they remain distracted because their leader is anointed. At the end of the day, when the leader prioritizes his calling before his consecration, he compromises and uses his Anointing as a deflection from being judged and being measured and examined by the people of God. "And there we have it:" the 21st-century Adam **Sin**-drome.

As a matter of fact, I recently and purposely attended a celebration service where the former, "trusted man" in my life was the guest speaker. In trying to protect me, I had been advised not to attend, probably because my covering realized that Satan knows your weak spot. And he looks to reopen an old cut that you thought you were healed from. Against his counsel, I decided to attend because I wanted to celebrate my covering. Ultimately, I wanted to convince myself and everybody else that, "I'm good." In reality, I wanted to see if my own head was really where it needed to be.

As usual, he was still bragging, but this time it was if to portray that no matter what you know or think about me, I still have my "celebrity" status, and I still have the favor of God on my life. This is what I do; this is what I have achieved; this is where I am at this point; and this is how I look (health-wise). The message kind of blind-sided me for a moment because it was almost like he was marketing himself as "the come-back kid." Somewhere I read, "Self-praise is for losers." I'm really not being biased here; my writings substantiate the fact that I absolutely love capturing a captivating Word.

I may give you a "courtesy shout" that don't count, but I am disappointed if I attend church and leave without taking notes. Sometimes, I'm like, did I get up and go through all of that to come here for this? Balaam or no, I don't care whose "ass" it comes through, I need to know, "is there a Word from the LORD?" Whether it makes me uncomfortable, or whether it makes me think, shout, or cry, I need a Word that's either going to make me change or bring about change? One might say that any word is better than no Word at all. "The devil is a lie!" "Let me boil this lobster while the water is hot." Because of humiliation and harassment from the pulpit, I have gone to church and left feeling more broken than before I went. I don't have the energy for that foolishness! Can you not see that my time is valuable?

Moreover, my first line of defense is my mind, so I must barricade it with an authentic Word of God! "Can we talk?" Oh I see, "you-not ready for me!" Although "the come-back kid" made a good presentation, and the goal was accomplished to raise a good offering, I failed at taking notes because none of it required revelation. The guest speaker (the EX-authority in my life) claimed that God changed his message once he got up to preach, or maybe it changed once he saw who he was preaching to. EX means: Thanks for the EXperience. Our time has EXpired. Now he has EXited my life (Alice 105.9). Whereas he became EX for some other folks too, he was known for his abrasive rebuke tactics and bullying people from the pulpit. Even so, I believe that's part of why I'm so disciplined today, even though my "Shannon" says I'm ancient, ancient, ancient.

Even if it did change because of me, I would tell myself not to "sweat the small stuff." But my friend, George, would likely tell me to put this divergence in my "don't-give-a-damn" column. *"BUT as he which hath called you is holy, so be ye holy in all manner of conversation."* So rather than following the lead of my friend, I'm going to stay with 1 Peter 1:15. "How about that?" In the event that a rebuke was intended, allow me to address the validity of its justification. To myself, I thought: "God if you blessed him as much as he claimed, after he tried to cover his "**sin**-drome," You must be getting ready to blow my mind. Would you be interested in knowing why? I have continued to confess my P.M.S. (stronghold) in an effort to prevent others from coming down with the "**SIN**-DROME."

Often, God will allow sorrow to lead or force you to repentance, but only **godly** sorrow worketh repentance (2 Cor. 7:10). "Self-justification and self-defense are the opposite of 'godly sorrow,' asserts Pastor Larry Stockstill, in his 2014 article, *Restoring Integrity in the Pulpit.* Not many men since King David have genuinely said, "I'm sorry; I was dead wrong." Some folks refuse to apologize to you because **you** represent the part of **them** that they refuse to **acknowledge**. Immediately after the vague and ambiguous confession, the former, "trusted man" in my life ushered his flock into an overnight Solemn Assembly (shut-in) to downplay the 21st-century Adam "**sin**-drome" (indiscretion) that **he** had initiated and committed for the past fifteen (15) straight years. "I mean, really?" Some folks should have protested with their feet and got up and walked out. Why? After the 24-hour Solemn Assembly, it was back to church/business/S.H.I.T. as usual.

TEACHING MOMENT/TRUE EXAMPLE: As maintained by Sutton and Jordan (2013), restoration is usually a communal act. Therefore, in an effort to bring healing to a congregation whose pastor's affair was revealed, a national church consulting group was hired to recommend improvements in communication, protections against future, illicit relationships, and even a change in the church's leadership roles to prevent burnout of the pastoral staff. The group or team was commissioned with the task of reviewing the offenses of the fallen leader. Following the assessment, an agreement was made with that leader for a psychologically-healthy, restoration plan (Thomas, 2011).

In this particular case study, the fallen pastor admitted to the congregation that a true pastor is not just a position that you occupy in a church. Rather, it is a place of trust, a place of leadership, and a place of love in the lives and hearts of the members. Considering adultery as a betrayal of the worst sort, he felt that he had betrayed the members' trust, violated their love, and profaned what is holy. In line with Thomas (2011), offenses definitely create barriers, but sincere apologies are quite successful in removing those barriers and opening the door to forgiveness and reconciliation.

As a result of this conviction, Thomas led the fallen pastor and congregation into a reconciliation service. He sent an email to inform the members that the consulting team was planning this service in an effort to move all parties toward the healing of a festering offense. He wrote that over the past, several months, they had been in a process to reconcile the pastor's relationship with the church, which had been broken since he resigned. The email went on to say that the fallen pastor had asked for a time to publicly apologize to those he had hurt. And they wanted to extend the opportunity to any of the members who wanted to participate. Then, the leading consultant asked any of those members who sensed God's leading, to join him in praying for this time that God would show **all** of them any place of unforgiveness in their lives and lead them in the path of reconciliation. He indicated that he saw that service as a beginning step to opening the door to reconciliation and healing (Thomas, 2011).

In the military, you are demoted or dishonorably discharged for adultery, as this is simply against military standards and is considered their code of honor. Professionally so, they have a code of ethics. But you mean to tell me that both have higher standards than the Church/code of "LOVE?" In the church where we should be upholding truth and establishing righteousness, our code is John 14:15. It's so simple:

"If ye love Me, keep My commandments." Yet, our leaders still get rewarded and elevated to senior positions, **after** they are caught in adultery and observed "getting 'mo' tail than the toilet seat." "Can we talk?!?" Apostle "Mo-tail" and Bishop "Ho-tail" keep right on preaching and establishing churches, and the evangelist and the prophet keep doing what they do: evangelizing and prophesying.

On the other hand, Elder "Whoe-no-mo" gets a praise break at the end of his sermon because he escaped herpes, and didn't get caught when he flirted with the choir members and the office workers. Because nobody called him out when he made "the other woman" commit an abortion, he's just thankful that he was able to get away. After all, they use for justification that Moses was a murderer, and he saw God's hinder parts. David was an adulterer, and God used him too. *"Because sentence against an evil work is not executed speedily, therefore the heart of the sons of men is fully set in them to do evil"* (Ecc. 8:11).

Since few people have read my Trilogy, allow me to borrow another excerpt from Part Three. "Why is I-chabod (the glory has departed) written over many of our churches? God is against anyone establishing Him a house that is full of strife and contention and unrepentance. Psalms 24:3b-4b says: *'Who may stand in His holy place? He who has clean hands and a pure heart'...* A good way to acquire a perspective on new construction is to examine God's heart toward David. Although it was in David's heart to build God a house, God did not permit him to.

He had fought too many wars and shed too much blood on the earth (read 1 Chron. 22:8). Rather, God chose David's son, Solomon, because he was a man of peace and rest." (Reid, 2010). Just in case you think you've gotten away, some of "y'all" closet freaks **and** homosexuals need to take a "slick leave" from the pulpit. "Real talk." You can't just cut the tree at the trunk; you need to get down to the root of your issues.

I have two, other points to make in this regard. First of all, adultery is an intentional experience, not a mental activity. Secondly, continual sin is not a mistake or an indiscretion. In the final analysis, more often than not, folks sin with their eyes wide open. Toddlers fall down and get back up. For those who desire to learn to walk in the Spirit, this is for you: *"Now unto Him that is able to keep you from falling, and to present you faultless before the presence of His glory with exceeding joy"* (Jude 1:24). On the other hand, if you refuse to get off the "waterslide," we will all know by your decision to go for the "plunge." How much you really and truly love God determines how committed you are to bringing your flesh under subjection.

After a sincere apology, the next step would integrate coming to a place of true repentance (change). Maybe if some of these unrepentant preachers would go ahead and take their collars off, the "yoke" won't keep them from breaking free. It is not my assignment to minimize or trivialize a person's humiliation when they get in trouble and are genuinely repentant. In many cases though, the preponderance of being sorry because one gets caught is that, had he or she not gotten caught, they would still be caught up and enjoying the "**sin**-drome."

While cheating is often connected to pain and sometimes marriage issues, some people make immature decisions that feel good at the time, but they later regret it and come to a place of repentance. Others have infidelity issues due to their character issues, so they recklessly contribute to the cheating population. Then, they want to blame the victim because they were not protective of their image. Let me give you my version of, "Charity begins at home and spreads abroad. "Eros love starts at home and should **not** spread to other broads." Ask me why. It is a state of the heart and is colored and underpinned by deep and beautiful procreative urges that's intimately related to sex.

For many, my situation was not easy to watch, but what is important to see is that this was **not** simply a case of an individual who had a sudden impulsive weakness for which he immediately confessed. Rather, this was an individual who had a long history of covering his "**sin**-drome" for an extended period of time, with not only me but others in the congregation. Many times, when you are left dealing with the damages of a breakup, that other person has already moved on to another relationship (wink,-).

According to Stockhill (2014 with emphasis added), "The doctrine of grace is certainly needed by all of us sinners, but 'grace and truth' is required for those who stand before others as a spiritual leader. To begin with, there is a stark difference between an indiscretion and a moral failure. You don't need a hammer to remove a splinter. An indiscretion requires discipline, whereas a moral failure may require **disqualification**. A moral failure is more often deeply rooted and long-standing. You cannot simply bandage a malignancy. Those in charge of the restoration process must recognize that there is a need for skillful surgery that deals with even the margins and borders of the cancer.

However, the pastor must be **willing** to surrender and submit to the requirements of authority, without **changing** to a different authority during the process of restoration. But when there is **no** restoration process and the pastor is allowed to immediately resume his role to preserve the church's financial stability and to save his image, the same weight and pressure that contributed to his demise will be back on his shoulders again. **After** a leader's sin has been carefully discerned by an overseeing body and there are **clear** 'fruits of repentance,' only then can true restoration begin. If his failure was simply an indiscretion (wrong judgment, poor financial stewardship, marriage and family problems, doctrinal issues), it's possible that he can be given a season of **discipline** (such as a sabbatical) to recover without forfeiting his position.

If, however, his sin was a moral failure, then the recovery of his marriage is in question, the trust of his congregation has evaporated, and he has placed himself in a position of being disqualified. At this point, the need to facilitate **deliverance** is **crucial**. The primary requirement for moral restoration is true repentance **and** deliverance. True repentance is 99 percent of deliverance. A renouncing of soul ties, breaking of all contact with the person he was in an immoral relationship with, closing doors opened from **childhood**, and praying and fasting for **roots** of sin to be discerned and removed are all critical to restoration. It is important for the overseeing body to not only recommend, but also to facilitate this type of deliverance" (Stockstill, 2014).

I hope that Pastor Stockstill helped you to arrive at an understanding of the essence of this experience. A special thanks to him for agreeing to weigh in on this matter. Even as we are destroyed for the lack of knowledge, those facts should have answered any lingering concerns. However, these are the kind of articles that seem to escape the Black church. But I came on the scene to keep you from missing it! Stop avoiding reality, and start embracing God's correction! As these principles provide meaningful ethical points of reference, the process of full repentance (confessing and forsaking), cleansing and restoration was **NOT** applied in my case. And that's how we ended up here with a chapter, entitled, *The 21ˢᵗ-century Adam "Sin-drome."*

Finally, here is the moment of truth – had I not initiated the break-up; the despicable practices would have continued INDEFINIELY! Here was the "acid test:" afterwards, when I asked him whether he was ever planning to sever these soul-ties, he honestly replied, "Probably not." Bottom line: lust spirits, sex addictions, and generational curses do NOT die with age! If you do not deal with the root, the fruit keeps growing. Whereas truth and exposure have a way of bringing one's true self to light, "leading while bleeding" is tantamount to knowing that you are indeed, infected with while having unprotected relations. I'm sorry, but I am truly appalled by leaders that are determined to live wretched lives; yet, they are eager to dash the pulpit, not only speaking into the lives of God's people, but laying their hands on them and transferring spirits that they need to be delivered from.

Never allow God's mercy to cause you to disrespect His holiness. God commanded Moses to take off his shoes before coming into His presence, to yield his right to lead as he wanted and to have authority in the Holy Place. Often, "God has to put up a 'fence' because He does not want us tracking our past in the presence of the God of our future" (Dr. Jamal Bryant). "That's deep!" Just as Sodom and Gomorrah were destroyed because their sin was very grievous, can you clearly see now why exposure was ultimately necessary? Maybe God allowed me to cross his path because He knew that inevitably and relentlessly, I would be the one to expose the "**sin**-drome" that has radically taken over the Body of Christ. As mentioned in Trilogy-Part One, if you don't want your sins exposed, simply stop sinning.

Hey, I respect your decision, but just for the record, "I am not afraid of my truth anymore. I will not omit pieces of me to make you feel comfortable. Love me for who I am or not at all. Decide if you are part of my history or part of my future. I AM WHO I AM!" Thanks Awakening People; that was "spot on." It's not personal. It's just my mandate to be a part of the Kingdom's "human resource" department. We make sure that the only instructions we utter are those that come directly from the Holy Spirit. It does not matter whether I get caught, you or your man gets caught, or whether your mama or your daddy or your preacher or your bishop gets caught, "sin is sin, no matter who it's in." Metaphorically speaking, I am just another Balaam's ass with a message to save "us" from premature death. Where is God in my mess? In Trilogy-Part Two, I prove that I didn't get lost; I was led into this "wilderness."

"And the LORD God called unto Adam, and said unto him, Where art thou?" (Gen. 3:9). At the core of such a misguided approach to restoration, did the members need to be called into a Solemn Assembly, or did "Adam" deserve to go out and face God alone, at that point? He should have had a cooperative attitude and asked for help way before the church discovered that he was "naked." Because "misery loves company," people involve others in the consequences of their actions to gain their support and talk their way back into some level of respect.

Did anybody really take the time to question the motivation behind this particular resolve? Oh no; rather than remaining firm in their convictions, most chose to defend rather than mend. Indeed, I was demonized for walking away, along with the classic victim blaming. When God uncovers what has been concealed, your job is to openly go through the healing process and allow Him to do what He does best: restore, recover, renew, and rekindle the fire that shall devour and consume the works of the enemy. I tried to tell you in an earlier chapter that God's got this! In any case where sin has already been brought to the light of the world, those sins must be confessed and repented of, before the world. In doing so, we only reveal in order to heal.

To be able to walk in the full coverage of God, you must realize that "the destiny that's for you is greater than the dirt that's on you!

Deliverance comes when you realize that the dirt is designing you – not destroying you" (Pastor Manwell Faison). Listen to the wisdom of Bishop Avery Kinney; he says: "A person that refuses to admit their mistakes and is rebellious toward authority is not a good candidate for leadership. In leadership, you will make many mistakes, and you will always be under someone's authority. So with that said, let's make them a candidate for deliverance first; then, we can revisit leadership. Some of you pastors and leaders are skip-tracing spirits now that dappled the radar! I'm trying to save you from that unnecessary warfare!" By sharing these important insights, my intention is to keep the devil from making drama out of our defeats!

Upon completion of the previous final changes, as I was preparing to finalize this series for another resubmission, I discovered a significant element that needed to be inserted here. As I now began to release myself from the written aspect of this project (for real this time), here is my prayer: "Father, help me to see the man whom I trusted as the authority figure in my life, as You see him, so that I can love him in the way that You love him. Do not allow me to continue to see him for what he did; allow me to see him for who You created him to be.

In spite of whatever happened in the past that made us both, resort to an ungodly lifestyle, heal us. Restore unto us the joy of Thy salvation, and uphold us with Thy free Spirit. Then, will we teach transgressors Thy ways; and sinners shall be converted unto Thee (Psa. 51:12-13). As You deliver us from 'blood-guiltiness,' I ask that You clothe and cover us as You did Adam and Eve, in Genesis 3:21. Finally, before it's too late, help him to renounce his pride and arrogance in an effort to realize in humility that this is no longer about us and what we did. It is about saving the generation that's coming after us, in the matchless name of Jesus Christ, I **sincerely** pray. 'And the Church said, 'Amen'." In a "nutshell," "that's my story, and I'm sticking to it."

Many times, the enemies that tried to kill you are kept alive so that they can actually see the purpose for which God has designed to use you. They need to see God's glory on your life, and they need to see Him spread a table before you in their presence. Sometimes,

He also leaves them here as an act of God's mercy toward them that they might consider their evil ways and repent. At any rate, you know that you have forgiven yourself and the offender when you make an honest attempt to help him to forgive himself. Helpful resources are revealed with the intention to help him and others to fight for their own freedom. You know that you, yourself are healed when the scar is still there, but the pain is gone for real.

While wounds were never intended to look good, a fall is not supposed to feel good. We judge it or assess it, not to bring condemnation; we expose it to bring healing to the Body. In this season, my honest objection is to help somebody. In your humanistic reasoning, don't judge my season from the season you're in. Allow me to serve where my season demands. *"And let it be, when these signs come to you, that you do as the occasion demands; for God is with you"* (1 Sam. 10:7 NKJV). Bottom line: we can't fix it unless we face it; we can only rectify what we identify. An underused but valuable protocol is Nietzsche's famous maxim: "What does not kill me makes me stronger." In this sense, it's time to turn and keep the plan.

CHAPTER NINE

FOR BETTER OR FOR WORSE: TURN AND KEEP THE PLAN

Despite what has happened in my past and what is likely to happen in the future, "my shock absorber" is divulged in Romans 8:28: *"And we know that all things work together for good to them that love God, to them who are the called according to His purpose."* No, I did not ask for this assignment by my own volition, but since I am committed to it "for better or for worse," Jeremiah 29:11 reveals my "road hazard insurance." *"For I know the thoughts that I think toward you, saith the LORD, thoughts of peace, and not of evil, to give you an expected end."* Either way, "I'm good" because the way God prepared me to handle my own was by training me to handle somebody else's.

It is only by careful examination of your experiences that God's plan becomes apparent. Once you have properly confronted the necessary evils, Bishop Avery Kinney gives this advice: "Don't waste your time trying to deal with things that you are going to pass through anyway? Pass through it and outlive it! Some anointings are stirred and birthed based upon your ability to outlive what was designed to take you out!" In amplifying this point, my brother, Bishop Brandon B. Porter, made this observation: "If your thorn in the flesh is not making you more like God, it's not from God. Remember, the thorn has a point to it; it's not in vain!" The point that I want to make from his point is: if God knows it, who cares who else knows it? That was the purpose of the cross!

Indeed, unhealthy attachments create false notions of truth and reality; however, bad things people do to you are not always personal. Sometimes, you just happened to end up in what seemed to have been the wrong place at the wrong time, but you remained there, "for better or for worse." Your arrival did not surprise God; "for better or for worse," He already had an exit. Now crossing the threshold of a completely different experience, forgiveness is giving up the right to hurt others, just because they hurt me.

Even as this particular book was never intended to be a reflective process to elucidate my personal experience of P.M.S., "for better or for worse," I felt compelled to take on the challenge of explicating the phenomenon of spiritual abuse and persisting to the point of exhaustion. Conclusively, I feel like I have finally reached a point of saturation and the stream of unpolluted consciousness. With an internal sense of closure, I feel satisfied that the explication is complete, and the story has been given adequate evidence regarding its existence.

After 15 years of being influenced by clergy-perpetrated sexual abuse and co-signing the inappropriateness of its emerging issues, the common thread here is that my process seems to become pronounced and guided by 15-year developments. In 2015, God instigated a big surprise for me that led me into a season of rest. And the fact that perceptual closure is realized around my years of experiences, this spontaneous sense of tranquility and anticipation has awakened some deep feelings in me that amplify the phenomenal arrival of another new season. After 16 years of wrapping my mind around explicating the phenomenon, I feel an internal readiness at this precise moment, to enter freshly into the "rest" of my future, beginning now (December 2016). I am talking about the kind of rest that I don't need to go sleep to experience.

"For better or for worse," the continuing correlation in this existing body of knowledge, is for the sake of those who may have experienced this phenomenon and are intensely interested in arriving at a comprehensive and integral meaning that embraces the whole of my experience. Thus, the phenomenal analysis is clustered into common themes and meanings that are used to develop continuing descriptions of the experience. The challenge in discovering these hidden meanings is that you must reflect on your personal experience or whatever it was that conspired toward our joining or connecting with one another. Inherent in this process, the one thing that I concur with Jerry Springer is that, "Love begins when we learn to carry each others' baggage."

Years later, as I have found myself submitting to the backlash of being on display and taking a stand in pursuit of the purpose that God has destined behind my pain, God is placing a demand on all of us to *Restore Integrity in the Pulpit!* "For better or for worse, we must do it in love. Just as I have chosen God's plan for my life over my own, and taking a road less traveled, I must continue to stand up for what is right, even when it seems like wrong has won. Most times standing alone, but self-determined to pioneer new realms of obedience, I have never, truly been recognized for doing the will of the LORD. I have yet to get a handclap for walking it out. "For better or for worse," as long as I know that what is in my heart is from God, I will continue to work from the inside out.

Most recently, I was led to attend some friends' church where I was looking forward to hearing from the pastor. However, the friend, Albert Crozier (2014), ended up downloading a personal "email" to me from God. To illustrate it as a model of helpful instructions, the topic was: *Turn, and Keep the Plan.* He went on to say: "No matter what they heard about it, no matter what they said about it, no matter how they feel about it, no matter how the nay-sayers interpreted it, do not give energy to that! If God told you to say it, say it! Even when they won't support you and listen to what you have to say, if God told you to say it, say it anyway! If it does not look like it's getting through, say it again!"

Needless to say, since his message had also changed at the last minute, I took it extremely personal, especially at a time when I wanted to forget this assignment and start living my life as a normal human being. Elder Crozier (2014) continued: "God says: 'I am not asking for their opinions; I only want to know, if you will trust Me.'

If you hold on to the promise rather than give energy to what is affecting you, this is what will happen after while: *'And he shall be like a tree planted by the rivers of water, that bringeth forth his fruit in his season; his leaf also shall not wither; and whatsoever he doeth shall prosper'* (Psa. 1:3)." Almost three years later, and I'm still feeling that!

At this juncture of the message, the pastor's absence was totally inconsequential. I knew without a doubt that I was in the right church on the right Sunday, in the right month and in the right year and at the right hour. By the time that I was compelled to walk down the aisle to the altar for prayer and strength, he said that he could see me in a room in a whirlwind. Consequently, it is my bedroom that I consider my personal sanctuary, and that happens to be where my writings and all of my struggles take place from the bed. I felt like God had changed this message because He knew that I was on the way. He knew exactly what I needed for such a time as this. In the voice of Tamar Braxton: "Won't He do it!?!"

The speaker assured us again that God was going to keep His promise, if we "turn, and keep the plan," Even when things got better, or even when they were worse, this tailored Word from God brought me tears of joy and anticipation in the days and weeks ahead. A few hours after revisiting this message and finalizing this chapter (the time before the last time) with the previous prayer for my former leader, my publishing consultant agreed to discount the resubmit fee by 30%! Then, I turned to the Word Network, just in time to hear Bishop T.D. Jakes say, "Your provision is in your purpose!" Wow! "For better or for worse," that made my "baby" leap again! Now that closure has taken place as far as I am concerned, allow me to get back on point!

Apart from Stockstill's (2014) pastoral leadership position, I was also inclined toward the philosophy expressed by the authors of my Ethics text, Sommers-Flanagan and Sommers-Flanagan (2007). They wrote: "Holding to the letter of the law but ignoring the spirit of the law is doing an act for your own sake and not purely from a sense of duty. You can purposely do what you know to be wrong. You can do what you know to be right but only because other people are watching. Or you can struggle to do what you know to be right just because you know it is the right thing to do. Some people are simply not motivated to take moral action."

Since everything done in the dark eventually comes to the light, pastors, more than most, should realize the central importance of accountability, even "for better or for worse." Values and ethics are different across cultures, age, and time, but since the majority of my readers are from my same culture, our values likely have the same moral weight. In this sense, you might agree that "saving face is taking preventive actions not to appear to lose face in the eyes of others" (Rosenberg, 2004 as cited in Sommers-Flanagan & Sommers-Flanagan, 2007). Just as both Adam and Eve admitted that they "did eat," likewise, I felt that open confession was good for my soul. Accordingly, I should not have been denied the authenticity of my confession.

As I have illustrated thus far, "hatred stirs up strife, but love covers **all** sins" (Prov. 10:12). Seeing that Adam was explaining and not blaming, most 21st-century Adams do **not** cover the woman that is caught up with them in their "**sin**-drome." Given that this kind of relationship is not based on true love, they will only cover themselves. Guess what, woman of God, disloyalty and betrayal are some of the treacheries of linking with another's spouse who has stepped outside of the sacredness and boundaries of holy matrimony (**please** read Trilogy-Part One).

J. Lee Grady's (2010) profound implications may be key in understanding my apparent and continuous need to address clergy sexual misconduct. He conveys: "Of course no minister is perfect, and every Christian has access to God's mercy when he makes mistakes. But a spiritual leader is held to a higher standard of accountability and disclosure. Those who assume a public ministerial role incur a 'stricter judgment,' according to James 3:1. That means a leader can't have a moral or ethical breakdown and then just hide it, ignore it or laugh it off.

It also means that he can't spin the statement to his advantage. The church, of all places, should be a no spin zone. We must take full responsibility, and that includes publicly owning up to our failures – and stepping down from the pulpit, if necessary, for however long it takes to find healing. Yet in this season of moral and spiritual crisis, we must appeal to all of those in public ministry to handle their charge with care. Of all the people on Earth, those who preach the Gospel of Truth must tell the truth." "For better or for worse," that really sums it up from a theologian's point of view.

From a moral philosopher's point of view, "Kant argued that even though there will be compelling practical or emotional factors in a given situation, it is our duty to consider the action through the lens of 'always, everywhere, for everyone.' Regardless of the circumstances, and regardless of the outcome, there are moral actions that are always right or always wrong. Of course, Kant recognized that we would not always be able to comply with what was truly correct, but he believed it is important that we not excuse our actions away, but rather take responsibility for our less than idea choices" (Sommers-Flanagan & Sommers-Flanagan, 2007, p. 30).

Even as these past, few chapters have resulted in an extensive rainbow of evolving reflections, I just discovered why God still had not released me to resubmit the final manuscript. In re-envisioning this phenomenon that I am seeking to understand through a more balance approach in my doctoral research, read **and** hear the painful story that was just shared with me by another victim who made the decision to speak out on clergy abuse. As a reader who may be forcing yourself into the interpretation, you may find meanings that are hard to grasp. Just as his textural descriptions will be formulated into a synthesis of the experience as a whole, perhaps this will help you to understand the rationale that triggers my urgency to engage in such topics.

Quoted with permission, Mr. Smith writes: *"It's hard to write about because there is so much to say and so many feelings to deal with. Fortunately, it has been a long time and we have moved on, but so much was lost during that period. We lost our church family, to some degree, we lost our faith. Our younger children lost their church home and never really understood why. What the poem is about [that's shared in Trilogy-Part One] is that the stark choice that faces an abuse victim and their family is silence or action.*

You are really faced with three choices – remain silent and leave the church (keeping the reason a secret), or remain silent and stay in the church (keeping the abuse events a secret), or to speak out and lose everything you have with the church and your church family – destroying or altering these relationships permanently. We really had no choice but to speak out, and all hell broke loose. The youth minister was, of course, very popular and charismatic, and much of the congregation 'believed in him.' His followers were so emotionally involved and dependent on him that nothing we could have said, no evidence we could have shown, would have shaken their faith in him.

Other congregation members who were also emotionally dependent on him were capable of a more detached, rational examination of the evidence. Officials brought in from the denomination were not under his spell either, and issued a forceful letter addressing the allegations. The whole process ripped the church apart and made our family the focus of much negative attention and anger. We no longer felt safe or loved in our church, as the anger and bitterness of the abusers' supporters overwhelmed us. So we left the church that was so important to our family and fought through the aftermath alone.

We have never joined another church, and most likely never will. Our ability to trust, to open our hearts, to allow ourselves to be vulnerable was deeply shattered, and the process of growth and rebuilding has been slow and difficult. We may join another church someday, but I don't know why we would. Without the ability to trust and open up, it would be a formality, a cynical waste of time. So our younger children lost their church family and lost the lifetime benefits of growing up in a religious setting. This has harmed them in ways we'll never know, and has shaped them in who they are today.

Our oldest daughter has gotten on with her life, but she will bear her burden the rest of her life as well. She lost a group of very close friends at an important time in her development, and her faith journey stopped cold in its tracks. She is grown now, and her family doesn't attend church, and her children don't have any real knowledge about Jesus or the Bible. So did we make the right decision to speak out and risk destroying a large part of our lives and everything we knew?

171

Adamantly, I have to say yes. I don't know how we could have lived with ourselves any other way. Silence was an option, but the damage done to ourselves and our beliefs would have been much more devastating than losing our church, our friends, and our faith. The damage would have been to ourselves and our souls, and that was an impossible price to pay for a few friends and a little fellowship" (D. Smith, personal communication, February 16, 2014).

Literal tears here. This totally tears my heart apart, each and every time I revisit it. Please remember the Smith family in your prayers. "Prayer is the wireless connection that never loses its signal" (unknown). After arriving home from the previous church service that I wrote about earlier, this was the missing element of the story that I viewed as distinctive and fundamental to helping you to understand the serious consequences of clergy abuse. "For better or for worse, it absolutely amazes me how this book has come together, little by little and piece by piece, even down to the final hour.

My question now is: If the Church is supposed to be a safe place for saved people, why are there so many soldiers missing and wounded in action? What if I had walked away and never looked back? Let me hit the "reply button" on that. Sometimes it's not a bad thing to look back and dig up what the devil thought he buried. He buried me, but he didn't realize that I was a seed. As a matter of fact, "Hagar," what are you going to do with your seed, "Ishmael?" Ishmael represents our past, our mistakes, our bad decisions, but should we always kick "Hagar" out of the house and put "Ishmael" up for adoption? No, we need to find a way to minister to them and restore them back to the fold. Without our past, there would be no memories to help us fast-forward to our future. In order to experience good, you had to have known what bad feels like. Thus, "you shouldn't hold grudges. You hold memories that keep you better prepared for your next encounter" (origin unknown).

How Pastor Shannon was strategically placed in my life to deposit the seed for the book that you're reading was over the conversation that we had about my mistake. What if he had talked me into aborting my mistake, rather than giving life to my ministry? The decision to birth my mistake is what gave life to my ministry. If God allowed the seed to be birthed, does it not have the right to live? Even though it left me with very little "child support," few spiritual resources, and a whole lot of rejection, the seed eventually became my gift. And what the Bible says about your gift is that it will make room for you.

Sometimes we hold on to what we should let go of (bitterness and grudges), and let go of what we should hold on to (gifts and treasures). "Ishmaels" often become Presidents of the United States, and "Hagars" become Ph.D. candidates and potentially, best-selling authors. "Ha!" If God had wanted to, He could have circumvented the plan, but when He allows you to have a past, you must learn to respect the process. Thus, in the words of Elder Crozier (2014), we must "turn and keep the plan." When I obeyed God, they kicked me out of the "loop" and never wanted anything else to do with me. But look at God; "for better or for worse," He cleaned me up and anointed me anyway. Not only did He give me my dignity back; He is restoring everything I ever lost.

"What shall we say then? Is there unrighteousness with God? God forbid. … I will have mercy on whom I will have mercy, and I will have compassion on whom I will have compassion. So then it is not of him that willeth, nor of him that runneth, but of God that sheweth mercy" (Rom. 9:14-16). Again, "Hagar," what are you going to do with your "Ishmael?" As the young folk say: "Let it do what it do." Just as Mr. Smith's perception is clear, alive and vivid in bringing to life the dynamics of our experiences, there is a deeper layer of meaning that unfolds. And that is: having a personal relationship with God is important to establishing a stable foundation to get through something that is so tragic as spiritual abuse. For years now, since first discovering his poem on a clergy abuse website (which is now written with permission in Trilogy-Part One), I figured that Mr. Smith probably still existed.

After desiring a response as to the accuracy of his experience and any changes that would present more clearly or fully the experience, God immediately led me to look for him on Facebook. Just as this resubmit was set to go back to the press, I was speechless and very overwhelmed by his surprise inbox. My mandate to expose spiritual abuse doesn't even make me feel good to be an author, but a part of my motivation is being able to connect and minister to people like Mr. Smith. His reflective poem, *Who Will Speak For Me?* and the above correspondence articulate many of my emotional sentiments and validates the integrity and legitimacy of The Twin Ministries Empowerment Network, Inc.

In an effort to allow my ministry to unmask what is hidden behind the objective phenomena, here is another portion of the experience that's most worthy of including in this section: "To those who ask that we forgive and forget, please understand...the survivors, each of us in our own way, have spent our lives trying to move on, always weighing those two options. For some of us, suicide, substance abuse, or violence ended the struggle early... But we cannot escape the effects of the betrayals that were committed against us in God's name. They are inexorably woven into the texture of who we have become. That betrayal may not be a chargeable offense in a court of law. But there is no statute of limitation on its impact. And there should be no forgetting" (Boston Globe, 2002, p. 9).

The one truth that I have attempted to communicate with integrity for 16 years is that our leaders must be accountable for their actions, whether "for better or for worse." Otherwise, Mr. Smith's story and many other stories alike are the realities and the heart-wrenching tragedies that God will ultimately make you leaders responsible for. Particularly those whom God expects to walk worthy of the vocation wherewith you are called, the Church and its leaders have both spiritual and ethical obligations to minimize this universal chaos that many are experiencing. As I immerse myself in incidents that stand out in the experience, I hope that you will join with me as a truthful seeker of knowledge and understanding with regard to the phenomenon of CPSA.

Meanwhile, Bishop Avery Kinney posted another message that exudes from my heart; it says: "Everything concerning you has the potential to be something major in the making. So make the most of it and not a mess of it." While no one has ever, literally covered The Twin Ministries, "for better or for worse," the upshot of the story is that somebody has to be the sacrifice that serves the common good and foster the culture of the community. Whether you feel my heart, understand my logic, or agree with my method of disclosure by now, with or without you, I am committed to this assignment until God releases me from it. "For better or for worse," and "by any means necessary," I **will** finish my course. As stated by Jermone Glenn, "You can't stop me because you didn't start me."

I think it's not important enough a point to describe any more evidence here because there comes a moment when you simply have to disengage. In my conclusion, allow me to say this while I still have the "mic." "It is worth considering that the most basic communication principle is that you cannot **not** communicate" (Wilmot & Hocker, 2000 as cited in Sommers-Flanagan & Sommers-Flanagan, 2007). Enough about the 21st-century Adam's "**sin**-drome;" let's make the shift, and see where the first Adam was with regard to the "for better or for worse element.

As Adam was a good steward who dwelt with Eve according to knowledge, He gave honor unto her, **as unto** the weaker vessel (1 Pet. 3:7). Do not ever forget the special emphasis there! Being heirs together of the grace of life, this is what I feel Adam advocated: "God, because of the simple fact that You created me in Your image, You know that I would not have recklessly participated in ignorant activity. At the same time, You would not have expected me to come back to 'court' and divorce the woman that **You** gave me to keep, in sickness and in health, and *for better or for worse*. I did not go out and find this woman on my own; I was in a deep sleep when **You** created her from the bone that was closet to my heart. **You** did not authorize me to keep her for as long as she made healthy decisions and was not tempted.

You gave her to me *for better or for worse*. Should I have **not** set the precedence for the second Adam? After all, if it took an Adam to mess things up, would it not take another Adam to clean up the mess? Since the ultimate plan was for Jesus to die and save the world, I just assumed that it was my obligation with all diligence, to save and protect the woman whose seed would produce the first generation. Because we were no more twain but one, I did what I did, because she did what she did. She did what she did, because Satan did what he did. And you allowed Satan to be Satan so that Jesus could become Savior. "Shundo!" Did you feel that?

In the final analysis, I decided that it was in my best interest to give up my immortality for the love of the woman that **You** gave me. Since she unintentionally fulfilled her purpose to produce evil so that You could carry out Your plan to demonstrate Your goodness, her sin should not count against her." "Now what?" Equally, this is what I feel that Eve inquired of Adam: "Since God gave you the permission and a mandate to love, cover and protect your wife, are you going to stay with me *for better or for worse*; or, are you going to allow the 'Judge' to kick me out of your house?"

Eve never had any preconceived notions of gaining independence from Adam, and neither did Adam have any perceived consequences of what it would be like to live without her. At a minimum, the results highlight the fact that not only did she **expect** Adam to speak up for her; he did what he felt obligated to do. What's more, I believe that he did what God **required** him to do! To say it another way, in order to **MAN-UP** and protect her from the consequences of disobedience, he had to take her place before the "jury" and become her, as it was in God's plan for him to *"take the stand and be the man."* #**man**imizingtheplan

Here is an interesting irony: Adam's demonstration of love had more to do with the decision that had to be made, than the transgression that Eve chose to commit. Besides, the law was given to Adam, not Eve. If Eve had only eaten the fruit, then Adam could have asked God for another Eve. But since Adam ate the fruit, God's plan was to send another Adam. "P☺W!" That blessed me, right there! Given the fact that Adam had free will and was given choices, either, he could have resisted her impulse to eat the fruit and have her thrown out of his house. Or, he could participate and cover her in her sin, and they both leave the house together as one.

In my estimation, what God really wanted to know was: "Will you **marry** her, now that I am no longer calling her your help meet? After seeing that it was not good for you to be alone, I went beyond the limitations of a help meet and created her as a suitable companion. Now that I consider her more as your wife for the purpose of procreation, than just a helper to assist in the garden, will you now take this woman as your lawfully wedded **wife**, who in sorrow shall bring forth children? Followed by the fact that you now have rule over her and her decisions, will you keep her and stay connected and teach her how to make better decisions, even if the 'jury' finds her guilty and evicts the both of you from My garden?"

As a husband (man of God), what He truly wants to know from you is, "Will you love your wife as Christ also loved the Church and gave Himself for it?" Following the human example set forth by Adam, Christ is now your spiritual example. There is no greater love in the eyes of God than a pure, covenant relationship between a **male** and a **female**. To demonstrate reconciliation and the complete love that He had for Israel (although they turned to other gods and engaged in the spirit of prostitution), God used Hosea to take unto him a wife of whoredoms and children of unfaithfulness. Out of all of the charges brought against Israel (Hos. 4:1-19), Hosea was commanded to display his love to Gomer in the same manner that God loved a people that were as stubborn as a heifer. "You-'gone' work 'wit' me?"

Eventually Church, there will be a marriage supper of the Lamb in the holy city, called the New Jerusalem. What God actually wanted to know from His own Son was: "Would You submit to being dethroned from the throne of Your Father, to being deposited in the womb of a woman that You helped to create? More or less, will You make the ultimate sacrifice and die for **Your** own Body" (the Body of Christ)? Naturally, when Jesus went into the garden and looked into the cup, He hesitated. Could these have been His thoughts? "Since I am already God, this is really **not** My will. Do I literally want to give up My godliness to become sin? Really Father?"

Yet, the only way to **help** us was to become **like** us. Becoming both God and man, God's whole purpose in Jesus' one decision was to demonstrate the universal law of love, John 3:16: ***"For God so loved the world, that He gave His only begotten Son, that whosoever believeth in Him should not perish, but have everlasting life."*** Because the sun protects the earth, the high-soaring eagle with brilliant leadership characteristics, is designed to look to the sun. Likewise, she directs her eaglets to face the sun. As we venerate the eagles as living symbols of power, freedom, and transcendence, one of their positive leadership traits is that they are nurturers. Similarly, as Eve was designed to look to Adam for direction, man was designed to look to the Son (the Head of the Church). *"Looking unto Jesus the Author and Finisher of our faith"...* (Heb. 12:2a).

The woman will inevitably make some destiny-altering decisions. But as a son of God and the savior of the woman's body, she is designed to look to her nurturer for protection. Man + direction = the woman's protection! For the woman whose man has left you stranded and abandoned, Dr. Jamal Bryant raised the following question: "If he was dumb enough to leave you, why aren't you smart enough to let him go? It's better to be with no one than to be with the wrong one!" My leading inquiry remains: "Adam, 'where you at'?"

If the man in John 8:3 was where God expected him to be in his logic, the scribes and Pharisees would not have had an opportunity to put the woman that was caught in adultery on display. In coming from an afro-centric perspective and being true to my Black history, race, creed, color, **and** pedigree most definitely impact the way I read and interpret the Bible. Thus, "the word on the street" is: if she was caught, it stands to reason that the man was still at the scene with his pants down too! This is the perfect scenario to reiterate the famous lyrics: ... "Looking like a fool with your pants on the ground!" ☺

Of course, the same man that is confused and dealing with rejection issues himself would likely label this woman as a tramp. For argument's sake, let's go ahead and assume that because of his **"sin-drome,"** the 21st-century Adam is probably more upset that he did not belong to the "tramp's camp." "Ha!" That's why Jesus commanded all of the accusers to drop their stones because NONE of them were without sin. My point is this: **if the woman was good enough to get him caught, he should have been man enough to "carry the can:"** **"Yes I CAN, *'take a stand and be the MAN'!"*** "Somebody 'betta' help me up in here!"

When all's said and done, "We need to teach our DAUGHTERS the difference between a man who FLATTERS her, and a man who COMPLIMENTS her. A man who SPENDS MONEY on her and a man who INVESTS in her. A man who views her as PROPERTY and a man who views her PROPERLY. A man who LUSTS after her and a man who LOVES her. A man who believes HE is GOD'S GIFT to women and a man who remembers a WOMAN was GOD'S GIFT to MAN. And then teach OUR SONS to be that kind of man" (origin unknown).

Logically so, it may <u>seem</u> illogical for Adam to take the blame for Eve's sin, but spiritually-so, it was the only, right thing to do. It is tantamount to a couple being arrested for a crime that they committed together. Wouldn't it be more reasonable for the man to say: *"For better or for worse*: allow me to take the blame. Put me in jail, and send my wife home to care for the children?" Under normal circumstances, do you ever wonder why the courts are **expected** to protect the woman as much as possible and allow the man to take the brunt of the blame? "Bam!" There it is – it is the long-established, divine order of God. That is why we live by the Word and not by logic. Hey "Adam," *for better or for worse,* what we need to know from you in the whole scheme of divine order – "where art thou," even in the likelihood of a dishonorable discharge?

CHAPTER TEN

DISHONORABLE DISCHARGE: CERTAIN RESTRICTIONS APPLY

Whereas Adam seemed to have been willing to live with Eve **outside** of the garden, I am convinced that God instituted eviction to keep them from living as <u>mortal</u> beings **inside** of the garden. Being spiritually dead and now knowing both good and evil, He could not have allowed them to live in an eternal element that was only created for immortal beings. Because *certain restrictions apply* in property-managed locations, the punishment involved driving the unauthorized users out of the garden. Therefore, the "Property-owner" cursed the ground to prevent them from living forever in Paradise while they were in a sinful/physical state of being (see Gen. 3:17-19, 22-24).

If Adam and Eve had not been evicted (after eating from the Tree of the Knowledge of Good & Evil), and would have later eaten from the Tree of Life, they could have still lived forever, as this tree was God's eternal provision. In other words, if they had eaten from the Tree of **LIFE** with sin in their lives, God would not have been able to discipline them, whether in the garden or out. That particular tree would have sustained them perpetually in a physical body that was not intended for for external existence. What happened to the tree of life after the fall? Christ made it available to us through Holy Communion. Whereas life is in the blood, He heals us at no charge.

Since God had a plan for Jesus to redeem man back to Himself, He could not allow Adam and Eve to deprive Him of His glory by eternally leaving them in the garden in a state of sin. Because *certain restrictions apply*, another central theme to this entire storyline is this: if God did not allow Adam and Eve to commit sin and still live forever, what gives 21st-century Adams the audacity to think that they can **continue** in sin and not suffer some consequences? "Really, Church?"

I know that the grace-abusers may beg to differ, but come on now. Like I stated earlier, grace does not give you time to prolong sin; it gives you the supernatural ability to wipe it out! Moreover, God does not love us any more than He loved Adam and Eve. It's something about that first child that a parent has a certain affinity to. Even when His own Son became sin for us, He turned His head. That's when Jesus asked, "Why hast Thou forsaken Me?" If God could not bear to see His own Son become sin for the rest of His children, what makes Him so blind to your sin that you feel like once you're in, you're never out? "Perish the thought!" I keep trying to lay emphasis on the fact that we cannot build a mentality around our conditions.

If He punished Adam and Eve for their disobedience, and we punish our children for their disobedience, what makes us exempt from reaping what we sow? Since karma is the new fad word that has found its way into our top culture lexicon, allow me to highlight that for **every** action, there is a consequence. Karma may have spewed from Buddha, but it really sprung from Scripture! My point again: there is a reciprocal or opposite to **every** law; for instance, because there is light, there is darkness. Because God created male, the female came next. For every truth, there is a deception. Then, can you not agree that divine order declares that since there is a Heaven to gain, there must be a hell to avoid?

You simply cannot take the wrath of God from the message of the truth! Besides the six Scriptures in Leviticus that command the children of Israel to be holy, the New Testament message is the same in 1 Peter 1:16: ***"Because it is written, Be ye holy; for I am holy."*** "Real 'talkerization'!" You may attempt to shut the mouth of the messenger, but the message remains the same. Since there is no "get out of hell free card," we need to make our hearts receptive to the truth and either, "get right, or get left!"

A mantra that we tend to embrace now, more than ever, is that we live in the dispensation of grace. But I would rather sow to the flesh and go to hell with "gasoline drawers" on, before I allow compromising pastors to have me sacrificing my hard-earned money for them to send me to hell on the church bus. Jesus didn't condemn the woman caught in adultery; indeed, He granted her grace. Here is the "game-changing" Scripture that came after the grace was given: *"GO, AND SIN NO MORE"* (John 8:11b with emphasis added). "How you like me now?" I know you did not expect me to go there!

Grace gives you a chance to catch up to the "Son," but it does not give you a license to continue in darkness with Satan. Like the Light, Gas & Water Company, if you keep refusing to catch up on your balance, eventually, grace is going to run out and, you may find yourself lighting some candles. I concur with Ravenhill (2012) that it is a false and perverted spirit that has managed to captivate the hearts of thousands, instructing them that regardless of their actions, grace forever turns a blind eye to their sinful, willful ways. From Malachi to Matthews, God was silent for 400 years. All of a sudden, in His wisdom, He cracked open the New Testament era with a prophet, and what was achieved by a prophet in the Old Testament was picked up by an apostle in the New. Because there had been silence, nothing could be erected until there was repentance. The prophet didn't preach, "it's my time;' he preached, "TURN!"

The first message (Mt. 3:2) was repent, and Jesus' last message in Luke 13:5 was repent. When Peter and the rest of the Apostles were asked, "What shall we do to be saved?" in Acts 2:37, how did he respond in verse 38 (with emphasis added)? ... *"REPENT, and be baptized every one of you in the name of Jesus Christ for the remission of sins, and ye shall receive the gift of the Holy Ghost."* Because the Church is being built over drama and over lies, and over sin and over deception, it has to exist in the strength of its foundation. For this reason, the Church is in a sin cycle because she wants to do everything **but** repent.

Grace abuse is a topic that deems its own chapter; for now, allow me to say this while I still have the "mic." Grace is not to sustain our stupidity; it is to make us better and bring us back to our senses. Since there are already too many drunken church folks in the world already, we must be a part of the remnant who's committed to thinking sound and soberly. Knitted in the fabric of Pentecostalism, we have always prided ourselves on standing for holiness and being different from the world. What have you been drinking, to all of a sudden, believe that hell does not exist?

The reason that no one wants hell to exist anymore is because that would make them accountable for their actions. So rather than repent **from** their sins as Paul instructed, they reinvent a new Gospel which gives them a license **to** sin. The Ark was stinky and full of animals, but Noah and his followers chose to be in the Ark with the animals than in the flood without God. Personally, I would rather live like hell is real, than to take a chance on dying and finding out that Universalism and the gospel of inclusion were wrong. Enough of this foolishness!

As far as the topic at hand, Adam had the right to renounce sin, reject Eve, and resume his life; yet, he was more willing to die **for** her than to live **without** her. Once he took her by the hand and they left the garden as one, "Eve" became known as the mother of all living (Gen. 3:20). Talmage (2010) gives an additional, profound indication of God's conclusive plan for the woman to become the man's savior and deliverer. He notes the following (with emphasis added): "Even Adam, whose physical body was not created by a daughter of Eve, was saved and delivered by a woman. For it was through a woman, Mary, that Jesus Christ came to conquer the bonds of death and sin and atone for Adam's transgression.

Without a woman to bear the body of Christ, mankind would have been lost and fallen forever, and Adam's work and purpose on the earth would have been meaningless. Mary was the gateway that made Christ's work possible and her nurturing the catalyst for His success. Even though Eve didn't give physical life to Adam, **she literally saved him from spiritual death by opening the way for the Savior and Redeemer to come into the world.** Salvation, in the form of Christ, literally came through the earth as a woman."

Despite the fallout, had Adam and Eve been fruitful and multiplied while **in** the garden, there would be no need for salvation outside of the garden. It was not until they left the garden that "Adam *knew* Eve, his wife, and she conceived and bare Cain" (Gen. 4:1). At that point of intimacy and consummating the marriage, she had taken full possession of the man that proved, "I got your back." Getting to "know" Eve in the fullness of time, his soul was completely tied to her soul. As this was the beginning of soul-ties, an interesting parallel that is being expressed here is that the oneness of soul is what God wills for every **husband** and **wife**.

It may be simplistic to point this out; however, marriage is not for children or immature grown-ups. In view of the fact that "foolishness is bound in the heart of a child," I concur with Taylor Moore's adage: "You can't find a man's love in a boy," no more than you would find a homeless person selling real estate; or, a sex addict reinforcing celibacy! I know that "certain restrictions apply," but I'm going to take a chance on "pulling out all the stops." Hey "Sis," you can have sex with a boy if you want to, but at the end of the day, you're "gonna" need a real manly-husband to share in some passionate, all-night, "chitty-chitty, bang-bang," love-making sex. You know a boy can't handle "no" real "hot-ass" intimacy. #unfiltered-revision!

You can close your mouth now (wink,-). It is always my desire to carry an excellent spirit, but even as I am a God-fearing "sistah" and filled with the Spirit, writing is all about what's true, what's ugly, what's real, and what is revealing. It gives an author the leverage to speak his or her mind and write what they may never speak otherwise. A few of my readers are drawn to my sense of uniqueness because of the mere fact that humans are so curious. So don't judge me for taking a breather and sharing my uniqueness; it's my safe place, especially since I warned you on the back cover that "reader discretion was advised."

Giving validity by my own consciousness and putting my whole heart and soul into this project, this **Rated-R** *Rebirth* revision has given me a chance to go back and say everything that I ever needed to say. Although I cannot allow my freedom and my personal feelings to overly impact my professional behavior, don't be so concerned with **how** I'm teaching. Appreciate WHO I'm reaching. The problem with some people is that they don't respect your Anointing because they can't control your deliverance.

Here I go digressing again. One of my previous editors advised me that I needed to write more like I am working on my Ph.D. and avoid sounding like a non-Christian (☺). He recommended that I clean up my writing to appeal more to the traditional Christian and make it sound like I am "evolving" into an orthodox minister. Traditional? Orthodox? Sorry, this is not Burger King! Did not I also warn the readers on the back cover that I could not guarantee a predicted outcome to a balanced approach of their reading experience? Yet, my editor advised me to keep it real at the same time (L☺L). Keeping it real is certainly not being traditional and orthodox. #LMA☺ #lettingmy-anointingoperate "Gotcha!"

Inconsistently, the same editor suggested that I make Part One a true tell-all book by calling names and bringing it to the pulpit. Intentionally, most people remained nameless to conceal their ignorance. This is not Charisma Magazine! Divulging names is not the name of my game. Even as God has already disciplined us in His own way, my projects are intended to be more of a teaching tool than actual "tell-alls." God-approved rather than people-tested, I deserve the right to utilize necessary components of therapeutic effectiveness. Thus, I must continue to allow Him to strip away the layers of other folks' expectations in order to reveal the beauty of what He has crafted me to be. He alone is the guarantor of my destiny, which is not about a person; it's about a people!

Of course, I certainly value my editors' opinions, as they help to keep me well-grounded. Certain restrictions do apply, but when it's all said and done, I must strive to please the Father – not the editors, not you, or anyone else. To conclude this editing issue quite briefly, my objective is not to "wear" my story; the ultimate goal is to carry the glory. Every now and then, I do feel the need to embrace my roots – anything wrong with it? Until the 7th grade, I grew up in the projects of north Memphis. Although I later moved to south Memphis, it was not an enormous upgrade from having lived in "Scutterfield." For future reference, if you were still expecting the typical author, let me say this in my best Ebonics: "it 'ain't-gone' happen!"

In reality, I do come across as someone who is categorical and uncompromising; the reason being: I happen to be committed to the cause with stronger conclusions. At this level of my educational pursuit, my candidacy challenges me to communicate on a professional level that uses accurate grammar, concise, balanced, and logical flow, APA format and citations, and in a manner that respects the dignity of all populations. As I continue to smooth off the rough edges, just keep in mind that I did not sign up for this. (-_-)

Yet, God worked the wrong into my purpose and made it an open door to my future. You know that you have matured when God anoints you to do something that nobody understands but Him. The strategy in this project is to make the "appetizer" so alluring that you will want to engage in the full-course "entrée." In the event that I have failed the test at any juncture, I have made a special effort to see that you got the "memo" from every angle that I have been instructed to post it. Any part of the core message is too important to miss!

Although I have been working on this current piece for six years now, Part One is really my "baby;" equally fascinating, this book is my favorite. A 16-year project/process, I have yielded to accept Trilogy-Part One as the "Trauma," Part Two as the "Transition," and Part Three as the "Transformation." And due to the sentimental value that this current book holds for me, I feel like I have finally found my "Treasure." There is a "Turning Point" that's on the way, as well. At some point, I vow to *turn* my efforts and energy toward some "me" time – a point in time when God will *turn* my mourning into dancing and my sorrows into joy. Now taking a praise break, while I listen to Tye Tribbet's song, *He turned it!* A victory lap is never out of order!

Okay, I'm back (I needed that)! To say the least, I am exhausted but still not empty; I'm tired, but God is not through! While my "trauma" (Part one) was the longest procedure during this entire process, the rationale is that your struggles are what identify your stability. As it turned out, this current project developed into the intersection between the Trilogy (Parts One, Two, and Three) and the new projects that are strategically forthcoming (please see resources offered at the end). Despite the fact that it is a challenge for men and women to reclaim God's purpose for our male descendents, I hope that this God-given tool will ultimately be used as a spiritual reference when training the sons of this generation to maximize their masculinity.

"If future generations are to remember us more with gratitude than sorrow, we must achieve more than just the miracles of technology. We must also leave them a glimpse of the world as it was created, not just as it looked when we got through with it" (Lyndon B. Johnson). Now that we have replaced Bill Cosby with "Madea," the "she-ro" representation is toxic to society's idea of a man's masculinity and true identity when "it" portrays the image of a woman. God is not pleased when society and particularly, certain television talk shows make allowances for it. With this type of "shade," how can we expect our men to escape the inevitability of experiencing an identity crisis? Oh, by the way, Samuel anointed David (1 Sam. 16); just when did David anoint Samuel? That likely went right over your head.

Recently, I took my "old-school," old-fashioned, holiness-driven dad to a special service with me to get him some help for his complaint, from an apostle who does not mind "busting the devil's head down to the white meat." My dad felt like his ex-wife had tried to poison him. Oh my God; he was really taking me through and acting like what my Mother who works for the Social Security Disability Office would call a "2960." But what was I thinking to take him to a church where they wore dreads, tight jeans, skinny jeans, and did all the "edgy" things that today's Christians do in the contemporary church culture? I know it's about the souls and not about the clothes, but back then, even as they were being controlling with their doctrinal brainwashing schemes, they were also teaching us how to represent who we were re-presenting.

My dad totally thought that this church was out of control. He refused to stay for prayer and admitted that he could not receive from those people and did not want them laying their hands on him. :'(For the next, few months or so, he would not allow me to live it down. He said: "Come out from among them, and be ye separate." And when warning me about attaching myself to the wrong spirits; he insisted: "Some of these folks got a ghost, but it 'ain't' the Holy Ghost." In the middle of every conversation, I wanted to say: "Daddy, I'm 'gonna' need you to switch to decaf." I literally dreaded his phone calls after that. Despite the gravity of what had happened here, I did get a revelation from it. Not all traditions are bad, neither, are they all good.

Especially when you are in the context of trying to affect people from all walks of life, the crux of the matter is that some things may not even be considered sinful. Yet, they may not be profitable for you, as they simply could be distractions for the people that you want to attract or need to reach. I am not referring to reaching out to attract people like my controlling, hard-core, "old-school" dad, of course. But believe it or not, we serve an "old-school" God. He's not with all these new definitions and new terminologies – New Age Demons! It's a matter of being good or wicked! Indeed, God ordered things to work in cycles, but there is really **nothing** new under the sun.

That's why Jeremiah 6:16 says: *"Thus saith the LORD, Stand ye in the ways, and see, and ask for the old paths, where is the good way, and walk therein, and ye shall find rest for your souls. But they said, We will not walk therein."* Because they would not hearken to the sound of the trumpet, God went on to say: ... *"I will bring evil upon this people, even the fruit of their thoughts, because they have not hearkened unto My words, not to my law, but rejected it"* (vs. 19). Stop "cherry-picking" the Scriptures to accommodate your lifestyle.

After four, negative, content evaluations from my publisher, God brought me back to that Scripture and a few other alterations. Could it be that the way my dad felt the night of that worship service is somewhat intrinsic to how God feels? It may just be that the daddy experience worked together for some good. Before I went off point again, I started by saying that I could relate to my dad regarding the men that he noticed with dreads. Originally, could they have foreshadowed a time when men were really competing with women because they were confused about their sexuality? Anyway, after that night, every time I imagined certain men in my life wearing dreads, I would get so tickled that I could hardly get back on track. Those moments gave me pure "comic relief."

Regardless of my traditional upbringing, let's have a "Scripture-refresh." Does not Corinthians 11:15 validate the fact that long hair is supposed to be the **WOMAN'S** glory, or did I read that wrong? I'm getting ready to come for the "juggler" again. "Different strokes for different folks," but when a man invests the time and energy into allowing his hair to grow down his neck and past his shoulders (all matted up and twisted together), he may have **literally** gotten it "twisted!" It has to be mentally demanding because he has to program his mind to deviate from the norm. "Don't hang up on me now;" GOD is taking me somewhere with this. If you have a problem with it, try hanging up on Him.

First, here is my personal theory. Maybe long hair was the tradition of slaves because they couldn't afford the luxury of barbers to provide regular haircuts. **Now** that you can afford barbers, 1 Corinthians 11:14 ask the question: ***"Doth not even nature itself teach you, that, if a man have long hair, it is a shame*** [dishonor or disgrace] ***unto him?"*** (1 Cor. 11:14 with emphasis added). In line with Simpson (2014), Paul's argument is that men were not to be known for hair that looked like that of women. Jesus likely had hair shorter than Jewish females of that time. Most Jewish men kept shorter hair to distinguish themselves from women, as well as for practical purposes. On a personal note, I realize that in some cultures, dreads are a sign of strength. Still, it just looks more masculine when a man cut his hair. If you expect us to shave our legs, we expect you to cut your hair. "Hey 'Adam,' where you at?"

Particularly, if you are the woman who's dainty, prom and proper, you may find yourself shaking and slinging your "glory," and then taking your finger and placing it behind your ear. Since this book is intended to help my Black people, it's just not a good look, in my opinion, to see a Black man "slanging" his hair all over his head. I don't even like slinging my hair, and I'm all-woman. Often times, I would prefer to wear a pony tail or an "up-doo" to keep it off my face. So when I see a man slinging his hair, I'm ready to ask: "You got a problem or 'somethin'." I'm "gonna" need you not only to think like a man. I need you to look like a man, talk like a man, dress like a man – act like a man. Then, "take a stand and be 'da-man!" "I can't hear 'nobody'!" That's okay; "good meat makes its own gravy."

Now here is where God was taking me on this. The White man (Esau) came out like a hairy garment (Gen. 25:25). As I prayed for something profound to validate my whole argument, He immediately opened my eyes to Genesis 27:11. Jacob (God's chosen/Israel) said to his mother, Rebekah: ***"Behold, Esau my brother is a hairy man, and***

I am a SMOOTH man." "How you like me now?" That even blessed me! Generally speaking, "Chosen one," how "you-gone-be" smooth-talking and silver-tongued when you "gotta" stop talking to sling your hair every few minutes to keep it off your face? I may not have any honor in my own country, but the weight of my irritation is unequal to the gravity of concern that I have for God's people. With that in mind, let's proceed with caution.

Since Esau, the White man's hair has always grown faster, longer, and straighter. But since Jacob, the Black man looks much more polished, persuasive and sophisticated when he is clean-SHAVENED and unpretentious. One reason that former President Obama (a class act) had stage presence was because he had a **"smooth"** look. As a result, he was hailed as being suave and the most debonair President that the United States has ever witnessed in office. You must admit that this revelation is "banging!" His refined charm and gracefulness was persuasive, and he **effortlessly** presented the Black masculine image with no extras. A **luxury** car doesn't need the extras; adding a spoiler to a Mercedes takes away from its elegance and its incomparability. Mature men should always maintain a position of strength and superiority. Some of our Black men do too much! Do you understand the words that are jumping off this page?

Wait! God is not finished! For the purpose of #damagecontrol, there are absolutely too many overrated, reality stupidities when it comes to mentoring our youth in their formative years, and particularly, being exemplars to our young Black men! Here is another "larger-than-life" example of my contention. I was extremely disappointed to see one of our most successful, Black men on a popular television talk show advising mothers that it's nothing wrong about allowing their young sons to dress up in the mothers' heels, and I guess, play with dolls and purses too. In my goddaughter, Lydia's voice: "What 'ya say now?" NO! NO! NO! That's "cray-cray," and wrong on so many levels.

Just because you are comfortable around that foul spirit, do not speak that over my nephews! That is not the kind of voice we need in our children's head. Role models, you need to either, "come clean, or stay away dirty." In fact, why can't you encourage the mothers to convince their boys to dress up in their daddy's neckties? Here is what you should have told the millions that were watching around the world: "What's in the root shows up in the fruit" (Mt. 7:20). Now that's Bible!

More or less, he went on to sanction that if your son turns out to be a "drag-queen," then, so be it. "Are you kidding me?" That's when my (=-O) "uh-oh" meter really went off. That was totally not acceptable because God's purpose for your son is to become a REAL man. Spokesman, ask yourself how it would make you feel for your son to grow up and be a "drag queen." I thought that was one of the most distasteful, inconsiderate, insensitive, uncharitable, careless and most thoughtless endorsements that I had ever heard. "The doors of the church are open!" "Get thee delivered!" It's ironic that Bishop G. E. Patterson just said on a Sunday afternoon telecast that "being rich doesn't stop you from being foolish!"

This foolishness right here has forced me to go way back to Part Three of the Trilogy and borrow the following excerpt from my well-documented battle of clergy sexual misconduct. Albeit another shameless plug, maybe, this *Rebirth* revision will result in the one book that actually gets read. "Since every seed produces after its own kind, I have relatives, friends, acquaintances and strangers, whom I am predestined to push through my 'birth canal.' When we do not accurately reciprocate what God has given us, we forfeit our generation. Will we die in the wilderness with an old generation? Will God have to wipe out a generation and appoint a new priest, or will we rise to the occasion to affect and raise a new nation of worshipping warriors? By changing our priorities, we may be able to reduce the incidence of 'birth defects.'

Keep in mind: a baby being developed depends on the environment that surrounds it. When deprived of essential nutrients or exposed to certain toxins, abnormalities may not become apparent, until much later. Thus, timing is critical, where toxins are concerned. I am a part of a generation who declares that the curse stops here. I will not be responsible for fabricating new iniquities in my family. I am a part of an army of warriors, who declares, 'That's it, enough is enough; we refuse to be silent!' As I was constrained to remain silent for 15 years, the 'trusted man' in my life was totally in control. Now that my books speak for me, the Holy Spirit has put me in control over the thing that had power over me. [Is your platform doing the same for you?]

If I do not speak out now, this trait could show up in my nieces' generation. ['NOT ON MY WATCH!'] The iniquity trait worsens after each generation. One reason is that silence grants permission. 'Behavior tolerated is behavior perpetrated.' [The enemy is familiar with the fathers' weakness, and his job is to take that weakness and pass it down to the next generation.] Will your children be forced to wander around in the wilderness because of your personal disobedience (read Num. 14:31-34)? Sending out the future of an oncoming generation, someone must deal with the way that you are living right now. Joshua said: 'As for me and my house [generation], we will serve the LORD!' When God saves you, He owes you the favor of saving your house.

Hannah validates the fact that you can call your children's Anointing before they are actually born. She told the LORD that if He gave her a male child, she would give him back as a prophet. Samuel did not have a choice in the matter. Rather than asking God to give you a 'Michael Jordan,' or a 'Tyler Perry,' or some other famous son, ask Him to give you a prophet to whom you can pass your mantel. It does not matter how much reefer he smokes, or how much marijuana he sells, or how many clubs he frequents. If you call the end from the beginning, one of these days, he is going to operate in the prophetic!

We must stand in the gap and band together, to shield our babies from the sins of our generation. 'A **GAP** is where the man takes the stand, until **G**od **a**nswers **p**rayer.' Having allowed too many babies to slip through the cracks, we are the repairers of the breaches and the restorers of paths to dwell in (Isa. 58:12). **We can no longer mask the pain.** We must fix the problem by being involved enough to plug in some gaps and close some doors. If Moses had killed the Amalekites, Joshua would not have had to fight. If Joshua had killed them, it would not have been Saul's responsibility. If Saul had been on his job, there would not have been a need for Esther. From a personal standpoint, my daddy was acting out the sins of his father. If my granddaddy had reversed the curse, then my daddy would have had the power to overcome his enemy (read Ex. 34:7). And my past may not have become my story.

Since the curse did not stop with my daddy, I am willing to do the collaboration that authorizes Jehovah-Nissi to fight for my generation. If I can get through all of the preliminaries, I can help to reproduce a sound generation of women, by procreating life and snatching them out of immoral situations and unnatural relationships. It does not matter if your issues are generational, environmental, or whether you signed up for them. The reality is: you must become a conqueror and not a crutch for somebody else!" (Reid, 2010 with emphasis added). Likely, the fine, rich brother that I made mention of previously, couldn't care less, but I lost some respect for the manly man that I still had hopes for. "Hey 'Adam,' 'where you at'?"

Generally speaking, do you want to be seen, or do you want to be saved? In basic terms, you cannot be holy and be a homosexual simultaneously. "Don't make excuses; make adjustments." I'm sure to get some backlash from this book, but if you can do you on television, then, certainly I can do me in the book that I'm paying to publish. I may not ever be able to convince someone to provide the Foreword, but you don't have to patronize me. Since I'm in the Bible, God's got my back. At least my message suggests, that as men and women of integrity (born to affect our generation), we must walk circumspectly, not as **fools,** but as wise (Eph. 5:15).

During a storm, have you ever noticed that the young plants die first? Guess why. They have not become rooted! That is to say: the devil is not only after our Black men; he is after our youth! In this sense, you must consider that you have given birth to somebody's future father. You are raising some church's future pastor, or some woman's potential husband, so your paradigm and how you "lead the pack" will forever be etched in somebody's memories. Believe it or not, my sincere prayer is: "God bless my nieces with some godly husbands, EVEN if you don't bless me with one." I keep repeating myself, but I cannot say it enough: "A seed bears after its own kind."

In any event, by the time Adam and Eve started making love, the first couple had become totally independent; therefore, Adam had to "step up his game." Now that he was no longer in the garden where he had dominion over the animals, he had to leave his Father's House and cleave to his wife and learn how to take rule over a female and not a "bitch." That is definitely a learning process, in and of itself. After thousands of years, the decadence of this reality is that many men today still have not figured it out and are yet disillusioned by this process! I concur with Dr. Mike Freeman that "every lesson unlearned will be repeated."

You don't want us to be bitches, and we don't expect you to act like sissies. Personally, there has been only one man that I have ever dated that raised the bar for what I am willing to accept for the rest of my life (see Trilogy-Part Two). If you have never called me your "butterfly," then, you know that it is not you that I am referring to. *Certain restrictions apply!* Let's get back to Eden and bring this chapter to a close. While Eve had completely lost herself in her husband, I can envision her embracing Adam as a new bride would embrace her groom. You know how the ladies do it – with the "thumbs-up" sign behind his back, indicating, "not only have I found my true self, but I finally got him **to** myself." "It's a wrap!" He is officially mine, and he is **all** mine.

Once this day is over, the message intended is very personal. It goes like this: To all the ex (es), the mother-in-law and any other in-laws, I'm "gonna" need you to back up off of him, and let me handle the business. While societal norms coupled with the spirit of feminism teaches single women to be tough, efficient and independent, we cannot allow it to denigrate our need to be "male-nourished." Throwing our lives entirely out of divine order, we learn early to sustain ourselves. Either, it is because we believe that no one else will; or, we have not allowed the right "Adam" to cover us. Needless to say, through his <u>dishonorable</u> discharge, Adam demonstrated a love for Eve that was stronger than life and greater than death.

In light of the previous analysis, we are not dammed to hell because of one man's sin. In His infinite wisdom, God knew that we would fall and become vessels of dishonor. In this sense, I will end this chapter with an extensive question: ***"What if God, willing to show His wrath, and to make His power known, endured with*** *much longsuffering the vessels of wrath fitted to destruction: And that He might make known the riches of His glory on the vessels of mercy, which He had afore prepared unto glory, even us, whom He hath called, not of the Jews only, but also of the Gentiles?"* (Rom. 9:22-24).

CHAPTER ELEVEN

THE POWER OF ENVIRONMENTS

In the process of elimination, maybe this will be the chapter that gets deleted in the *Remix* on the next round, but for now, let's go for it. What had been so difficult for me to confine to a single chapter in Trilogy-Part One, I have insistently fulfilled the task that was massively inspired by Pastor Shannon who exemplified the kind of empathy that was anchored in advocacy. A journey terminated much too soon, he could not even die until after I made that last phone call. To be brutally honest, that final three-hour long discussion literally wore me out. As I was "antsy" and anxious to get off of the phone that day, I did not understand then what I know now. He was unrelenting in emptying himself because that was likely going to be his final impartation.

Wow, as I cherish the miracle that was awakened in me, I truly honor the strategic plan of our God. *"For My thoughts are not your thoughts, neither are your ways My ways, saith the LORD"* (Isa. 55:8). Indeed, this was the season that opened my spirit to new discoveries, to the excitement of exploration, and to the embracing of new eye-openers and revelations. Just as I am extremely intrigued by this God-ordained project and the divine connection that inspired it, I am optimistic and hopeful that this will be the element of my **16**-year journey that God will use to thrust me into the season of, "double for my trouble."

Certainly, my assignment via *The Twin Ministries* has not been an easy task under the best of circumstances. As the Anointing without money definitely leads to annoyance, the anticipation to all of my projects is that eventually, God is going to reduce my hold time. At any rate, writing has been a consistently rewarding experience, as it has brought a new kind of passionate involvement into my world and a way of actively participating in the lives of others. When you do not share or pour your legacy in others, it dies with you.

Since Pastor Shannon was one of the three people who unselfishly had immeasurable faith in my future, I feel indebted to honor his legacy and labor of love by mentioning his wife, Mrs. Myrtle Shannon. Artist Lester Kern and Evangelist Linda Macon were the other two. Before I update you on the power of my most recent environment, please allow me the time needed here to reflect on the divine connection between Pastor Shannon and I, and to make a few eulogistically remarks with respect to the deceased.

After being introduced to them by a mutual friend, the Shannons became guests in my home during the 2007 C.O.G.I.C. Holy Convocation. Then, a few months later, I flew in to St. Louis for a "round table discussion," just to collaborate a few hours about Adam and Eve. I flew there again, the second time, and they came to sit around my friend's table to collaborate about a different project, which was aborted due to the untimely death of the illustrator for my cover art. The final time was all so precious, when they came as the only guests to my graduation, as I received my Masters degree from Webster University (St. Louis) in 2008 – not to mention the extensive phone calls that Mrs. Shannon never once, distracted him from, as he poured into me, such powerful revelation.

Karen D. Reid (Ph.D. Candidate)

(2008)

Even as Pastor Shannon was always discerning of my purpose and potential, during all of those times, I never imagined that this divine connection and his investment would eventually evolve into a book of its own. "Look at God! Won't He do it?" While my effort is not my issue, exposure is what I'm lacking. There are some doors that won't be opened from where I am because of the "child safety lock." This big door can only be opened by the Father. And until He opens that door, I will keep praising Him in the "hallway." At the same time, I must only gravitate toward the people who have my back.

When I finally push out the destiny that God has birthed in me, I am going to thank some people for not showing up in the "delivery room." This time, only God will get the credit! As I have welcomed certain people out of my life, it is no indication that I hate them; it only means that I respect me. Even though my portfolio does not yet match any of the astounding prophecies that have been spoken over my life, it is because of what I know that I refuse to let go! *"I had fainted, unless I had believed to see the goodness of the LORD in the land of the living"* (Psa. 27:13).

As introverted as I naturally am, am I really prepared to receive all of the promises that God has made concerning my destiny? "Can I really stand to be blessed?" Please do not allow the validity of my

198

anonymity to be wrongfully held in low esteem. Just because I am not visible does not mean I'm not valuable. I am just a "limited edition" that's waiting to be put under the right "radar" and in the right hands. I am convinced that God has been hiding me out and protecting me from the "vipers." I have experienced enough of those in my life. Can I go ahead and be totally transparent for a couple of more pages? Maybe after the rant, I'll turn the next phase into another chapter.

Even as I have engaged my total self into what I am so passionate about, this is what I do and have done for the past 16 years. The bottom line is that I never, really had a midwife, except Pastor Shannon, who went home way too soon. As a starving author, I have had to lick my own wounds, as my gift was never fed. My destiny was planted, but it was never watered. Just as the next person who may have been given some unmerited favor, my gift deserves to emerge from obscurity, and my labor merits financial respect as well. Don't you get paid for what you do?

Whereas the weight of the glory of God has been a part of my consciousness both night and day, not only have I invested 16 years of my life. Also, I have invested over $30,000 into my projects just to bring a rich set of my experiences into focus. Can you imagine what my books would cost if you were paying me by the year, or even by the hour, like most working people are paid? And some people have the nerve to ask for a free book. "What in the 'hood' are you thinking?" "Oh snap," I almost went there again! But thank goodness for the "street-edge." It keeps me from giving in to the irritation to use offensive language. Can I be really transparent, right now? Experientially, I would like to show you, "for real, for real in real life" (Sophia Ruffin), what PURPOSE OVER PROFIT really looks like. Below is the kind of royalty checks that I have received since my first publishing in 2003.

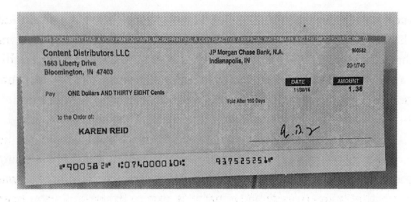

My sister, "Shannon," was more devastated seeing this check than I am receiving them. She was in total disbelief! Why even waste a stamp to send me checks like this for over a decade of my career? Resting in His sovereignty, I really believe that God was waiting until such a time as the present for me to be forthcoming with this project. One thing that I know for sure is that out of the past 16 years of my assignment, I have felt the Anointing on this particular revision, stronger than any other. I am actually thankful that the previous projects remained "under-cover." They weren't ready, and I wasn't prepared.

In 2014, Demetries Foxworth posted on my Facebook page that she had just finished reading this book in its previous edition, and it was exactly what she needed. She stated that it made her laugh and think at the same time. Behind her post, Lady Tihara Thomas commented: "Hello Karen. As we traveled this past week, I had the opportunity to read to my husband [Bishop Ladell Thomas, Jr.] your book... It truly blessed us. You are a proven work in the Master's hands. Never, that I doubted this at all. **Keep up the assignment. Millions will be changed through this riveting Masterpiece.** Love you in a million ways. Agape." (T. Thomas, personal communication, Sept. 29, 2014 with emphasis added). You can't even imagine how humbling it was to finally get some validation from noteworthy people whose words have merit!

I feel in my spirit that God purposely did not allow other, notable people to read this book because it was not time yet. There were still a lot of missing elements that were extremely important to its evolution. First, He had to allow my family to go **back** to Killeen for the second time, on a military duty. Then, as a result of one of my visits, God allowed me to attend the Thomas' Sunday morning worship, **after** Bishop Thomas, Jr. had become Senior Pastor since the passing of his father. Finally, by the end of the service, I felt compelled to give them complimentary copies of this book, along with Trilogy-Part One.

Even as it has not yet happened (as of Christmas Day, 2016), I believe that God allowed them to read this particular book that you are holding in your hands right now, so that Lady Tihara could come on Facebook after Demetries, to give me, what I believe was ultimately, a major prophecy that **must** come to pass. I have been given many, many prophecies, but what's so "God" about this one is that she didn't even realize that she was likely on a divine assignment to prophesy to me on Facebook. Did you notice what she wrote? ... "**Keep up** the assignment." At that time, either of us had no idea that I would be compelled to write a *Rebirth* edition. She goes on to say (with emphasis added): "MILLIONS **WILL BE** [not might be] CHANGED THROUGH THIS RIVETING MASTERPIECE."

It truly amazes me as to how strategic God is in His own timing and in all of His ways. After all, did not my cousin tell me recently that "my labor was not in vain?" Maybe labor intensive, but it's not in vain. Wherefore, a more challenging question might be: Am I really prepared for the real backlash and the spiritual warfare that my projects will likely present? Apart from the enormous potential that is presented by technology, my first competence challenge is finding a way to confidently and emphatically re-present the God in me and introduce to the world the gift that He has given me, in a way that makes Him pleased with me. That was probably the longest sentence that I have written thus far. ☺

Anyway, if it were left up to me, I would prefer to be nameless and faceless, as long as the results are measurable. Even as public speaking is my social deficit, I feel that who is driving and directing me is more important than who is watching me. Either way, I do not want my efforts to appear value-free. If by divine providence that this is the element of my series that reaches it's potential and does not fade in the background, I can only pray and hope for an Anointing that will make presenting just as effortless as writing.

To say the least, in 2014, when I was again in the process of finalizing a revision (but not the *Rebirth* edition, my threshold was at its very lowest. My current circumstances were killing my momentum because where I was, was intimidated by where I was going. David was getting closer to his throne when a jealous Saul started throwing javelins at him. Usually, when the warfare increases, it is an indication that your time is at hand. Besides, the enemy wages war on those who are a threat to his territory. If you are not getting hit by Satan, you are probably not in the "game." When God has handed you the "ball," you have a tendency to break when you've been hit the hardest. But if you break, your spiritual instability is exposed, and that's when you stop "playing the game," and praying in His name. You stop believing, and you start doubting. However, you don't get off of an airplane because there is turbulence; you stay the course!

During this particular "boil-over" (with thoughts of letting it all go), I would often medicate my pain and go to sleep, early in the day. I took what Vera (Will's alcoholic mother on Tyler Perry's Meet the Browns), referred to as preventative medicine. She said that it prevented her from "giving a damn." Sorry, I don't intend to use engaging terms for malicious intent, but those are my honest sentiments. The way I handle my stress is likely different from the way other Christians handle theirs.

Sorry to say, I do not always pray at the onset of stress; consequently, I take it to the bed and pray for strength as I sleep in an altered state of relief. Some people need power naps; I take reward naps. At the end of a long day when I am poured out and exhausted, an altered state of sleep is how I reward myself. I echo the Unicom commercial claim that "a stressful day deserves a restful night." There is really nothing like a Sunday afternoon, chemically-induced nap when I'm home alone in the rain. Even as my body has built up a resistance to my meds and I have taken enough at one time that would have probably killed someone else, the only reason that I'm not dead is because I'm not done.

Sometimes you don't want to die, but you get tired of hurting. Besides, some problems are just "sleepable." The LORD that keepeth Israel never slumbers nor sleep (Psa. 121:4), so there is no need of both of us staying awake. Psychologically, I often feel that if I can just sleep on it, I will feel rejuvenated enough to wake up and start over again. In the lyrics of Marvin Winans: *It'll be all over in the morning.* Whether I sleep it off or pray it off, as long as it comes off, "I'll be good." Irrespective of how I handle life while being overwhelmed by multiple projects at one time, here is my best advice: When you take the big picture and break it down into smaller images, the completion of the task doesn't seem as complicated. So how do you eat an "elephant?" Take one bite at a time.

Recently, when I told my goddaughter, Lydia, that I was unable to sleep for two, consecutive days, she goes: "Even Joseph went to sleep so he could dream again. I'm going to have to send up a custom-made prayer for you." L☺L! As I had recently gotten into the habit of falling asleep with the television on, God woke me up in the middle of the night while the station just happened to be turned to either, TBN or the Word Network. As I had been second-guessing myself again about my assignment and literally on the verge of giving up (for real this time), these are the only words that I woke up long enough to hear: "Don't give up now; your DUE season is on the way" (November, 2013). Ironically, I heard the same minister repeat these words a few months later, in a movie that I happened to be watching.

As these were the words that gave me the strength and tenacity required to keep waking up and starting over, I must concur with Bishop Avery Kinney (with emphasis added). He posted: "Obedience is a protected **environment**, but that doesn't mean it's a perfect climate! The very storm that tries to prevent your progress provokes God's performance! He will not let the storm outdo Him!" *"For his anger endureth but a moment; in his favour is life: weeping may endure for a night, but joy cometh in the morning"* (Psalms 30:5). Guess why; the "Son" shows up.

My associations with fruitless people and things have obviously impeded my strategies to produce. As a result, my recent appetite for growth has outgrown many of those selfish relationships. Why do people act like walls when all you need is a door? Since Jesus said in John 10:7b: ... *"I am the door of the sheep,"* I will not break or enter into any more doors that refuse to open for me. God has foreclosed those doors for a reason and does not want me chasing after anyone that He has chased out of my life. I refuse to miss my exit trying to recreate an entrance to a season that's over!

Fair whether friends will always abandon the "ship" in the middle of a raging storm, but as soon as GOD has successfully led the ship to safety; here they come, wanting credit for your success story. That's when it's time to hang up the "CLOSED FOR RE-GROUPING" sign! Bishop Avery Kinney advises: "When promotion hits your life, folk that have been in inactive status will try to become active again with an agenda! Watch out for people who all of a sudden get interested AGAIN when you start to go up! Be spiritually intelligent instead of deep and dumb. Umph!"

In case you're wondering why it has taken me so long to delve into the precise contents that relate to my chapter title, I was forced to do some restructuring in the end. What was only a section in the previous chapter has now become a chapter of its own. Let's start here. Perhaps the reason why I have not fully manifested everything that God put in me, or why my money, academic, relationship, or ministerial potentials are not where they could be, is that I was unwilling, even for a time, to be a part of a different environment. There we go; we're back on track.

Maybe I was unwilling to make the sacrifice, or to do the research, or to be ridiculed, or to be called a fanatic because everybody where I was, wanted me to be where they are. That was then; this is now. After I had completely finalized this chapter, I felt compelled to return and make revisions based upon Dr. Matthew Stevenson's periscope on the power of environments. It began to wake up a sort of echo in my consciousness. Accordingly, I understand better now why the Anointing was stronger on this particular project than it had ever been before. This powerful teaching may bless somebody.

Months before God coerced me into writing this *Rebirth* edition, the devil attempted to make me literally, sleep my life away. As I had become severely depressed and legally "drugging-out" every day, the way God woke me up was that He deliberately allowed water damage to become an issue with my apartment home. After being homeless almost seven years ago (for nine months) and being blessed to ascertain this apartment by a divine miracle with no proof of "no" income, I vowed that the only way I would move was either by coming into a lot of money or a lot of man. While neither of those things had come to past yet, I relished living in my residence for the first five years. Now going into my seventh year, I was in dire need for some type of environmental change to awaken the "sleeping giant" that was destined to release this project.

In the state I was in, the environment was not conducive for anything to happen for me, to me, or inside of me. Although I was coming out of a devastating seven-year famine, I still felt like I was in a mental season of drought. My motivation to write was frozen; my ambition toward ministry had dried up, and my expectations were at a standstill. Even my season as a foster parent had abruptly come to an end. When the last placement started acting like the seed of Belial, my response to future placements was "that's a negative." In being forced to confront the water damage, GOD woke me up early one morning and told me what to write in an email to my leasing manager. *"My sheep hear My voice, and I know them, and they follow Me"* (John 10:27).

Being the explicit writer that I am, my request to forfeit my remaining lease was granted, immediately. Not only was the reply an immediate yes, but they willingly deducted $400 from the current month's rent. My cousin, who had just relocated from California and became my neighbor, actually thought I was losing it. But I'm so excited that I'm learning how to tune out everybody else and follow the voice of my Shepherd with such accuracy and clarity, and with peace in my spirit! After God had so clearly spoken through the email, it was my confirmation that now was the right time to wake up and make this move. Refusing to remain in a fetal position, the mistake that the enemy made was that he had left me **half**-dead. Somehow, there was another part of me that still had the potential to be resuscitated.

While I had in no way prepared for this move, moving my things into storage was my next plan of action. Indeed, it was a bit confusing to a few of the people whom I was in direct contact with. Yet, I knew that it was a move of God because I resonated with myself in a way that I even had peace in packing. While I absorbed myself in this peace, there was such tranquility about the idea of even being in transition. Ironically, Lady Andrea Singleton had told me months prior that she had a dream of me telling her that I was moving to Dallas.

Well, the day before the actual movers were scheduled to arrive, I took a break from packing and attended a 12 noon service at Bishop Brandon Porter's Jurisdictional Workers' Meeting. After responding to the call for prayer at the altar, when Bishop Ronnie Webb (the guest speaker) arrived at the end of the row where I was standing, the first thing he did was started turning me around. His word to me was: "God is turning things around." To myself, I was like: "Great! It's about time; I just hope that it's not another one of those distant-future prophecies." Because I had been given so many prophecies down through the years that had not yet manifested, I was excited but not ecstatic. "You feel me?"

Once I told the family "prophetess" (Carolyn Wright) that I was preparing to move, she made a commitment to go before God for direction on my behalf. A couple of weeks later, I text her and asked: "Cuz, have you heard anything yet?" She replied: "The only thing I could hear was: "He's turning things around." Now, I'm like really becoming excited. In recent months, I had been posting on Facebook with intentions of encouraging somebody else. One post in particular, went like this: "Why are you worried about making the right move when God is in the turn? If you make the turn, God will be responsible for the turnaround." What I didn't realize is that God was giving me a Word for myself.

By this time, I had gotten to a point where I had literally stopped posting on Facebook because while I was always speaking faith, a lack of manifestation was making me feel like a fool. On the other hand, as I was in the middle of this transition with feelings of rejection, I could hear God say things like: "Don't talk until you can testify." "Be still and quiet until I do something big and loud." Remain in "H.U.S.H." mode – "**H**ush **U**ntil **S**omething **H**appens." If somebody asks where you're moving to, just tell them what "Shannon" suggested: "T.B.D." – **T**o **B**e **D**etermined. L☺L! For years, my sister had been trying to persuade me to relocate and come live with the family because she was always aware of my financial struggle. It was deep.

I kept trying to believe God for miracles and manifestation; yet, every few years or so, I would always end up in bankruptcy court. It was a zone that I could never seem to avoid. Sometimes I would wonder: did my ex-leader really cast a spell on me, when I obeyed God and decided to walk away. Whatever may have been going on in the spirit realm, in July of 2016, I told "Sis," "I'm coming for real, this time. I have turned my notice in (again), but this time 'it's a wrap'." As there are only 12 numbers in my Favorites cell phone list, I only told the few, faithful friends whom I was directly involved with. Not even clear to me yet, I was not only in transition; I was going on a mission. Since the conclusion was dependent on my environment, I kept my move on the "D.L." because I did not need the enemy to "blow my cover."

Moreover, I was too exhausted to entertain any foolish questions from nosey people, particularly, like the one whose cruel rejection was confirmed by her crushing remarks. You talking about somebody feeling persecuted. Here I was, minding my own business and doing the will of my Father, and my own folk shot me down with a "bullet" to the brain. Man, did she interrupt my flow. I can't even repeat the words that came out of that person's mouth, but I just did a "skip" to get back in step.

Relentlessly, I went back and forth to Dallas as a temporary means to an end. Now with clothes in three places and feeling fashionably-challenged, "Shannon" convinced me to start working out with her at Lifetime Fitness. While she was looking all cute and coordinated, I was looking homeless and feeling discombobulated. After she persuaded me to upgrade my workout gear, it was now the power of environments that God convinced me to upgrade this book. One of the untold stories of the K.R. is my phobia of animals, particularly dogs; I'm talking traumatized, terrified, and jumping on your dining room table, terrified. One reason is that they grossed me out.

At peace with my decisions and now enjoying a rent-free/worry-free environment in a beautiful 4,000 square foot home where I virtually have the upstairs to myself, I am ever so grateful to my family for taking me on, basically as their other dependent. What I force her to take every month; I couldn't "beat **anywhere** with a licking stick." I often think of the money that I could have saved if I had moved here when she first offered. But it wouldn't have worked.

"Timing is everything;" I had to wait until I heard the voice of God. For the inquisitive folks that are trying to figure it out, my "back-home-home" is just as blessed. "Enuf said."

Now all of a sudden, after I have been spoiling my dad to life and killing that meanness with kindness, he loves me so much that he claims that he can't get well because he's worried crazy about me traveling back and forth to Memphis on these dangerous highways, where people are getting killed every day. After he has enjoyed his life and done whatever the hell he wanted to do for 81 years, he's begging me to come home and stop trying to live like I'm President "Crump's" daughter. He claims that God keeps trying to warn me through him. That "ain't" God; that's Daddy! Basically, I told him that if I'm at peace with it, save your energy for something else. If truth be told, he really wants me to get a place, move him in with me so that I can "daddy-sat" him for the rest of his life.

I'm about to be 56 years old, and I am not about to subject myself to living under my parent's rule and allowing him to run my life. At first, I considered it because I felt obligated for the mere fact that he's my father. But after I "slapped" myself back into reality, I told the devil that he was a liar, and my daddy is too. That would not be a good "power move;" that would be more like a "power outage." After all of the hell I've been through for most of my 56 years, "BUMP THAT!" It's my time now, and I dare not get **stuck** in a house to subject myself to listening to him preach all day about that old time religion. To make it even more tormenting, he hollers, "HEY," every few sentences, as if he's in the Spirit. "What the world?!?" My dad may as well adjust to old age, and at the appointed time, I will assist him with finding an assisted living facility, or a home for the elderly.

Ultimately, he became obsessed with trying to control my life and where I lived, and was convinced that it was okay for him to talk to me like a child. I'm not sure if he was delusional or just being unreasonable, but Daddy may have earned his own book: *Daughter-Daddy Senior Care: Was It Dementia; Or, Was It "De-devil"?* If you want to know the truth about it, every disease and disorder that we have given a name to is from the devil. The Bible calls it "legion." Anyway, after my dad ranted for months because I would not acquiesce to his demands, he admitted that if something happened to me, he was not going to cry. You see? That "ain't" God; that's the devil! Sadly, he had said the same thing when I was 15 years old, that if I died, he would not attend my funeral. Only this time, he came back with a vengeance and said everything that had been building up for the past 40 years.

Since he doesn't know what "bougie" is, the reality is that I'm too "klassy" for him. An encore of my childhood torture, he hates my lifestyle with a passion. Literally, he wants me to have a poverty mindset and advises that since I came from a poor family, I should come down off my "high horse;" stop being in love with money and live like I'm still poor. He expects me to live in the ghetto and always look like I'm going to the gym. "The devil is 'be-damned!" What father does not want the best for his child, or want his child to do well in life?

He became so angry that he took my name off of his affairs to avoid leaving me his inheritance. But what God has in layaway for me is far bigger than what he could ever leave me. If he is offended by my lifestyle now, in a few months, he won't be able to stand the ground I walk on. After accusing me of taking $1,000 from him, he now claims that everything I've done for him was for the wrong reason. I refuse to keep going out of my way for someone who does not appreciate it. However, some of my last words were: "If you need me, call me."

When I refused to receive his curses and declared that I was covered by the blood; he goes, "How you covered by the blood and living in sin?" Now mind you, according to his theology, I was living in sin because I was living with my sister. Yet, he had married an unsaved woman because he was burning in his pants. Now he claims that God just put him back with the woman that he accused of trying to kill him. Since he was suddenly called to be my personal prophet, I wanted to know how did he miss seeing his own demise. He had the nerve to say that God conditions things. I said: "If God can condition things for you, He can condition things for me!"

He could not handle me defending myself. He claimed that he was the same old now, as he was when I was born. In other words, he had the right to still talk to me like I was a child. No disrespect, but I'm not the same young as when he was the same old. Same relationship but different roles; he is no longer changing diapers. In reality, I'm 56 years older than when I was born. "When I was a child, I spake, understood, and thought as a child" (1 Cor. 13:11). Oh, I felt so accomplished for finally having the courage to speak my peace. As a matter of fact, I had gotten so emotional and out of character that before I knew it, my blood pressure had gone up to 176/109. At least, when I was forced to introduce him the sanctified "clickum," I had enough respect to put a strong goodbye in front of it.

What Vision Strategist, Clarissa Joi, recently said about James White who made history for winning the Super Bowl Game in overtime is that there will be people nagging us at our heels, **right before** we score that final touchdown. I can so relate to that, but what really affected me about this whole situation is the fact that for years and years, the two men who claimed to be my daddy have done nothing but tried to curse me and tear down my self esteem. If I had allowed it, their toxic words would have easily become my actual reality. Okay, enough of him/them and their brainwashing schemes! #purefoolishness!

Both claiming that they loved me; however, when you love something you should make a conscious effort to set it free. Sobering but liberating moments, I cannot allow my decisions to be predicated on my daddy's dogmas. "When he forsakes me, then the LORD will take me up" (Psa. 27:10). When he went so far as to change his cell number, I was released from my daughter duties. My sister, "Shannon," said that after he had pouted and went on like a child, he put himself in "time-out." She guaranteed me that he's going to need me before I need him. And guess what else: I plan to be right there for him.

As the book had been submitted for almost two months, and I was still dealing with technical issues and uncommon delays (labor pains), since I know that it's "time sensitive," I stopped being bothered about it. Since somebody has to witness my resurrection, keep it coming devil; bleeding is only a sign of life! Ironically, on the day that I am about to submit this project again, this time to the Assistant Manager of Operations, I overheard Bishop T. D. Jakes say something to this effect: "If you see your setbacks as failures, then, we'll bury you. If you see them as opportunities, then, we'll resurrect you." I was like: Wow; look at God! This was just after I had finished inserting the passage about my resurrection and going over my content issues with the management. Needless to say, at every possible occasion for delay, I have taken the opportunity to make worthwhile changes to this content.

All the same, what was really happening is that Satan was trying to intensify the warfare in order to block the inevitable. And since truth has no revisions and transparency has no restrictions, I was even forced to come up with a pen name (before I reminded them of my First Amendment Right. However, the labor pains were only an indicator of the size of the miracle that was being pushed out. The irony is: the intensity of Satan's warfare is a gauge of the multiplicity of God's "well-fare." "That was a good place to shout, right there!"

Even school became a daunting challenge, and probably the most stressful quarter that I had ever had. I was like: "Life is too short for long-term stress," particularly, busy work and undue/self-inflicted stress. I was even hoping to be denied of another gradplus loan, which was my only recourse for continuing the new school term. At least that would give me justification for threatening to quit again. To no avail, I was approved immediately.

The very morning of the final countdown, I revisited a chapter in Trilogy-Part Three, entitled, *The Power To Give Birth: PUSH, And By All Means, Don't Stop Breathing!* What I had been experiencing was the prelude before the song, the warm-up lap before the race, the misalignment before alignment, the chaos before order – from preparation to conception. ***"Thou art wearied in the greatness of thy way"...*** reveals Isaiah 57:10. Whenever you are shouldering greatness, the magnitude of the load is determined by the vastness of the vision. Although it had not yet manifested, the awesome responsibility of what I am personally carrying in the womb of my spirit was heavily weighing upon my shoulders.

Hagar was in the middle of a transition, when Abraham, the same man who loved her, urged, "You **and** your child must go." You are not really causing the breach; it is that "baby" of yours. You could stay, if it was just you. The real fight is about that "thing" that you pushed out. It is not you that the devil wants to kill; it is what's inside your womb that is causing the ruckus. You and your ministry must go! You and your anointing – get out! Take your gift and get out of this office!

Take your testimony and leave this church! Honey, they are just upset over your "baby" – your destiny, your fruit, your future, your promise, and your prophecy.

Don't even think about it; it is too late to abort! The MIRACLE has already been set in motion. (Reid, 2010). Wow; an oldie but goodie. Just as Clarissa Joi said in her periscope: "If you are not pumped up by now, check your pulse." Maybe that's why I almost allowed them to convince me to use the pen name, "Destiny's Miracle." From my own writings, I had to remind myself of this: "Do not make it to the door of your miracle and become too exhausted to <u>push</u> it open (see Isa. 40:29-31). You are only a few breaths away. 'BREATHE! BREATHE! BREATHE! AND BY ALL MEANS, DON'T STOP PUSHING'!" Hey AuthorHouse; "where you at?" "Destiny" is finally ready to give birth to her "Miracle." After weeks and weeks of one delay after another; this "baby" is finally on the way! #03/21/17 (all significant numbers for me)

Temporarily, this is how I'm living until God says different. My daddy needs to GET OVER IT and stop pulling at my heartstrings! He is so **not** used to **not** having a woman around to control that he was determined to reduce me down to a live-in "daddy-sitter," to substitute or compensate his need for female companionship. Not out of disrespect or to sound condescending, but he provoked me to "bull dog"-tenacious rage so that my loud voice would dodge his "bullets" and the word curses that he released toward me. I later apologized for getting out of character. At the same time, you must do what's right <u>concerning</u> people, but you can't put yourself out, <u>because</u> of people. Finally, he teamed up with my oldest brother for reinforcement, (with his "oxygen-deprived brain"), who had the audacity to send me threatening text messages at 4:00 in the a.m. Two people can hate each other, but they will come together with one thing in common; to "hate on you."

Meanwhile, while my family was "hating on me," I fell in love with my sister's "white" Maltese dog, whose name is "Baby." Sorry to say, I was biased and had very little to do with Cherish, the black Chi-poo. Unless she was hustling me for treats, she had an attitude and was always "mean-mugging" me. So I understand the White man's plight. If you took me serious, then, you must also believe that the Pope is Baptist. Anyway, the white dog was allowed to roam the house, "foot loose and fancy free," even when nobody was home. But the preferential treatment had nothing to do with color.

The black dog was kept in her kennel most of the time because she had forgotten how to "poop" outside and not in the house. As a result of her personal issues, almost everyone in the house treated her differently. At 10 years old, my Mother, Clarice Moore, suggested that Cherish may be coming down with dementia. Or, it may be her only way of retaliating and letting us know that she does not appreciate, not being treated equally.

This "chick" right here, made the book! I had to come back and give her a larger "billboard!" Because she has to "feel some kind of way," seeing that the white dog gets the most love and attention. But then, when I would try to play with her, it would scare her because she was so used to hearing me holler, "OUT! Cherish." Every time I try to be nice and let her out of her kennel to go outside and "potty," she runs away and hides under the bed. My sister referred to her as the "runaway slave." She's so stubborn that they have to pick her up and force her to go outside. And while the white dog never complains about being outside, Cherish has the most annoying shriek, when she's outside longer than the time needed to "potty." Whenever she's bad, that's considered her time-out, which she absolutely dreads. I'm surprised that she hadn't jumped into the swimming pool and tried to commit animal suicide. No, I'm kidding; it's not that bad.

Whenever I did decide to give both of them treats together, I always made sure that the white dog was given the larger treat. Do you not see how easily it is to be prejudiced? =^-^= But then, "Baby," the white dog, seemed to have started swallowing her treats and hurrying back as though she was entitled to get more treats than Cherish. The spirit of entitlement: does that not sound like "Esau?" On the contrary,

"Jacob" (the black dog), hid under my bed and tapped me on my leg, trying to "deceive" me into believing that she was the preferred dog. After finding a new home for her, I actually started feeling sorry for her and tried to convince my sister to give her another chance to reconcile. Unfortunately, it was too late to save her at this point.

In contrast, every move I made, "Baby" (the white dog) was on my heels, until she finally stole my heart. To get my attention, she would not stop staring me down until I made eye contact with her. Once I made eye contact and talked to her in my "Baby" voice, she knew that she could get anything she wanted. It's a wonder that I didn't "treat" her to death. Even when I went to the bathroom and came out, she was right there "ear-hustling" and hoping that I came out with a treat. If they were both in the room together whenever I came home, they would run out as if they were running a marathon. I thought, "God, what if Your people ran after Your voice like that?" My friend, Renee, claims that I will come up with any occasion to get a revelation.

Hinged on the premise that my worse phobia was animals, I have come a long way where dogs are concerned. Forced to come around them at my sister's house, I eventually learned to tolerate them by dressing up in my "dog gear" (always long pants, boots and gloves, no matter what time of the year it was). But you should see me now. I still have to put a sock on my hand to pat them – as long as I'm making progress, right? I would have never dreamed in a million years that a dog could melt my heart, like "Baby." I even made up a one-line rap song for her: "What my 'Baby' want?" "What my 'Baby' want?" She dances to it, and I absolutely love it.

It's the power of environments! While destiny will literally pull you like gravity, your obedience triggers **every**thing in your environment to supply you with what you want and need. If you are without, you might want to examine the extent of your obedience level. God is not obligated to supply resources for those who procrastinate. I can prove it to you by the Word. ***"For because ye did it not at the first, the LORD our God made a breach upon us, for that we sought Him not after the due order"*** (1 Chon. 15:13). Personally, I have learned to be passionate in my willingness to obey God the first time, even if

215

I am forced to go into that mental place where I have to block torture in order to stay on task.

In any event, this book literally evolved from taking notes around a table to a chapter in another book, to barely, 60-typed, double-spaced pages in a book of its own. Now to hopelessly trying to avoid exceeding 200 pages with my many "ecumenical" changes, I feel like I'm "busting the devil over the head, down to the white meat." The power of environments has taken this book from an odd number of nine chapters to an even number of 14! I'm going to tell you about my "even now" moment in the final chapter.

After16 years of writing, from the bedroom that became my office, the bed that became my chair, and from my lap that became my desk, I really felt like God was keeping me hidden in a closet with all the lights off, and where there were no resources or recourse. In coming out of my night season, this book is undoubtedly why the enemy tried to take me out (emotionally, mentally, spiritually, and physically). Despite what all has gone into this process, I am so thankful that none of those "rejected editions" got off the ground. And for those of you who had counted me out – maybe not by popular demand, but "Baby, I'm back!" You may be irritated that I'm back, but one thing you can't deny is that I am anointed. At times, the Anointing on this project was so heavy that I felt like Jeremiah; "it's like 'fiya' shut up in my bones!" (Jer. 20:9).

On reflection, the Anointing really didn't hit me until **after** I made that attempt to sow into a much heavier Anointing. How can an empty attempt to sow a seed work for my good? Wow! It's the power of sowing and reaping! Because I obeyed and sowed into good ground, God honored what was in my heart to do. At the center of my transition, sowing that one seed put me on the "fast track" like I cannot believe. Their rejection may have caused them to miss their harvest, but I'm already reaping mine. Evidenced in my life, He never "leaves me hanging!" I knew it was on, when God started taking my sleep again and talking to me in the middle of the night like He did when I first started writing. One of my most, recent prophecies maintained that God was going to give me back my first love.

Then, my brother-in-law surprised "Shannon" with a new, 2016 Mercedes, CLS400. As I witnessed this "no-special-occasion" surprise, God whispered in my ear that in this environment, He was giving me a glimpse of what's about to happen in my life. Just like I have continued to do for my own expectations for the past 30 years, my sister spoke her blessing into existence. When the principle is spiritual, God has to get in the middle of it to cause it to manifest.

In those moments when you're up high enough, you can see far enough, to appreciate where you are and how far you have come. Sometimes God is moving you so fast that you don't understand your travel. Just since I have been in this environment, God has redeemed the time, and in five months, I not only completed this "Rebirth" edition; I produced a complete manuscript for someone else (publisher-ready). At the beginning of the year, whereas it took me two quarters to pass one, dissertation Milestone, I just completed three Milestones in one quarter. Out of the past, almost seven years of my pursuit, I don't ever recall finishing the quarter, a week and a half early. It's the power of environments!

By the end of this same, challenging week (November, 2016), after I was required to orally present myself to my doctoral committee for the first time, I received a surprise phone call from the beautiful, Lady Catherine Saulsberry of Memphis. While my faithful God had brought me before her in prayer, I didn't even realize that she knew me well enough to single me out. After encouraging me, she left me with Philippians 1:6: ***"Being confident of this very thing, that He which hath begun a good work in you will perform it until the day of Jesus Christ."*** That blessed me! Was that ironic, or was that GOD?

So far, I have defied my mentor's claim, every time that she claimed that I was at the stage where most Ph.D. candidates flunk, give up or drop out. Consistent with her experience, I might not finish, but in line with my faith, I'll finish strong. Now at Milestone 8 (writing Chapter One), but four months ahead of my Plan of Action, she informs me that some candidates take up to nine months to write one chapter. "Really?" I'm trying to convince her that this "ain't" about me! It's all about the Christ **in** me who is now on the "fast track" to restore back my dignity and bring honor to my name. Since I'm not really into titles, so it's "gotta" be all about Him.

The essence of who I am is not determined by my education. However, in connecting my identity to my profession, I must be able to be successful, even when I can't do what I've learned to do. I want to display myself as a vessel of honor so that my character garners respect, not a Ph.D., or the kind of house I live in, or even the kind of car I drive. "Bar none," my most intensive desire is to be a trophy on display for the Christ that lives in me. Yet, since this Ph.D. pursuit is a rite of passage, I don't mention it to boast of myself. I always boast in God because I am totally oblivious without His wisdom.

The two things that I KNOW that God has had His hand on in my life are this book and my education. He has proven to me (over and over), that He has ordained these two journeys. At this point, being happy is more important to me than being a doctor. As a result, I have threatened to quit school so many times, but He has proven to me, over and over that as long as the grace is on me to do it, I can't give up. Even when the funds ran out and I didn't know how I would cross over into the next quarter, He assured me with "miracle money" that my steps were **ordered**. Some of my peers with much better credit than mine were unable to access the same funds that I was approved for in a matter of a second (three different times to date). That's another testimony within itself! But it also serves as a reminder of my favorite Scripture, Ephesians 3:20: *"Now unto Him that is able to do exceeding abundantly above all that we ask or think, according to the power that worketh* **in us."**

In my transition and this same environment, I started a new editing project for which I am being compensated, and also a surprise project that I will mention at the end. I even committed to being on the local church's "Special Edition" Souvenir Booklet committee for the Pastor's Appreciation Celebration. Still "on the outside looking in," I couldn't say no to someone who has always had my best interest at heart. While I had only planned on getting it started and drafting up an Ad letter, the Bishop requested that I take the "driver seat." And if you know me, I try not to "co-sign" anything that does not "scream" perfection.

In my element and in my zone, I am seeing some powerful breakthroughs! My case in point: while I was only having meltdowns before, I'm now producing Milestones. It's the power of environments! Whereas little planes start in little places; I suddenly feel like I'm on a "747." At the beginning of the year, my spiritual battery was so dead that even a "jumpstart" seemed far-fetched. "When your dreams start to believe for you" (Tyler Perry), God will put His "foot to the medal" and accelerate your pace. I had to experience certain losses so that God could give me certain wins that made it worth the pain, the wait, the tears and the talk.

His response to where you are is based on His Word, not your emotions. I learned from Pastor "J" of Memphis that He is not moved by your tears, but He does hear your cry. There is a difference! Since God is of no respect of person and has already spoken that He's turning things around for me, Dr. Stevenson's (2016) periscope teaching left me with a sense of clarity. The unification and the interweaving and the rhythms of the following excerpt created a harmony and an understanding of this entire transition. The power of environments!

To miss half the journey is to miss some of the experience. You don't realize how important it is to deliberately involve yourself in environments that allow for the full maturity and the full exposure of even who you're supposed to be. A lot of what God wants to do in your world can only take place in certain environments. I know that you are of the persuasion that God will do whatever He wants to do with you wherever you are, and that it doesn't matter what city you live in, where you go to church, or whether or not you involve yourself in a local assembly, or watch church online.

Those are erroneous beliefs because the Bible is replete with examples about how God would shift the environment before He would either add a person's dimension, give clarity about who they were supposed to be, or give them the next point of what He wants to do in their lives. So environments are very important. God wanted to deal with Abraham, but before He would allow for His dealings to begin to take their full course, particularly about his assignment, his destiny, or who he was going to be, God mandated that he migrated to a different residence. God would talk to him as He shifted his environment.

There are certain things that God will withhold from you when you are in the wrong environment. Your comfort zone often affects your conversation with God. When you are in the place of your pulse or the place of your assignment even, sometimes that affects how well you hear from God. It also affects how you process what God is saying to you. The world around you has the ability to affect your ability to accurately perceive what God wants to do within you.

God spoke to Abraham in Genesis 12:1-2 to come out from his father's house and unto a land where He would show him. There He would bless him and make of him a great nation. We see another time where God spoke to Abraham about his destiny. He was in a tent when God had a conversation with him. After taking him outside of the tent, which was the context of his assignment and the context of his comfort zone, and even his safety mechanism, God continued the conversation as Abraham was willing to come from outside of the tent to see the stars. Sometimes, in order to see the stars, you've got to leave the tent. Oh my, I felt that!

The same is true with the disciples who followed John, and then left John to follow Jesus. In John 1, they asked, "Master, where are You staying?" Jesus said: "If you follow Me, I'll show you where I'm staying." They left one residency/training initiative to follow Jesus into wherever He was residing. After they resided with Him that one day, they came out convincing people that He was the Messiah. In the first residency, they saw Him as Teacher. In the next environment, He was no longer Teacher; their new testimony of Him was that He was the Messiah. The way they saw Him and the manner about which they saw Him shifted because their environment shifted first. This teaching is resonating with me like "white on rice."

Now does the environment dictate God's conversation? No, but for whatever reason, there are times when God wants to talk to you on His terms and not yours. There are things that you can never hear on the lower parts of the valley that are more easily perceived on the top of the mountain. So, some of you are missing information from God because you want Him to talk to you on your terms. You want Him to talk to you in the context of your comfort, your convenience, your contentment, and your complacency. But what I know on a new level; continues Dr. Stevenson, is that the most powerful instructions from God only come in moments of discomfort.

God does not speak your most challenging assignments or your strongest mandates in seasons of comfort because comfort has a tendency to be distracting. When you are comfortable, content, complacency and everything is going right, or you are around everybody that knows you, you don't have the threat of departure, or the threat of having to go somewhere you have not gone before. Often it affects the urgency whereby we hear God. But when things are uncomfortable, inconvenient, or when you have had to apply sacrifice to journey somewhere with God that you are not accustomed to, often, God has our attention in a way that He would not have had it in the area of our comfort zone. I'm having an "O.M.G." moment, right now!

People are not invested in environments because they have developed adhesive attachments and emotional, sentimental, romantic, psychological, spiritual, or solace attachments to those things that give them safety. Friends, churches, relationships, and jobs become pillars in our lives that uphold us and give us a sense of safety. We end up trusting what is around us because they are predictable and consistent. Predictability often gives us permission to trust. However, when it comes to purpose or potential, or manifesting your assignment, what ends up happening is that God does not always do things how and/or where He wants us to do it.

So sometimes, people don't always want to go into new environments because of unconfronted trust issues – either with God or with themselves. Journeys also reveal where your trust is, the last place you put it, and the last thing you invested it in. Many people say where they are, environmentally speaking because they don't want to have to go through the strenuous and sometimes excruciating process of having to unearth the energies to trust at a level that they have not had to trust before.

When you move and when you shift, whether that is a physical migration, an emotional migration, or a relational migration, any change of scenery that provokes God to speak to you on the next level, you will find that you're going to have to trust Him on a level that you may or may not be aware of. And that trust is going to be scary because one of the reasons why trust is formed is that it actually affects your fear. The beginning of trusting at a new level is the confrontation of fear. Until your fears are thoroughly confronted on every level (justified or not), you will be unable to trust at the level you need to. Environment is important, and maybe you should reflect upon when the last time you deliberately immersed yourself into a new environment. "My GOD today!"

When it comes to destiny, sometimes the law of exposure is the law that leads you to the next place in your life. An underexposed person won't know the possibilities of what you can be and what you can do. One of the greatest investments you can make in yourself is to have a shift of environment; it doesn't always have to be permanent. As with me (the author), it could be going somewhere long enough to proceed at the next level, or to understand at the next level, or to retain at the next level.

When you are a soldier, for example, you don't go to Basic Skills Training in your bedroom, or at your grandmama's house. Nor do you go outside and decide to run in place and think that's going to be how you qualify to be a soldier. No, you literally have to prepare your life to be drafted to a different location where the information that you need to progress you is what governs that location. What governs your location is your habits, your beliefs, and your familial. What govern your current location are your own desires and your own fantasies. But when you are drafted and forced to go into another environment, there is another set of protocols, another set of information, and another body of principles that governs how you are trained in a different place.

When you are not trained on your own turf, you are trained in academic environments, often away from everything you know to be true, or everything you know to be safe or predictable. Every skill that you employ for life is not always learned at home. It's often learned in the shifting of environments. As soon as you graduate in life, you prepare for a career. To make money, you prepare to make a memorable impression on whatever sphere of society that you are going to develop a career in. Again, you do not do it on your own terms. If you are going to do it and do it well, you must leave and go away.

Residency training; why? I believe God, the Master Educator, knows the power of immersing you into the world of your future, in order for you to look around and perceive what you are to be and become in order to be the recipient or the candidate of a level of information that matures you for what you are about to achieve in your future. You don't go off to shift environments or your past alone. A shift of environments is strictly for your future. You are supposed to take away from that environment and be added to, by the things that are around you. You're not supposed to deflate because of it, and you're not supposed to be defeated because of it. You're supposed to be immersed in the world of your future.

You ought to be able to look around at your friendships and your relationships, or your local church or careers and determine if that environment was sent by hell to keep you comfortable, complacent, restricted, or outside of resource. When an environment is ordained by God for your life, you should be able to see your future in it somewhere. If there is no route or road to your future, God is not the One who put you there. Why? God has never punished a man by making him live in the past. The LORD does not deliver you, save you and free you for you to relive where you have already been, or what you were loosed from or taken out of. His blood not only gave you entrance into Heaven; His blood gave you entrance into His future for your life. It's predetermined, and it's a pre-existing plan for all you were to do and for all you were to be.

When Jesus reverenced going to prepare a place for you, He was not talking about going to create Heaven for you. When He said that in Scripture, which was to His disciples, the Heavens had been created since the first Chapter of Genesis. Jesus was going to create places for us in the unseen world and in an unseen way that would allow for us to have the opportunity to fully become, to fully learn, and to fully submit to. There is a place for you that you never have to fit in. In the environment that God has called you to, He has ordained that you be there. "Shundo!"

I will conclude this insert with the same implication that Dr. Stevenson started it with. Perhaps, the reason why you're not fully manifesting everything that God put in you, or why your money, academic, relationship, or ministerial potentials are not where they could be, is that you are unwilling, even for a time, to be a part of a different environment. Maybe you are not willing to be mocked for the mandate on your life, or simply for manifesting your version of yourself from your highest potential. Consider what you need in a change of environments and what God can do for you, just for a moment in a different environment. Is this environment worth investing in? The answer is a brutal yes. Being at the right place at the right time has everything to do with what you believe God is about to do with you next. #thepowerofGODthroughperiscope For all intents and purposes, that scope was epic.

The morning after God had instructed me as to how to rework this chapter, I quickly noticed three, small words across my computer screen before I instinctively clicked on the log-in button. My eyes focused on a message that said: "The wait is over." Whether or not I was supposed to take that as a personal message from God, I'm not sure. But those words became life to me. It may sound a little bit out of sync, but the following is the rest of the chapter that was written before the insert.

As I have been an "underground movement" while Earth has been waiting for me to show up, God is bringing me into a season of performance. But first, He is requiring me to "de-board" all of the "Jonahs" in my life that are causing my "ship" to sink. The sooner I can get them off and land on some good fertile ground [obviously, in a different environment], I will be able to make the right connections and take that inevitable flight toward an expected end. "The sad truth is that there are some people who will only be there for you as long as you have something they need. When you no longer serve a purpose to them, they will leave [on their own]. The good news is, if you rough it out, you'll eventually weed these people out of your life and be left with some great friends that you can count on" (unknown). I think that I'm finally in the place that I heard Mike Murdock mention: ... "When He gets ready to protect you, He deletes people from your life."

The reality of it all is that when man promotes you, there is always an expiration date attached to the platform. Listen to this significant truth that was posted by Pastor Manwell Faison: "You will never know what you are capable of being if you remain connected to the people that you're depending on. The greatest enemy to your potential is not the bad people you avoid but the good people that you are too dependent on." "Why work so hard to fit in when you were called to be set apart?" (origin unknown). I refuse to be dishonorably discharged for being found in the wrong environment. Since I am trying to get away from really, really long chapters, let's "fast forward" and find a new title for what would have been the rest of this chapter. After going ahead and reading the next, few pages, I decided to go with, *I-chabod, The Glory Has Departed.* Toward that end, join me, and let's see how I can tie this in and make it work. By now, I should have it down to a science.

CHAPTER TWELVE

I-CHABOD, THE GLORY HAS DEPARTED: "OFFICERS' BOOTCAMP" WITH SPECIAL GUEST "PRESS OFFICERS"

Eden was perfectly designed for perfect people. Before the fall, Eve never had to go through a menstrual cycle or the normal process of a nine-month delivery. In actuality, they didn't even need clothes because they wore the glory of God. "Oh, the glory" ... Unfortunately, they lost the glory as a result of the transgression. Man or woman of God, don't ever lose what you already have for something you can live without. "Did you hear what I had said?" There are some sins which I vow to never participate in. The temptation will dissipate if you don't participate! I don't want certain spirits to possess my soul and take control of my body. I simply refuse to try another woman, just because I had bad experiences with men. I irrefutably refuse to try Heroin because my body chemistry has become resistant to Hydrocodone. I would totally decline to give up on Heaven because "church-folks" have shown me the other side of hell.

Here is a simple analogy that came to me in the shower. Because of the soapsuds effect that I get from a certain brand of soap, I refuse to buy any other brand. If I am that scrupulous about sanitizing the flesh that's made of dirt, shouldn't I be even more conscious about sanctifying the temple that houses the Spirit of the living God? If

Adam and Eve do not teach us anything else, I hope that the results of their transgression and disobedience have taught us how to operate in temperance. As I mentioned in Trilogy-Part One, the Bible did not imply that Joseph did not <u>desire</u> to have sex with Potiphar's wife; he **REFUSED**! Did you catch that? If he refused, he may have given it a second thought; yet, he chose something higher (temperance).

Being truly connected to God in our character is what gives us the ability to "stand fast therefore in the liberty wherewith Christ hath made us free!" (Gal. 5:1). Some things you must refuse in order to maintain the glory. After Eve's transgression took them to another dimension of ecstasy, the glory departed and Adam's eyes opened. What happened next is that he was able to see Eve in the flesh. Ever since this eye-opening exploration, the woman's flesh has been the man's most enticing exhilaration. Due to the female factor, flesh is the major component that has kept our leaders from maintaining the glory. Especially given that "church-folks" had been taught that all other pleasure was sin, the woman must have tipped the balance toward that which was left to enjoy. I'm trying to make this work; work with me!

Having seen both good (an intimate relationship with God) and now evil, the process of pain came as a result of the curse upon the woman. Notably, Adam and Eve never brought forth children until after they sinned and left the garden. Although God told them to be fruitful and multiply at the beginning of creation, He must have anticipated them procreating once they left the garden. In my opinion, if they had engaged in sexual relations <u>before</u> the serpent came on the scene, Adam may have been too engrossed by the sex to yield to the sin. Maybe, "That's what's love got to do with it," but what about the glory? "I'm glad you asked." That is what brings us to this "Officers' Bootcamp" for leaders and the five-fold ministry officers.

One main, plausible conclusion that can be reached from my argument is that, originally, we were never created to engage in sex because perfect people have no need for sex. Man was created to live forever and to find pleasure in the things of God, not each other. Still, this argument cannot be responded to simply. The truth is: now that our spirit beings got trapped in human bodies, man can hardly live without sowing to the flesh. This further explains why we have to fight so hard to get the glory back. Seeing more evil than good, we are now so engrossed by each others' "nakedness" that we can hardly engage in the true intimacy of seeking God's face. "And the Church said, 'Amen'." Could this also explain why sexual sins (particularly in the church) are one of the main evils that provokes God to turn His face from us?

TEMPLE FRAUD

"And she named the child I-chabod, saying, The glory has departed from Israel" ... (1 Sam. 4:21). I-chabod, found in 1 Samuel 4:21, 14:3 was the son of Phinehas and the grandson of Eli, the priest of the LORD in Shiloh. Hophni and Phinehas died in battle with the Philistines who captured the Ark of the Covenant and took it away from Israel. Upon hearing the terrible news, Eli fell backward and broke his neck and died. Phinehas's pregnant wife went into labor and bore a son. The word, *I-chabod*, means that there is no glory, and in her pain and despair, the woman lamented over the loss of the glory of God from Israel.

Now that we have established the rationale for the new chapter title, let's call Eli, the priest of the tabernacle and his two sons who served with him, Hophni and Phinehas, to the "witness stand." Allow them to testify about I-chabod, the loss of the glory. You do know that "warning comes before destruction," right? God tried to warn Eli through the boy prophet, Samuel that he was going to tear down his entire lineage because he did not correct his sons. "Despise not the day of small things" (Zech. 4:10). While I was looking for that reference, God brought the next Scripture to my attention. ... *"My son, despise not thou the chastening of the Lord, nor faint when thou art rebuked of Him"* (Heb. 12:5b).

Before I went there, here is the point that I was about the make. Even though the prophet was a boy, and Eli was a priest, God visited the boy to give the man a word that the priest couldn't handle. Your level of maturity is going to be dependent upon your willingness to hear God, regardless of whose "ass" it comes through. As a result of sexual sin in the House of God, or what I am referring to as temple fraud, 30,000 men were slain, and the glory was departed from Israel. Here is where I must go ahead and spell out the repercussions for you because some folks are determined to criticize me for exposing the "temple fraud" that I experienced in the "house."

"Now Eli was very old, and heard all that his sons did unto all Israel; and how they lay with the women that assembled at the door of the tabernacle of the congregation. And he said unto them, Why do ye such things? For I hear of your evil dealings by all this people. Nay, my sons; for it is no good report that I hear: ye make the LORD'S people to transgress" (1 Sam. 2:22-24). "Officer," did you see that? "Ye make the LORD'S people to transgress!" That's "TEMPLE FRAUD" revealed! Men of God, if you want to avoid death and destruction, get back to real holiness and righteous living, and stop laying with the women that assemble at the door of the tabernacle of the congregation.

God's daughters are precious to Him. Don't force Him to take what's precious to you because you have tainted what's precious to Him. A reasonable assertion of judgment, here is a warning for those who are committing "temple fraud." Do not sacrifice the life of your ministry for a life of compromise, and do not sacrifice the lives of your family for a lifestyle that is out of control. Proverbs 25:28 adds an important amplification: *"He that hath no rule over his own spirit is like a city that is broken down, and without walls."*

We see perhaps, more strikingly why the Church is so weak today and not operating in power and in the Anointing. If you are not destroying any yokes off of folks' lives, you only have a gift. Beyonce' can "woo" a crowd, but after the show is over and the lights are out, "at the end of the day," were any lives changed?? Were any hearts healed; or, were any souls delivered and set free? *"For the gifts and calling of God are without the repentance"* (Rom. 11:29). Why? A covenant cannot be broken. Because God has not changed His mind about anointing you, you can be anointed and not fully operating **in** the Anointing. Most often, we confuse giftings and callings and emotional downpours with being greatly anointed.

Nevertheless, sex in His house is considered EVIL by God! Here is the logic that establishes my premise: it's not really the *Sex in the City*; it is the SEX IN THE CHURCH that is provoking exposure and pouring out the wrath of God upon His people! As it started in Genesis, the most observable exposure in the Bible involved sexual sins (see Gen. 38:11-26). For this cause, "I-CHABOD" is written across the doors of many of our churches and the foreheads of many of our leaders. Whereas THE GLORY HAS DEPARTED, many of you "officers" have been given a "dishonorable discharge."

"HEY APOSTLE, 'WHERE YOU AT'?"

After leaving on the wrappings of advocacy from previous chapters that remind the readers to "beware," that's the question that colors or directs my interview with the Apostle. I had considered omitting this section from the book because I felt that it was too much information and too many variables to being an apostle, to feed it to a general reading audience. But since the apostleship is the number one office in the Church, God would not release me from it. Maybe He will in the *Remix* on the next round. Meanwhile, my job now is to use my coordinating skills to piece it all together.

Fortunately, this book has been suitable for the father, the son, the mother, the female, the Blacks, the Whites, the Jews, the Gentiles, the saint, the sinner, the rebellious, the obedient, the disobedient. Unintentionally, this chapter turned out to cover the five-fold ministry, particularly, the office of the apostle. Either way, if you are an *officer*, I got you covered. And if you are an aspiring "officer," I really got you. If you have no aspiration here or feel that this section is of no benefit to you, I am releasing you to "fast-forward" until the Spirit leads you to stop.

In any event, this "bootcamp" may be a good place to learn about Kingdom protocol and some ecclesiastical order. As the "Officers' Bootcamp Conference Host," I will be "chiming in" off and on, and maybe a couple of others. However, my phenomenal guest "Press Officers" include: Dr. Matthew Stevenson, Prophet Floyd Barber, and J. Lee Grady. "Parasites want what's in your hand; protégés want what's in your heart. Parasites want what you've earned; protégés want what you've learned" (Mike Murdock). If you are a protégé, let's move forward with what's in my spirit and find out that which I have learned from my special guest "Press Officers."

The apostolic Anointing goes far beyond baptizing in Jesus' name. Some Apostolic Christians are broke; they don't cast out devils; they don't heal the sick. Some even have deaf sections in their churches. What would Jesus do if He came and somebody was signing at the front? He called it a deaf and dumb **spirit**, but you have a department for it. We have developed systems to cater to the devil! Stevenson (2016) declares that if you are doing sign language in your church, and if you have a sick and shut-in list, you need to sit down until you learn how to lay hands on the sick and cast out devils. "P☺☺F!"

We are not really apostolic, people. Belief is not the basis to what we become. Even demons believed, and they trembled. Jesus, a sent one, moved in deliverance and had authority over all sickness and disease. Deliverance happened on accident. While He would be merely walking up the street, demons would cry out from the graveyards: "Jesus, we know who You are." He didn't have to go look for them, they came to Him. 1 John 4:6 solidifies that ALL of the original apostles were "masterfully" skilled in demons and deliverance. They had insight and information on invisible war and invisible opponents. But we have made demonic spirits a team – the sick and the shut-in. What kind of Holy Ghost do you have that wants you to speak in foreign languages but not heal bones, or open blinded eyes, and unstop deaf ears, asks Stevenson (2016)?

The African American Church is very vocal; they love great oratory. It's an Anointing on us; it's how the Civil Rights Movement got started. It was the swag and the verbal velocity that was upon Malcolm X. The last Black man that brought a major revival to America was William Seymour. Somewhere, the devil made us drop signs and wonders for great speeches. We love wanting to be entertained, but nobody has power. And when a Black man does come up with power, we kill them. We ruin his life; we ruin his name and end his marriage.

We've got to put premium back on the supernatural. We should flow in miracles just as must as we preach. We should move in demonstration just as much as we declare. And if you can't demonstrate it, don't talk about it. The apostles' ministry was an authority ministry, not a power ministry (Mk. 6:7). Their sending represented their authorization, and when you have been authorized, you have authority over devils (Stevenson, 2016).

As the so-called "pen☺prophetess," my question is a long one: Could sexual sins be the rationale as to why I-chabod is written across the doors of many of our churches, and why we do not experience an evidence-based culture of miracles and blessings like the disciples did when they were so diligent in being sold out for Jesus and engaged in carrying the Anointing? That was not an essay question; it only required a yes or no response. *"And God wrought special miracles by the hands of Paul"* (Acts 19:11). With so many people calling themselves Apostles these days, miracles should be the order of the day.

The lack of signs and wonders cancels out about 90% of the people who call themselves, apostles. "It's like thousands of people were suddenly bit by a strange mosquito that caused them to come down with apostle fever. They're all over the place now! Yet, these apostles can't heal the common cold," exclaims Prophet Floyd Barber. Wait "y'all;" I need to stop and find a painful face to put with that. (>_<)

"And when He had called unto Him His twelve disciples, He gave them power against unclean spirits, to cast them out, and to heal all manner of disease" (Mt. 10:8). *"Truly the signs of an apostle were wrought among you in all patience, in signs, and wonders, and mighty deeds"* (2 Cor. 12:12). Dr. Stevenson, Prophet Barber & J. Lee Grady, you have a question on the floor: Why aren't we seeing diseases departing from people and evil spirits going out of them, according to the Word of God? Did not Jesus give the apostles specific directives: *"Heal the sick, cleanse the lepers, raise the dead, cast out devils"...* (Mt. 10:8).

Allow Dr. Stevenson to hit the "reply button." He who will cleanse the lepers must not be one. "Uhh-uh." If God caused apostolic men to touch infectious people, it must mean that they were not infected.

"P☹W!" You must have diplomatic immunity to whatever is contagious on the lives of the people. If you are going to deliver a homosexual, you must not be one. If you are going to deliver a lesbian you must not be one. If you are going to heal a marriage, you must not have a sexless one. If you are going to bring peace to homes, you and your spouse should not be sleeping in different bedrooms. All of that merits another face (now I'm blinking) #-)

You have no authority over covenant breaking spirits if you are breeched in your own house. And if a bishop should be a good husband, how much more should the #1 office in the church be a good husband? Many of you are not sent ones because you are not satisfying your spouse. Many First Ladies are muzzled, robbed of freedom and punished by your calling. You need to know that the Church is not your spouse; it's Jesus' spouse. And you cannot honor God by abusing your wife while you take care of His. You can't oppress your woman and try to resuscitate His. "Help us Holy Ghost up in here!"

What is the problem, Apostle? Simple: the level of your power is connected to your lifestyle. The real question is: Are you really an apostle, or are you an imposter? The apostles operated in the power of God to the point that Peter's **shadow** healed the sick (Acts 5:17). Amplifying this point, Prophet Barber adds: "Although others in the church (like Stephen) MAY perform signs, wonders and mighty deeds, an apostle MUST. These would include the ability to heal all sickness and disease, and the ability to heal physical deformities and raise the dead, along with bilocation at will. A TRUE APOSTLE CAN CAUSE AMPUTATED LIMBS TO GROW BACK! Why? Because he's an apostle!"

Paul healed every sick person on the island of Melita (Acts 28:7-9). That's because Paul was a true apostle. No faith is required on the part of the recipient because a true apostle is already appointed by God with all three Power Gifts of the Spirit (i.e. special faith, healings and working of miracles) to an unlimited degree. This is a part of his supernatural credentials as an ambassador for God's Kingdom." Hey Apostle, were you not aware of your job description? Miracles were not an addendum to Paul's ministry; they were mandatory for the apostle to function. When a bishop flows in miracles, it's by grace and not responsibility. Their responsibilities are more administrative and managerial than they are supernatural. You don't need an encounter with Jesus to return emails. You don't need an encounter with Jesus to hold convocations. You don't need supernatural power to oversee churches. :">

On the other hand, supernatural encounters are mandatory for anybody that has an apostolic calling. Paul had signs that were exclusive to his apostleship. Again, they were called the special miracles of Paul. You need supernatural power to have authority over HIV. Apostle, have you performed any miracles that we can actually **validate**? You also need an encounter with Jesus to have supernatural power over high-ranking witchcraft and Greek spirits. It's because of the absence of a sent one that you have pastors that mix witchcraft in their work by calling themselves Free Masons. They are allowed to come to the Kingdom and not lay down their Greek philosophies and Greek affiliations. You must be emancipated from your other gods. You cannot be in an occult and flow in miracles. An apostle must flow regularly, easily, and routinely in miracles (Stevenson, 2016).

Here I go with my questions again. Apostle, what is your shadow doing in the lives of God's people? Is it healing the sick or attracting sexual favors from God's sheep? Even if they are not innocent sheep; they are still sheep that are dependent on the integrity of their shepherd. Guess what; certain restrictions still apply! The word, apostolos, refers to God's special ambassadors, or "sent ones," who are bold enough to help the church to advance into new territory. Apostles are also commissioned to contend for pure doctrine, preserve unity among the saints, equip leaders, and model Christian character. God could not use John to birth a church because he was more interested in laying his head in Jesus' bosom and sucking up the revelation. In contrast, He used Peter because of his boldness.

Jesus' objective for the 12 Apostles also reflects the beliefs of J. Lee Grady, who "chimes in" with additional guidance for my research. He writes: "The apostleship is not just a fad to create networks of independent churches answerable to a governing apostle who takes ownership of their buildings to control their congregations. Paul sometimes made tents for a living in order to avoid the appearance of entitlement. False apostles prefer the primrose path over the Calvary road. [Bona fide apostles] are true generals in the faith, with a depth of character that matches their spiritual authority. They don't carry the sense of entitlement or egotism that is sometimes displayed by Americans who print the title, *Apostle* on their business card. May God grant us true apostolic anointings that is marked by New Testament courage, unquestionable integrity, and Christ-like humility."

To incorporate the dimensions of the apostleship, there is agreement that: "They read about the oracles of the prophets and the miracles of the apostles in Scripture and become fascinated with these stories. Then they begin to have delusions of grandeur – envisioning themselves as the next Elijah or Paul. Then, before you know it, they're running off half-cocked toward nowhere, talking about, 'I'm Apostle This or Prophet That,' with absolutely NO POWER! *'For such are false apostles, deceitful workers transforming themselves into the apostles of Christ'* (2 Cor. 11:13). Always be skeptical of those who have less revelation than you but who claim to walk in an office higher than you! That doesn't compute. They're donning the title for the prestige of it while not possessing the actual grace of it," adds Prophet Barber.

Stevenson (2016) reasons that if you are not called from your mother's womb to the apostle's office, no amount of experience as a pastor is going to make you that. There are reformations, fellowships/networks who toss seasoned or veteran pastors into this office. Because they have come to a certain place of achievement, they want to honor their successful tenures as pastors. Pastors are maintenance gifts, and to be veteran and/or to have another apostle pour into you does not make you apostolic. When you are a sent one, the thing that drives you is your assignment, not the accolades or applause of man.

Besides, the commission to start churches was given to the apostles as a by-product of the apostles' mandate. Since there were no churches before the apostles, you can't use the amount of churches to verify an apostolic spirit; the church came **out** of the apostles. That contradicts why Jesus ordained the original apostles. In fact, they hadn't labored yet; they were ordained and given the authority so that they could labor. Jesus told them that He was ordaining them so that they could be with Him and bear fruit. [You don't work hard to get a gift; you get a gift so that you can work harder.] When you ordain as a reward, it's fleshly, carnal, and anti-Bible.

I know that this may be a "gut punch" for somebody, but according to Stevenson (2016), your certified supervision only makes you kin to a bishop or a pastor, or maybe just an elder. If you build the church after Jesus-the Shepherd, and not Jesus-the Apostle, you may not be strong enough to send people into destiny. While pastors are placed in the Church to stabilize, they struggle just to keep people out of sin. There is a reason why, in 1 Corinthians 12:28, the pastor is not even listed, and why God set in the Church, first, apostles, secondarily, prophets, and thirdly, teachers. Pastors are neither listed in the whole Book of Acts. (#_#)

You can't stabilize something that hadn't started yet. What happens when a movement is headed by stabilizers? That movement stops moving. Since there is no room for the apostle, prophet, and teacher; pastors and deacons have "hijacked" most churches. Stevenson (2016) asks: "So what do you think the Church is going to look like being run by people who weren't even put in government in the Bible?" Every church doesn't necessarily have to be run by an apostle, but they need to be in relationship with one to keep them focused and to keep that grace upon the House.

Not to bash the pastors because we need them; we just don't need them in government. Whereas starting a church is the apex of most ministers' careers, every great preacher does not make a good pastor. And the fact that you can vote them in proves that you have taken the American democratic process, as wicked as it is, and decided that you are going to have a campaign to elect somebody over your soul and over your destiny. That's the election to be nervous about. Donald Trump is not going to answer for your soul. The one that has to give in account for your soul is your shepherd, whom the Holy Ghost has appointed as overseers. So how can you have more expectations for the President than you do for your Pastor? (SMH)

When you have a synthesized ministry, you don't make good movement decisions. You can't make good war moves because you're too worried about what people think, how they feel, and how they may hurt. You're too afraid to offend or advance; you apologize for progress. But not the apostle! If you have not been discipled and constructed, or taught for a season under one who is more superior or senior than yourself, you cannot be sent because you don't have a sender. You have an assignment and should not be allowing any hands to be laid on your head, or "no" kissing of the rings because it's OFF (Stevenson, 2016)!

This is totally me talking now; you may be able to recognize the transition. Church is the only thing you can start without any real knowledge of what you are doing. All you need is some zeal, a building, a sign, some chairs, and a musician. You don't need a real Word, no Anointing, no miracles, signs and wonders. And they will really come if you offer free breakfast. The last time I saw a ministry in my hometown giving away free snacks on Third Street, I was hungry after just leaving church. Yes indeed, I stopped to get that free food as I had a couple of other times before, but this time, my intention was to specifically avoid buying lunch. Just for that, God made me take out a $20 donation. I'm just saying; Black folks will make sacrifices for **free** food.

Paul says in Romans 11:13, "I magnify my *office*." That means he was installed in an official responsibility. According to Stevenson (2016), when you are set in an office, people should know what to expect from you. What is your job description? If you say that you are a sent one, the next question should be: To whom and why? Apostle of what? What are you going to do when you get to your assignment? Christians are the only ones who don't ask questions. Paul said in 1 Corinthians 9:2: "Ye are the seal of my apostleship." If you have no signs and wonders and testimonies following you, you are NOT an apostle! "And there you have it." <@> <@> Look at me! I think that I did a wonderful job of piecing all of that together. "And the Church said, 'Amen.'"

INSIGHT INTO THE HARVEST

When you have no seal, rather than raising people up, you build your church all around you. You are not producers but idolaters of the microphone when you hate to give it up to anybody else. You don't like to multiply because you feel that if you teach somebody else how to prophesy and cast out devils, then, you are not important anymore. "What am I going to do if I allow someone else to become more powerful than me?" That's not an apostolic spirit; apostles are reproducers who reproduce producers. And you doing good makes someone else look good. If you are not a reproducer, you are a supervisor or a manager. Consequently, God disseminates information based upon function, not office. So, He talks to apostles and prophets differently than He does the teacher, pastor, and evangelist (Stevenson, 2016).

At any rate, nobody has an excuse to have a storefront church. As long as people are dying and going to hell, you should always need a new building. We recycle disgruntled church people because we don't know how to harvest. Maybe you need a revelation of mercy. Before your mama got saved, she may have been that mistress that you frown upon. The point is: you "religious demons" need an insight into what the harvest looks like. The harvest doesn't wear choir robes yet. They may not look normal; rather, some will have their faces tattered up. Some will be strippers, fresh out the club. They may need to be "quarantined" and cleaned up, but if you try to clean the fish before you catch the fish, your church will always be the size it is. You simply cannot have evangelism before discipleship.

The #1 enemy to the apostolic is the spirit of religion. When Jesus gave His disciples insight into the harvest, He didn't teach them about the Law or offerings of Moses, or about linen and 1st Sunday communion. He taught them about how to get the harvest, which means that He never intended for His Church to be small. The first new members' class in the Book of Acts had 5,000 people. After that, the Lord added to the church daily such as should be saved (Act. 2:47b). Thus, every apostolic church is supposed to be mega; it was God's idea. So when you make statements like: "People don't come because they don't want to hear the truth," it means that you are not anointed. Jesus was truth and is truth, and He never had a problem gathering a crowd.

Jesus life was a seed for a harvest, but it's going to be produced by your works, preaching and teaching. All the same, it is the absence of the apostle that has us abusing the word, evangelist. If you "gotta" keep saving saved people, then, you are probably not an evangelist. Being an itinerant or a traveler does not make you an evangelist. There are missionaries in the Church who don't even have a mission or a passport. We must have a vision for more than teams and departments. We must be gripped by visions to reap a harvest and build something that outlives us (Stevenson, 2016).

The city is your responsibility; you are not just a pastor to your church. When the city is your responsibility, there is no competition. Basically, when people leave out of "Pharaoh's" house, they need somewhere to go. So when your growth is only by church transfer, these people come to you because you refuse to labor. When you are sent, you have an uncommon work ethic. The spirit of prayer gives birth to the apostolic spirit and release the apostolic Anointing. You can't be sent with the absence of intercession in your midst. Jesus was an apostle who prayed all night. There was no getting tired, sleepy and burned out because He didn't do it in the flesh.

Laborers were few, but the apostles were Jesus' answer to the problem. He told them to pray, not get up and get ordained; not go and learn some Greek. PRAY! If you are still struggling to get people to come to corporate prayer, you are probably not apostolic. Prayer was the lifeline of the early Church. When they prayed, there were certain species of angelic voices that came to respond to the prayers of those that were sent. When you are a sent one, you have a delegation of angles; when you are a "went one," you're on your own.

What's more, intelligence is native to the apostolic spirit. Jesus came to build something.... ***"And upon this rock I will build My Church"...*** (Mt. 16:18a). The Greek word for sent one is *architectile*, which means, master builder. To be able to design, an apostle cannot be dumb. A real apostle despise ignorance; ignorant faith, ignorant shouting, ignorant tithing. They don't want you doing anything that you don't understand why you're doing it. While others worry about your what, an apostolic spirit will interrogate your why. There were 12 tribes and 12 apostles for every tribe. Why? Jesus needed an apostolic spirit for every type of culture, so that there could be no speech or language where their voice could not be heard (Psa. 19).

Darkness is what mandates the arrival of a sent one. When you bash the dirty, and judge the undecided and folks that are already "RSVP" for hell, you are ignorant of what your harvest is. Apostolic leaders are harvesters; pastors are gatherers. Real apostles are hated by other preachers because they gather the ones they fail to reach. They draw the ones they walked past on the streets. Pastors require light because they can't shepherd you until you belong to Jesus. You don't shepherd sinners; you win them. It is no reward if you win somebody that was already won. Can somebody please say: "TEACH, Dr. Stevenson!"

We should not be competing over church members and playing church politics. We should be going after the "lepers." How can you be afraid to be seen among the "lepers" when Jesus came out the "gate" going to wedding parties where they were drinking wine? When you all made holiness about rules and all white, the devil distracted you. When you made holiness about wearing buns and long skirts, all you did was take on a form of godliness and denied the power thereof (2 Tim. 3:5). The reason God made you holy is that He wanted to send you to hell to pull out the unholy for the harvest.

You are not holy if all you are doing is staying away from the world; you are RELIGIOUS! Real holiness will launch you into some dark assignments and convert you so deeply that you can be around it and it not get on you. The Church should be filled with "lepers," but what I'm saying is: the ones that are there are likely saying: "Why sit we here until we die." When you want to grow a House, put a mercy seat in the middle of it. When you can accept people, then, you have the right to change them.

Another variable of a real apostle is that he spends hours of impartation. It is not biblical or valid for men to ordain or commission apostles whom they are not responsible for, or willing to answer for. Irresponsible "rogues" run the Body of Christ because they are ordained or commissioned by organizations that don't know them. Organizations who passively pass out credentials do not verify character. They don't know whether the recipients are crack-heads by day or whoremongers by night. Without the right hand on your head, you don't have a path to your purpose.

There are witchcraft apostles and Jezebel leaders that are trying to make you earn something that doesn't even belong to them. You are what you are by the grace of God, not because you pass some stupid test or know Greek and Hebrew. You were chosen from the foundations of the world, and that's what gives you a right to be who you are. *"Freely ye have received, freely give"* (Mt. 8:10). "I desire to see you," not so that I can collect your dues to buy me a new Rolls Royce. I desire to see you so that I may impart to you some spiritual gifts that you can be established. A leader that does not impart cannot establish; if you cannot establish, you cannot build. If you want to hear a speaker, turn on the radio. Flee these plantations and come out of her, my people. Leave these Jezebel spirits and find you an apostolic house (Stevenson, 2016).

"Hey Apostle, 'where you at'?" For those of you who were even thinking about calling yourself to be an apostle, did he not just teach the taste out of your mouth? ☹ As a result of the "ratched" lives that some of our apostles and other leaders are living today, do not be surprise if the evil spirits that they are trying to drive out, respond to them in the same way that they responded to the seven sons of Sceva, the Jew, and the chief of priests."*Jesus I know, and Paul I know, but who are ye?"* (Acts 19:15). While America is in a state of emergency, we need the apostles, prophets, teachers, pastors, and evangelists. We need all five; that's how revival is going to come to America. However, while others are jockeying for position, make sure that you are striving for purity.

Take note of this post that is so applicable to a power-deficient culture of Christian leaders.... "Jesus, the greatest preacher, had disciples, not armour bearers. And they were learning how to carry His Anointing, not His briefcase. Stop misapplying Biblical titles to make people your servant" (Pastor Manwell Faison). Jesus told the disciples in Matthew 9:37: *"The harvest truly is plenteous, but the labourers are few."* If we stop ego tripping and commit to doing the work without so much recognition, we will be rewarded for being laborers and not performers. Jesus later told the disciples in Matthew 20:4 (with emphasis added): "**AFTER** you go into the vineyard, I'll pay whatever is right." Now, who wants to be an Apostle? "Whew," I really dreaded this process, but finally, I can see some organization to my rambling and a "method to the madness."

It may seem as though I have been vacillating back and forth, but what I have intended to establish throughout this project is Hosea 4:6: *"My people are destroyed for lack of knowledge: because thou hast rejected knowledge, I will also reject thee, that thou shalt be no priest to me"...* Thanks for indulging my expedient impulsion to come on through, hopefully with conviction rather than condemnation. I told God that I was willing to be His "puppet," as long as I know that He was "pulling the strings." *"But when it pleased God, who separated me from my mother's womb, and called me by His grace"* (Gal. 1:15). Since it was God who decided who I was from my mother's womb, I discovered my destiny when I decided to comply with who He wanted me to become. If at any point that you have refused to open the gift, please understand that you have dishonored the Giver. #team-awesome

Well "officers," I had planned to ask Dr. Stevenson to stay over for the prophets' and pastors' session. But due to time and space restraints, I extracted from Trilogy-Part One, a general guide to adhere to when evaluating the efficacy of your call. Per Prophet Barber, "If you can't heal all manner of sickness and disease, then you're not an apostle! If you can't see into the past, present and future with sight beyond sight, then you're not a prophet! If you have no profound compassion for God's people, you're not a pastor! If you're not driven to win the lost, you're not an evangelist! And if when you teach Scripture, you're as dry as the Mojave Desert, then, you're not a teacher!" Study the job description before you advertise your title! Well, "are we there yet?" *"But he that shall endure unto the end, the same shall be saved"* (Mt. 24:13).

THE SCOPE OF THE BLACK CHURCH

At this point, I may as well remove Adam from the equation for a while longer and ask again, but with a different implication: "Hey Apostles and Prophets, Pastors, Evangelists and Teachers, where 'y'all' at?" An active attempt was made to help you recognize that the disciples did not absorb idle time that allowed them to become trapped in sexual sins. And neither were they caught up in turf wars – reaching for titles, fighting for positions, and competing for success. Since greed will drive you farther and farther away from the blessing, here is how Brian Rawls defines the scope of the Black church.

... "The world laughs at the Black church. In fact, so void of power and hungry for attention, we have become the tool to sell chicken, the pawn of rock stars, videos, and recording artists' concerts and the caricature of 'American Idol' Worship – in effect, becoming 'Sunday's Worst!' Where is the remnant that will obey and decry this aberrant monster we've labeled as the Church?" J. Lee Grady expressed a similar conviction by referring to our foolishness as charismatic sideshows, spooky stage drama, and mesmerizing manipulation. The "spirit of fascination" is what I call it.

"Who is left among you that saw this house in her first glory? And how do ye see it now? Is it not in your eyes in comparison of it as nothing?" (Hag. 2:3). If you really want to go back to the "old landmark," here is the key. When the power of love overcomes the love of power, the Church will experience the power of God! Before we broke through out mother's womb, we were with God. Father, bring back to our remembrance how it was when we were with You, so that we can get to the point that we are saying: "I'm sick of church as usual; I WANT GOD!" Sorry to say, the Church today is less concerned with efficacy and caring for people's souls. Rather, it is more about power, positions, money, marketing – sex and success!

"Church-folks," I know you hate to hear the truth put "on blast," but God put them on blast in the Bible for us to see. Now, He is putting the Church on blast for us to see ourselves! Don't get so preoccupied with repudiation and rebuttal that you reject the reproach and the reproof. While it seems that I have a message of condemnation; my message is really about confronting and correction! Exposing the human populace to the moral grandeur of Christian faith is part of my nature because that is exactly what I have been called to do. Prophet Barber offers this distinction: "There is a new genre of Christians on the rise! They humble themselves; they confess their sins. They renounce compromise; they reject worldliness and lay hold of the mighty hand of God! Them shall God cause to 'be strong and do exploits!'(Dan. 11:32)."

While I may have gotten out of sync with the chapter's original content, it parallels my consensus regarding the lack of discipline in our churches. Just because we are now in the Dispensation of Grace, it does not give us a reason to act ungodly!! When righteousness is in control, you can rest assure that your integrity is on cruise (read Rom. 6:19). Even if I were not going to mention that "the wages of sin is death," basically, here is my whole point. Bad children give their parents a bad name. And since God is all about His holiness, His name stands for righteousness.

Holiness simply means that we agree with Him. If atheists, who do not believe in God, have morals and ethics, why do we, who call ourselves Christians, look for excuses to throw our principles "out the window" and give the Church of God/the Body of Christ a bad name? You simply cannot have one foot in the Word and the other in the world! That is called "straddling the fence!" You can straddle the fence if you want to, but don't expect me to cross over! Wait! In my summary, the following observation is a relevant example of my contention with the Black church.

I thought that it was a disgrace to the Body of Christ to wake up at 3:00 in the a.m. and hear one of the singers on a R&B Reality Show disclosing that the strip club is the first thing that preachers look for when they come to Atlanta. "Are you serious?" While putting the pastors on blast for giving the girls their pastor's anniversary money, and likely building fund money too, she reveals that after they have blessed "it," the strippers hit the poles. Whereas the clergy should be charged with protection of the vulnerable and seen as representatives of God, you wonder why the world is not interested in coming to your churches. They don't want to see how you pretend on Sundays, if they have seen how you perform during the week.

God does not want His church to be wild and dress code-holy; He is calling us to pure holiness! How can we just allow this kind of negative attention to "roll off our backs?" No! No! No! No! Since she had no "shame in her game," why should I be ashamed of the Gospel of Christ and back-down on the weakness that He has allowed to become my weapon? I was called to speak out against the sins that are grieving Him the most. Just in case you didn't know, God **anoints** us in the area of our weakness! Like as with David, the giants in my life have overestimated their size and underestimated my ability.

"The Lord GOD hath given me the tongue of the learned, that I should know how to speak a word in season to him that is weary: He wakeneth morning by morning, He wakeneth mine ear to hear as the learned" ... (Isa. 50:4). Because His strength has been made perfect in my weakness, for over 16 years now, God has been waking me up in the "wee" hours of the morning to minister to me that which He wants me to minister to you. I guess that's why He allows me to "go to bed with the chickens!" Even if it is 10 degrees outside with snow on the ground (like now), rather than trying to sleep undisturbed (with no one beside me to keep me warm), I have given God permission to keep my life on "auto pilot".

Often being forced to get up while the Anointing is fresh and the words are straight off the press, I really **am** ready to be released from "y'all." If only for a season, I need to find another companion outside of my computer. Even as I have poured myself into something bigger than my past and willing to deal with the "cards" that I've been dealt, it's like I was dealt four deuces, and none of them was wild. Sorry to say; the "churchy folks" that I have had to confront need to take a spiritual laxative. Ask me why. THEY ARE FULL OF **"S.H.I.T."** Stop thinking of me in that tone of voice; consequently, I'm not saved yet. ☹ Even as Romans 10:9 states what will happen if we confess with our mouth the Lord Jesus and believe in our heart that God raised Him from the dead, it does not say that we are saved at that moment. That Scripture and the majority of those related, state that we SHALL BE SAVED.

Did not 2 Thessalonians 2:3 inform us of a falling away first? By the time that we are gathered unto Christ, some of you claiming to be saved now won't even be standing. So, here is the "game-changer:" *"But he that shall endure unto the end, the same shall be saved"* (Mt. 24:13). "How you like me now?" God knows that my flesh is a fool, but He also knows that I am really striving to be saved in the end. So what He has to say about my flaws and the foolishness that He uses to confound the wise is that: "I got you, 'Boo'." *"The harvest is past, the summer is ended, and we are not saved"* (Jer. 8:20). However: ... *"It doth not yet appear what we shall be: but we know that, when He shall appear, we shall be like Him"* ... So "holler" at me at the finish line; IF we get it together, we will be saved together. But as I am being saved, here is where I stand: *"And my speech and my preaching was not with enticing words of man's wisdom, but in demonstration"...* (1 Cor. 2:4). My question is: Do you want the truth, or not?

Unlike my "unwanted" editions, I tried to tell you that this was the "uncut" edition that had no censors. Seriously though, if you read shit and not S-period, H-period, I-period, T-period, that's on you. Whereas my books will eventually transcend different levels of people, for me, s.h.i.t. is not an offensive word. It's my signature acronym for my personal depiction of church folks. If you can't read my writing, it may be that you are the one with some of Peter's DNA in your bloodline. In developing a vocal strategy to reach the "in-too-deep" the "not-so-deep," the "cold," the "hot," and the "lukewarm," my books are for imperfect people who don't mind receiving from an imperfect author.

Besides, God selects the audience of our anointing. *"Him that is weak in the faith receive ye, but not to doubtful disputations. For one believeth that he may eat all things: another, who is weak, eateth herbs. Let not him that eateth despise him that eateth not; and let not him which eateth not judge him that eateth: for God hath received him"* (Rom. 14:1-3). Come on Paul and help me out again: *"To the weak became I as weak, that I might gain the weak: I am made all things to all men, that I might by all means save some"* (1 Cor. 9:22). The thorny exception to being one of God's "wild cards" is that to become like them, you must have a divine, apostolic flexibility to talk like them. You can't go to the weak talking as though you are above them.

One prophet, who did not know me, did call me out a few years back, whereas he prophesied that God had given me the ministry of reproof for His people. If you are not too deep to "roll" with me, I interpreted that to mean that I was being anointed to call out the **"S.H.I.T.!"** In the event that you are too deep, here is some "BREAKING NEWS:" I DO NOT CARE! Just kidding; seriously though, America and the

Church are in some deep **"S.H.I.T."** Now I understand why dead people (especially dead church folks) look so peaceful when they die; they no longer have to deal with church folks' "S.H.I.T.!!!"

If you are shaken by my audacity and wondering what the acronym represents, I understand your challenge; however, there is really an upside to this. SIN is the keyword. Does that make you feel any better about it at all? It is never my intention to use expletive terms for malicious intent. To save some, I only use a verbal velocity and a diversity of language to bypass my intellect and my degrees, so that I can strike you right at the core. All the same, I realize that in our culture, our system of rules does not allow for a few of my choice words to be included in meaningful sentences. Obscured by my real purpose, some words simply depict intense emotion and are not used to express debasement or disrespect.

With that in mind, can you guess the rest of the acronym? Okay, I will go ahead and "let the cat out the bag." S.H.I.T. epitomizes **S**in, **H**ypocrisy, **I**niquity & **T**ransgression. Now, can you make me one promise? Whenever you attend church, make sure you turn on your "bull-s.h.i.t. detector." I know I'm in trouble now. A few years back, I even printed a flyer advertising a "No More S.H.I.T. Conference." I just felt like telling the church folks to bring all their **S**in, **H**ypocrisy, **I**niquity, and **T**ransgression, and dump it at the altar. And don't just dump it; leave it!

Consistent with Dr. Stevenson, smart people are the best "cussers" because they know how to sentence structure. In being creative, they know how to put things together. Slow people don't know how to cuss that well because they don't put words in the right place. That's why you never see intelligent people [like myself] in fights. All we have to do is talk [or write] and insult you with our words. Really, that was not my intention. You may be able to accuse me of a lot of things, but you had better know that "my worship is for real" (Bishop Larry Trotter).

Anyway, here is the challenge to restructuring and fine-tuning this new chapter. The denomination that has come against me the most has become more notable for their immorality lawsuits than any other denomination that I am aware of, besides the Catholic Church. Thus, I feel that my acronym best describes my position in the Kingdom. Since I enjoy working clean, I don't know how I ended up with the dirty job, but somebody's got to do it. Somehow, I was anointed to help clean up the mess, and that concludes the rest of my rant. This chapter has taken on so many different angles that I almost forgot the title. After adding and tweaking the last insert, I decided to take a quick shower/Walmart break. After slipping on my work-out gear, I followed the little voice that told me to put on a little powder because you never know who you might meet.

After shopping and returning to my car, I ended up meeting a tall, nice-looking, 50 year-old gentleman who owned several construction companies. After he told me that he thought I was no more than 27 years old and a lot of other "blah, blah, blah," I told him that he needed to take off his glasses so that he could see straight. I engaged him, but evidently he had * _ * in his eyes. While he was most flattering, he complimented me on everything from my hair to my shape to my smile and pretty, white teeth. In a strange town and feeling like I had been disconnected from my world; that blessed me.

Now I understand why I woke up two hours late and was delayed by the computer glitch. Otherwise, I would have missed the moment. Admittedly, it was like a breath of fresh air, and the fellowship seemed quite sacred, for whatever reason. Oh, I know why. Lately, particularly since being in transition, I had been experiencing a lot of rejection and no responses, for no apparent reason. I couldn't figure out what was wrong with me that the saints were being so mean to me for simply reaching out to compliment them, or show concern. Even when I sent one person a simple text that said "Happy Holidays," and asked another person a simple question like: Can you confirm that you are speaking at this place tonight; I was totally ignored. #rude "God, help me to never grow so big or important that I can't say 'thank you,' or that I have respect of persons and avoid responding to them because I don't feel that they're on my level."

Yes, this "season of rejection" has really rattled me, especially when I was coming from such a pure heart. On the contrary, the gentleman at Walmart asked if I had ever been a First Lady and connected that inquiry with some wonderful qualities that he claimed to have perceived in me. What a refreshing moment. When I asked if he was prophesying or something, surprisingly, he quoted a Scripture. That sparked a real interest. I was like: "Oh, you're really talking my language now. The Word is what I live on and stand by." Congruent to this assertion, the door was opened for me to ask about his church affiliation here in Dallas. Jokingly, "Shannon Brown" said that even though I was not wearing my dress down to the floor, "blah-blah-blah," it was not hard for him to determine that I was a "church girl." She said I had "the look," not so much physically so, but the look that she was referring to is the poise and the presence that exude from my spirit.

I do not carry myself like a worldly woman (wink). Here was the clincher. While trying to remember the name of the church that I had visited that was identified with a certain acronym, I said, "You know; it starts with an "I." Trying to think of the name, "IBOC," he mistakenly said, "I-chabod." We "hollered!" I was like: "Really? The glory has departed?" That's when he made a joke out of inviting me to attend the "I-chabod Full Gospel Church" It was hilarious, but I thought that it was also ironic, being that I had just ended this chapter.

I know that I have some strange "characters" this time, but I think that God places certain people in my path, just to enhance my storyline. To say the least, he may have been late for "boot-camp," but "he made the book." At the end of the day, do not allow **"I-chabod"** to be written across the doors of your churches. Rather, be committed to seeing the reality of Haggai 2:9: ***"The glory of this latter house shall be greater than of the former, saith the Lord of hosts: and in this place will I give peace, saith the Lord of hosts."*** That being so, "If I perish, I perish," but not according to prophecy.

CHAPTER THIRTEEN

"IF I PERISH, I PERISH:" BUT ACCORDING TO MY LAST, MAJOR PROPHECY, I'M PROTECTED BY THE "SCRIPT"

When examining the impact of my horrendous failures and dreadful decisions and wishing that I were more advanced in the different stages of life, I am now attuned to the auspicious reality of God predetermining the end of the "script" from the beginning. Even as four of my major team members have been prematurely cut off, isn't it comforting to know that the "main character" never dies? Thank God that I am protected by the "Script," which says: *"I shall not die, but live, and declare the works of the LORD!"* (Psa. 118:17). Apart from mounting evidence that I am obviously ☺ still a piece of work, I am right now where He knew I would be.

Just as Eve was not on trial, I am not on trial for my fall with man. I am persuaded that part of the test was to determine whether the shepherd loved his sheep enough to restore her soul and lead her back into the paths of righteousness, for His name's sake. Despite the fact that the 21st-century Adam failed the test due to his **"sin**-drome," never once, as a consequence of my "P.M.S." has the Chief Shepherd separated Himself from me. After all, when Jesus came on the scene, He did not come in the name of Moses or Elijah. He came in the name of Adam, who had previously demonstrated the greatest love of all.

Conceivably and remarkably, I am convinced that what Jesus did was based solely on what Adam had done. For the sake of the uncompromising naysayers, allow me to say this "one more gain," while I still have the "floor:" ... *"Who is the figure of Him that was to come"* (Rom. 5:14b). Therefore, if we condemn Adam, then, we should condemn Jesus who became the last Adam and did nothing different from what the first Adam did. If we believe that Jesus made a greater sacrifice by dying for the whole world, we certainly should not criticize Adam who gave up immortality for one, single woman.

Jesus, who gave up immortality for a season was aware that He would resurrect in three days. He even made this statement: *"For as Jonah was three days and three nights in the whale's belly; so shall the Son of man be three days and three nights in the heart of the earth"* (Mt. 12:40). Adam did not have the assurance that if he became sin to remain with Eve that he would be able to return to his immortal state of being. Nonetheless, Jesus did much more for us than Adam did for Eve. Adam died, but the Son **bled and** died. Just as He was crucified and resurrected, what is more significant than considering who had more to lose in this intriguing process of redemption is the conclusion that is found in John 15:13: *"Greater love hath no man than this, that a man lay down his life for his friends."*

Joseph was willing to die for his people; likewise, Esther was willing to die for her people. She went so far as to proclaim, "If I perish, I perish." Accordingly, the respected civil rights leader, Dr. Martin Luther King, Jr., said in his driving force to push for racial equality: "If a man hasn't discovered something he would die for, he isn't fit to live." Ultimately, I have chosen Esther's position: "If I perish, I perish." We must be willing to lose some battles if that's what it takes to ultimately win the war.

Ironically, on Resurrection Sunday (2015), Bishop Craig Baymon sparked a "tweetable moment" that added fuel to my passion. In his message, *A Return on the Deposit,* he said that the first Adam was extracted **from** the earth. But the second Adam was placed **in** the earth, so that when He got up, we got up with Him. In other words, we are the return on the deposit. Yes, my past certainly influenced my prophecy. Whatever it takes to fulfill the purpose that has outlived my pain is the process that I'm willing to submit to in order to get to the promise. Why? I am God's return on His deposit!

Had I not added to this *Rebirth* revision, the 2nd line of the chapter title, which incorporates my last, major prophecy, I may have had a different trajectory when I said: "If I perish, I perish." But according to the inclusion here, this is my hour. On April 10, 2016, I was invited to The Awareness Center in Little Rock, AR, to attend a Dedication Ceremony for Derek & Jackie Smith's grandbabies. In an insistent attempt to forego the request to make this trip, there was something on the inside of me that pushed me to go against my decision. Before the close of that service, I was given my last, major prophecy before the *Rebirth* of this book.

I was so burned out from dozens of past prophecies, due to the lack of manifestations, until I wasn't even in the mood to be prophesied to anytime soon. To say the least, I was not pulling on Apostle Lawrence Braggs to give me a Word from the LORD. Yet, after seven years of being in a state of spiritual oblivion and a season of famine (in 2009 when I became homeless for nine months), this is the prophecy that changed my perception. Originally, this chapter had only four pages to it, but now I see that it was left short for a reason. Moreover, I understand now why it was so difficult for me to retrieve the DVD to this particular service. God had the perfect place for it here, and thanks to Kim of ACI for her unyielding assistance. Apparently, she felt my energy and became one with me, for "such a time as this."

And the Apostle says: "Karen, God told me to tell you that your seven-year sabbatical is over. The hand of the LORD is upon your life. This is your season. God said, after seven years, the famine is over, even in your life. When I called you, Evangelist, I saw the look on your face. But God said, 'I'm 'gonna' take you back to your first love.' You've been called by God; not by man's approval; not by the license of 'no' man, but by the Anointing that God has put on the inside of your life. [As I have resigned myself to being locked out of my car and having acquiesced to some final tweaking, I am literally crying "crocodile tears."]

God told me to tell you: the problem that you've had is that you have not aligned yourself with people who's on the level that God has taken you. Therefore, you've reduced yourself to be accepted. But God told me to tell you to thank God for that because that preserved you until it was time for your change to come. I want you to know, now is the time of your change. Seven years, go home and began to count back, and you will see, my God, where the enemy began his plot to stop and try to hinder.

But God told me to tell you, the price you've already paid is enough. Now is the time for you to go to the next level. Your word was ahead of the people. Now, the people are just catching up to be able to appreciate your word. For the hand of the LORD is upon you. The glory of the LORD is about to be revealed. **From this day forward, don't do anything to please and appease or to be accepted. Find your level and wait for those to come in and to underwrite – for those to come in and to help push.** [Wow; I just prayed these words yesterday, without even reflecting back on this prophecy.] God told me to tell you that many of them will not be in the church. He's going to go outside the church to bless you. [After just checking my vehicle one more time to see if there was a chance of me sticking to my agenda, to no avail, I continued reading this prophecy. As God's presence just began to envelop me, I had a huge meltdown.]

For this is your hour. There are some things you decreed and said: 'LORD, I'll never do this again; I'll never allow that again.' But baby, don't let the hurt of yesterday began to ruin your future because God's hand is upon your life. This is your hour. I want you to lift your hands to the LORD. And the LORD told me to tell you that I'm about to reverse everything... Everything that the enemy said, I'm reversing it"... (Braggs, 2016).

That was in April; by the end of July, one of the things that did manifest was change. God reversed my living arrangements to where it worked out for my good. I made the "crazy" choice to give up my apartment, eventually, making my transition to Dallas. Another manifestation that has taken place is that the seven-year famine is really over! I may be financially stable, but I'm still not clear on the *evangelist* element of the prophecy. Even though that was Apostle's third time calling me that, I don't see that "handwriting on the wall." I was nervous for three days because of a conference call presentation.

Even Jeremiah asked: *"If thou hast run with the footmen, and they have wearied thee, then how canst thou contend with horses?"* ... (Jer. 12:5).

Personally, I feel that my scribes Anointing is my mantel, and my books are more my platform than the pulpit. I don't ever intend to create a divergence for where God wants to take me. But IF I had a choice to do it my way, I figure that I can both educate **and** evangelize by using my pen to give voice to my passion. "God, I want you to have Your way in my life, but can I just please 'stay in my lane,' called comfort zone?" Either way, God has definitely taken me back to my first love. To date, this *Rebirth* edition was the most striking manifestation of my last, major prophecy.

Then, the first church service that I attended in Dallas was the Potter's House, which happened to be Bishop Jakes' first Sunday back from doing his new, talk show tapings in LA. Ironically, on August 14, 2016, he "came out the gate" talking about *Crazy Choices*. After illustrating a picture of the crazy choices that we make in general, Bishop Jakes' text came from Acts 23, when the apostles appointed two men to replace Judas after his betrayal and death. In part, he talked about how the lot fell on Matthias, and he was numbered with the eleven apostles. One of the points of the message was that for the fact that they could not stand to have an empty seat, they cast lots and prayed over the person. However, they did not pray over the process. They had just been filled with the Holy Spirit and were now playing with sticks to choose who would become the next apostle.

They did not consider that God might choose somebody whom they did not select. This process was the birthing of politics in the church and <u>manipulating</u> people to the forefront. Out of all of the people on the planet, they chose two people for God's consideration. Here is door #1 and door #2. To expound upon the process, Bishop Jakes added that you cannot force God to vote for your candidate. And you cannot limit His choices to your ideas because He may be thinking of something bigger than you. That's why He gets the "big office with the view." Since He is a little bit smarter than you, you must not limit Him to your choice because He may have a plan that you never thought of. Just because you're in a jam and feel hard-pressed to fill a slot, don't just snatch anybody to fill it because God's presence is in the gap in your life. It's in the void in your life, and He shows up, not in what is there, but in what is not there.

So here the apostles are about to rush into a crazy choice and choose a successor because they couldn't stand to have an empty seat, when an empty seat is far better than the wrong person. Sometimes you have to take the class of loneliness, rather than fill a seat with misery. Matthias, who ended up being man's crazy choice of an apostle, had not written any Books of the Bible. He had not delivered any prophetic utterances that we are certain of, and he had not performed any miracles that we have validation to. One thing for sure is that he never made any impact because that which is manipulated by man never has impact.

On the contrary, when God makes a move, it's worth the wait; it's worth being lonely. God's crazy choice is worth people laughing at you for a while. While they were trying to choose Matthias, God had even a crazier choice. He was choosing Saul, who was later called, Paul. Out of all the people that you would think that God would choose to become Judas' replacement, He chose the "Saddam Hussein" of the early church. He was an assassinator and a terrorist in Jerusalem; yet, God had found a man that He **promoted** to be the stronger leader of the New Testament Church.

Since His thoughts are not our thoughts, and His ways are not our ways, His crazy is always better than our crazy. Matthias made sense to the apostles; equally, it was crazy that God would replace Judas with Saul. In this crazy choice, he was the one that was earmarked to teach revelation knowledge of who God is. His crazy may not make any sense, and it may look ridiculous. It may even look impossible, but it will ALWAYS be effective. God took a Christian-killer and made him an apostle and an evangelist, and responsible for the largest portion of the Epistles in the New Testament Church.

Bishop Jakes insisted on talking to people who were ready for a crazy, ridiculous, supernatural "snot-back" miracle from the LORD. "It's 'gonna' be crazy," he said! But are you going with your crazy choices which have brought you to where you are right now, or are you going to get out on a limb and go with God's crazy choice that you are

255

scared to receive? Saul didn't come before the review board; he never met with the committee because Matthias made more sense to the rest of the apostles. He had been with them the whole time, and he was an eyewitness to the resurrection of Jesus, so they thought that he should be the one.

On the other hand, Paul wasn't even in the church; He never made any of the meetings. He wasn't at the Last Supper or the first one. He wasn't at the marriage in Cana of Galilee; he wasn't there when Lazarus died. He had no experience; still, he was God's crazy choice. How God is going to bless you is going to be crazy... "I don't know who I'm preaching to, but the LORD told me to tell you, not to be scared of it." ***"This is the LORD'S doing; it is marvelous in our eyes"*** (Psa. 118:23). Here comes the blessing that you've been praying for all the time. What do I see? I see a cloud the size of a man's hand. That's crazy! It may be crazy, but an abundance of rain is going to come out of that cloud, and unexpected blessings are going to come from unexpected places.

Now, the rest of this message is where it really became even more personal for me. "Come on through," Bishop Jakes. The stone that the builder rejects always become the chief corner stone. If you hadn't been rejected, you can't be selected. There are some people in here, right here today, that if you knew their whole story, you wouldn't have betted on them being where they are. But in spite of how crazy it may look to somebody else; it's crazy, but I'm here. It's crazy, but I've made it; it's crazy, but I survived it. It's crazy, but God brought me out. I "wanna" preach to my haters; I "ain't" mad at you. I get it; it doesn't make sense. It doesn't look right; it shouldn't have happened. But in spite of how crazy it is, He blessed me anyway. I understand why you hate me; I'm a crazy choice.

Then, Bishop Jakes told all of those who've had everybody against them, and those people said that you would never survive, but God chose you anyway, to give Him a praise. If you are a crazy choice, then you ought to expect a crazy blessing. A crazy blessing is a blessing that blows your mind, and that makes no sense, and that comes out of nowhere and slaps you upside the head. Today is the day that you stop being afraid of crazy opportunities that God brings into your life.

Out of the crazy things that He tells you to say to people that you think will not work and the crazy doors that He tells you to step into that you feel intimidated by, I want you to understand that you are God's crazy choice. **You've "gotta" become comfortable with your craziness.**

God's going to do something for you that you can't explain, that you didn't see coming, that you never thought would happen at this age, or stage, or season in your life... God is going to prepare a table before you in the presence of your enemies, and you're going to ask, "How can I eat around my enemies?" God's going to say that it was your enemies that made Me prepare the table in the first place... Somebody said that you could not live without them; somebody spoke and said that you would never be anything, and that they were the only reason that you survived. Somebody said that you would never get upon your feet, or that you would ever have good credit, or that nobody would ever love you. But God said it's "gone-be" crazy.

The glory of the LORD is in this place right now to minister to every area in your life where you feel like, I can't do it. I don't understand it. I don't see it. Be comforted by the fact that He chose you. He called you. He sent you. God wouldn't put you in a place and not give you what you need to function in the place where He put you. You're the woman for the job; you're the man for the job. Stop doubting yourself and wondering whether or not you can stand up to what's being thrown on you. "Greater is He that is in you, than he that is in the world." He chose you! You didn't just come here. You didn't just walk into this; this just didn't happen. Believe what He has done. Receive it. Accept it; walk into it. Stand on it, and trust it. Don't doubt yourself; don't doubt what God did in your life. Don't doubt what He called you to. Don't doubt what's possible; He chose you. It's yours because He chose you, in Jesus' name (Jakes, 2016 with emphasis added).

Wow; were my steps not ordered, or what? It was not ironic but by another divine appointment. After all of the previous chapters, inserts, prophecies, and divine appointments, it was evident to me that God was really taking me somewhere. But was I really ready for it? NO! A few days before the end of 2016, I had to have a big, private

"RELEASE PARTY" between HIM and me. Sometimes you can't have the vision party until you have the release party. You know the kind of party that you release people, places and things; thoughts and feelings that you were still trying to hold on to. I had to "rewrite some rules" in order to reset some boundaries. #reset-ready

When you allow what's in front of you to become stronger than what's holding you, only then do you release God to reset you into what He has called you to. I was reminded of one of my favorite messages of all times by Pastor Andrew Singleton, entitled, **"I'M READY FOR IT NOW."** The thought came from Ezekiel 21:27: *"I will overturn, overturn, overturn, it: and it shall be no more, until he come whose right it is; and I will give it him."* Is that not one of the most dynamic Scriptures in the Bible, or what? Just as Bishop Jakes' previous message was designed for me, this one was too. I can distinctly remember the messages that have taken me **all** the way in, like "behind the veil," in. These were two of five.

"Turn down for what?" "Hannah," you don't have to fast and pray, weep and work, or stress and strain to birth this "baby" another day. Now that you have released it, you can relax now because **"there will be a performance."** Those are the words that I received from Bishop Herman Murray, as I was channel surfing, earlier this week. When I made my transition five months ago, you can say that I got my fight back. Then, you could see that the fight was back on. Without exaggeration, the fight is not on; it is now 2017, and the fight is really over!

You are not going to believe what happened after my release. First, I had some serious complications that made it impossible to save and retrieve the final changes and editorial <u>corrections</u> that were made to the manuscript. I could pull up the file, but every word, page and chapter had been suddenly wiped out from the hard-drive. I mean, there was not even an auto recovery file. Totally devastated, I was determined not to go out without a fight. By faith, I told God that if He could turn water into wine, surely, He could turn a blank file into a "Word" doc. If He could make a donkey speak, I just believed that He could create words on paper.

I don't know about you, but I'm at the point in God that I need to know Him in a real way. I'm tired of believing Him, just because of what I've read; I want to know Him because of what I've seen. Finally, after I shut-down and waited for a few days, I had to make a quality decision: do I deprive my reader of what is left, or do I make the best of what I have? You know by now that I hate to leave a "stone unturned." But after trying to trigger memories to piece it all back together, I can't say what's missing, but I resolved to feed you what's left. But here is what came after the "storm." Are you ready for my big reveal? Are you prepared to be a witness to some real signs and wonders?

Well, unfortunately, since this book has already been extended to the "max," and Pastor Clinton Bryant has just convinced me to eliminate about 50 additional pages, I have been forced to make the reveal a part of my "next chapter." Still a bit "over the top," we'll figure out how to further reduce the "Remix" on the next round. Obviously, I have comprehensively and meticulously exhausted what was in my "belly." In order to precisely and methodically hear the incomparable conclusion of the whole matter, you will have to purchase my other, latest book, entitled: *My 70-Day Journal To Living On The W.O.W.W.W. Side* [Woman of Word, Worship, Wisdom & Wealth]. Also, I will disclose my other, 2017 undisclosed, surreptitious secret, as soon as you get to the final chapter. I said all of that to arrive at one word: "WHOOSA."

Meanwhile, as far as ministry is concerned, I thought that I would never hear myself say this; but I'm willing to perish for this Gospel. Whether it is in the jurisdiction of an evangelist, an author, or just one of God's daughters, I'm over the antics, and I'm here for HIM. Thus, if He is clever enough to choose me, He is sensible enough to sustain me. While there are some missionaries in third countries that are actually dying for the cause of Christ, under normal circumstances, God is not precisely demanding that we lay down our literal lives anymore; though it may eventually come to that. But fortunately, brother or sister, the ultimate sacrifice has already been paid.

While both the prophecy and the message exponentially increased my awareness that I have been called, these are the simple questions that I believe are emerging from the heart of God: Would you be willing to give up your selfish pride, to draw men unto Me? Are you willing to put your reputation up for discussion, to convince somebody that it is all about Me and not about you? Are you bold enough to tell the Church that there is an enemy in the camp; and then, tell them to put away from among themselves that wicked person, as in 1 Corinthians 5:13b? Are you humble enough to become an overcomer by the mere words of your testimony? Are you willing to make the shift in letting go of your 'stinking-thinking?' Evangelists, rather than being confined to the walls of the church and re-saving people that are already saved, are you assertive enough to go into the 'hedges and highways' and compel sinners to come unto Me?"

When it comes to dying daily to our own fleshly way of thinking, or being martyred for the sake of the Gospel, those are the questions that God is asking us to consider in this hour. Additionally, and only as an intensifier to denote disdain, here is a more relevant question in relation to ALL of my projects: "Shepherds, would you be disciplined enough to feed the sheep and NOT *sleep* with the sheep?" To avoid being offensive, I went ahead and relinquished my rights to say the word I really wanted to say. Finally, are you willing to cover the sheep and not control the sheep? I hope that we can all respond to these clear-cut questions with this consensus: "Yes LORD, here am I, send me." When you're ready for God to move, you must "turn up" when He calls you out.

Although I was indisputably undressed by man, I was conclusively addressed by God (Trilogy-Part One). After He prepared His Son a body, Jesus pulled off His robe, left the portals of Heaven and stepped out of eternity down into time. He came down through forty and two generations, the seed of Abraham, the root of Jessie, burning bushes and kinsmen redeemers, daystars and bulwarks, the blood of bullocks and goats. As Bishop T.D. Jakes says it best; "He then wrapped Himself up in the flesh that He found in the dressing room, called Mary, and landed in a little town, called Bethlehem."

Born of a virgin, Jesus became the other Adam to address "the other woman." Oh my, I felt that! As with the woman with the issue of blood, He looked at me and acknowledged my issue with the right attention. Like I insisted earlier, even after my menstrual cycle had continued for eight, consecutive months, "can't 'nothing' stop a cycle like a seed!" Now that part of my story is in another book. Even so, my enemies tried to bury me, but they didn't know that I was a seed. Whoever had hindered my progress, and whatever had put my life on hold for all of those years, Jesus caused those ugly scars and every bloody issue to completely dry up. Now He says, *"Daughter,* go in peace and be whole of thy plague." I finally had the opportunity to become a "Daddy's-girl." Thank God for the last Adam and the precious blood of the Lamb!

As far as the first Adam is concerned, like the classic Christian and the typical woman, I admit that I was totally oblivious to his role as a real man. As a result of being taught this contrasting point of view and an exceptional revelation, I hope that it was worth the brain-teasers that I drew from, for you to absorb some of it. Either way, I have gained a whole, new respect for Adam. Proper interpretation is the indispensable element in any investigation. Despite your consensus, *"All that ever came before me are thieves and robbers"...* (John 10:8). Even within this context, a paradigm shift is clearly on the way. For now, all I can say is: I may have been a woman with some serious female problems, but Adam, "Bro," "you 'da' man." ... *"Who is the figure of Him that was to come"* (Rom. 5:14b). Then, by far, Jesus Christ, Sir, indeed, YOU ARE THE LAMB!

If you call yourself a **Christ**ian and Jesus is not your Lord, or you do not believe that He's born of a virgin and that He died on a cross and shed His blood for you, or that He rose again from the dead and He's now the Savior who is coming back to reclaim His Bride, then you are **not** a Christian, and you need to become one. A **Christ**ian simply means that you believe in Christ. If you do not know Him in the pardon of your sins as your personal Savior, pray this prayer: Lord, I've failed You; I have not believed Your Word. Jesus, come into my heart, and save me. I'm trusting in Your shed blood; cover and take away my sins today. Come into my heart Jesus, and be mine today. In your Holy name Jesus, Amen.

In this final analysis, are you still trying to figure out why I ask so unsophisticatedly, "Hey Adam, 'where you at'?" If you are not a real man or a good shepherd, "I'm 'gonna' need you to back up off of me, and go toward the 'Light'." Somewhere on this huge planet, there is only ONE man whom my soul loveth; *"I sought him, but I found*

him not" (Sol. 3:1). Aren't you about ready for a new storyline? Well, that's the rationale that leads me to my final inquiry: Why **DIDN'T** I get Married? Let's have some comedic relief and reality television, and some private one-on-one. Brace yourself for an intriguing ride! I have even added room for my "Baby."

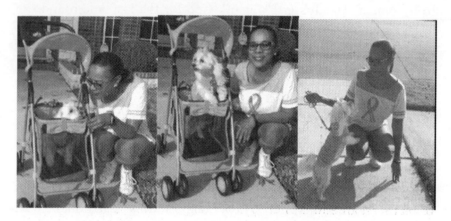

WHY DIDN'T I GET MARRIED?
I WAITED ON PURPOSE

"Ooops;" "my bad." In the final analysis, there was a change of plans. In an effort to obey some last minute instructions, I was persuaded to make Chapter Fourteen a book of its own. Obviously, there are a lot of layers to my story, so here is your opportunity to stay in the "loop," or leave the "hullabaloo." If you decide to stay, please go to Amazon.com or your favorite online book distributor and order my two, latest books. Whereas I have been working on the previous, three projects, concurrently, if one or the other is not readily available, it is definitely forthcoming. Now that the first and last Adam has set the House in order, "let's get back to Eden!" Hey "Adam," "where you at?"

REFERENCES

"HEY 'ADAM,' 'WHERE YOU AT'?"

Baymon, C. B. (2015). *A return on the deposit.* Memphis, TN: Holy Temple Cathedral of Deliverance C.O.G.I.C.

Blackissue.com (n.d.). Malcolm X. Retrieved from http://www.blackissue.com/malcolm_x.htm

Bibletools (2016). Commentaries: Forerunner Commentary. Retrieved from bibletools.org

Braggs, L. A. (2016). Sunday Morning Worship. Little Rock, AR: ACI-DI.

Bryant, J. E. (2016). I'm not ashamed of the Gospel of Christ. Ft. Worth, TX: Greater Greater Gospel Kingdom C.O.G.I.C.

Crouch, A. (2016). Speak truth to Trump. Retrieved from www.christianitytoday.com/ct/ 2016/October-web-only/speak-truth-to-trump.html

Crozier, A. L. (2014). Turn, and keep the plan. Memphis, TN: Powerhouse Ministries Revival Center

Cure B. (nd). Esau & the Edomites. Retrieved from www.yahspeople.com/esau.html

Garland, D. R., & Argueta, C. (2010). How clergy sexual misconduct happens: A qualitative study of first-hand accounts. *Social Work & Christianity, 37*(1), 1-27. Retrieved from SocINDEX (48314305)

Guinness World Records (2017). Best-selling book of non-fiction. Retrieved from guinnessworldrecords.com

Graham, R. (2010). Women pastors. Retrieved from http://www.standingforgod.com/2010/08/women-pastors/

Grady, J. L. (2010). Private pain, public trust: Why leaders must be open about failure. Lake Mary, FL: Charisma Magazine and Strang Communications. Used with permission from http://www. charismamag.com/index.php/fire-in-my bones/26333 private-pain-public-trust-why-leaders-must-be-open-about-failure

Jakes, T. D. (2011). The blood speaks. Dallas, TX: T.D. Jakes Ministries.

Jakes, T. D. (2016). Crazy choices. Dallas, TX: T.D. Jakes Ministries.

Jakes, T. D. (2016). Is it well with your soul? Dallas, TX: T. D. Jakes Ministries.

Jones, S. (2015). Spirit of Jezebel (Pt. 3). Memphis, TN: Safe Place Ministries.

Mount, H. (2014). Is this proof Jesus married and had two sons? Ancient manuscript said to be 'lost gospel' with a sensational twist. Retrieved from dailymail.co.uk

Moustakas, C. E. (1994). *Phenomenological research methods.* Thousand Oaks, CA: Stage Publications.

Olar, J. L. (2000). Just what do you mean... "WEAKER VESSEL"? Retrieved from http://graceandknowledge.faithweb.com/vssel.h

Parnitzke Smith, C., & Freyd, J. J. (2013). Dangerous safe havens: Institutional betrayal exacerbates sexual trauma. *Journal of Traumatic Stress, 26*(1), 119-124. doi: 10.1002/jts.21778

Ravenhill, D. (2012). The danger of abusing the grace of God. Retrieved from charisamag.com/blogs/prophetic-insight/15505-the-danger-of-abusing-the-grace-of-god

Real Israelites (2006). Who are the Black people that were sold into slavery? Retrieved from realisraelites.m.webs.com

Reid, K. D. (2014). *God, why didn't he cover me?* Minneapolis, MN: AuthorHouse.

Reid, K. D. (2010). *From man's abuse to the woman God loosed.* Minneapolis, MN: AuthorHouse.

Reid, K. D. (2010). *From mistress to ministry: He got me pregnant on purpose.* Minneapolis, MN: AuthorHouse.

Rutter, P. (1997). *Sex in the forbidden zone: When therapists, doctors, clergy, teachers and other men in power betray women's trust.* New York, NY: Random House.

Simpson, J. (2014). Why is Jesus usually depicted with long hair? Retrieved from Quora.com

Sommers-Flanagan, R. S., & Sommers-Flanagan, J. S. (2007). *Becoming an ethical and helping professional*. Hoboken, NJ: John Wiley & Sons, Inc.

Stevenson, M. L. (2016). Empty: I never knew you. Chicago, IL: All Nations Worship Assembly.

Stevenson, M. L. (2016). The ministry of the sent one. Memphis, TN: Living Word Ministries.

Stevenson, M. L. (2017). Bring back the preacher! Chicago, IL: Fire Conference.

Stevenson, M. L. (2017). Prophetic word for 2017. Chicago, IL: Fire Conference.

Stockstill, L. (2014). Restoring integrity in the pulpit. Retrieved from http://ministrytodaymag.com/index.php/ministry-leadership/ethics/20596 restoring integrity-in-the-pulpit

Sutton, G. W. & Jordan, K. (2013). Evaluating attitudes toward clergy restoration: The psychosomatic properties of two scales. *Pastoral Psychol, 62*(1), 859-871. doi: 10.1007/s11089-013-0527-7

Talmage, J. E. (2010). Women in the Scriptures. Retrieved from http://womeninthescriptures.blogspot.com/2010/11/real-meaning-of-term-help meet.html

The Boston Globe (2002). *Betrayal: The crisis in the Catholic Church.* Retrieved from archive.boston.com/Globe/Spotlight/abuse/betrayal/chap1_7.htm

The Washington Post (2016). U.S. owes Black people reparations for a history of racial terrorism, says U.N. panel. Retrieved from washingtonpost.com

Thomas, D. L. (2017). *A new perspective of the Book of Genesis.* Minneapolis, MN: Authorhouse.

Thomas, J. (2011). Case studies. *Journal of Psychology and Christianity, 30*(3), 250-252. SocINDEX (0733-4273)

Wallis, J. (2016). It's Embarrassing to be an Evangelical this election. The so-called "Evangelical vote" has some explaining to do. Retrieved from https://sojo.net/articles/it-s-embarrassing-be-evangelical-election

Will,? (2009). Is the Tribe of Judah the original Israelites~and Black? Retrieved from http://educate-yourself.org/lte/tribeof judah24nov09.shtml

Williams, A. R. (2013). The glory of God (Pt. 10). "The love of the Father." Memphis, TN: World Overcomers Outreach Ministries Church.

Zambia, Z. (2012). What does it mean when the Bible says, "the man is head of the woman?" Retrieved from http://zibanizambia.com/2012/11/21what-does-it-mean when-the-bible-says-the-man-is-the-head-of-the-woman/

ABOUT THE AUTHOR
A "P.M.S." SURVIVOR

In addition to surviving eight, **major** stomach surgeries, Systemic Lupus, and breast cancer, Karen D. Reid also experienced "P.M.S.," an acronym that she coined as the, **P**astor's **M**istress **S**tronghold. While living in this emotionally-abusive relationship for 15 years, she even encountered racial discrimination and sexual harassment violations in the workplace. Having filed multiple bankruptcies as a result of unwavering and unshakable financial adversities, Ms. Reid is definitely a **survivor**.

She earned a Bachelor of Science Degree in Education from the University of Memphis (formerly known as Memphis State University), and a Master of Arts Degree in Management and Leadership, from Webster University. She is currently a Ph.D. candidate at Capella University, with an expected 2017 completion. Having maintained a 4.0 GPA in the School of Social & Behavioral Sciences-Counseling Division, her major is Human Services with a specialization in Community Services. Chronicled in the leading biographical, reference publisher of the highest achievers and contributors from across the country and around the world, her profile is often recognized in the International Who's Who of Entrepreneurs, Marquis Who's Who in America, Who's Who in the World, Who's Who in Finance and Business, and Who's Who of American Women.

God-employed as a full-time author and ministry-gift to the Body of Christ, Ms. Reid is previously an 11-year employee of Pinnacle Airlines (a wholly-owned subsidary of Delta Airlines). She was the recipient of the 1st Annual, Recognition Award – Employee of the

Year, for her professionalism in Customer Service. Having found her forte as a committed author and entrepreneur, and foster parent (for a season), she currently serves as an Editorial Specialist, Ghost Writer, and Ministry Consultant. Other aspirations involve setting up a Retreat Facility for Ministry Leaders, establishing Transitional Housing for foster children, and ultimately, launching a multi-ministry Safe Place & Empowerment Center to accommodate The Twin Ministries Empowerment Network, Inc. *"Verily, verily, I say unto you, except a corn of wheat falls into the ground and die, it abideth alone: but if it dies, it bringeth forth much fruit"* (John 12:24). From an abuse victim to a cancer survivor, Karen D. Reid ultimately becomes "more than a conqueror," and the sum total of a working project in progress – life after death.

OTHER BOOKS & RESOURCES BY THE AUTHOR:

TRILOGY: PART ONE
GOD, WHY DIDN'T HE COVER ME?
UNDRESSED BY MAN BUT ADDRESSED BY GOD

TRILOGY: PART TWO
FROM MAN'S ABUSE TO THE WOMAN GOD LOOSED
PAIN, POISON – PURPOSE

TRILOGY: PART THREE
HE GOT ME PREGNANT ON PURPOSE
FROM MISTRESS TO MINISTRY

MY 70-DAY JOURNAL TO LIVING
ON THE "W.O.W.W.W.W." SIDE

WHY DIDN'T I GET MARRIED?
BOAZ OR "NO-AZ," I'M WAITING ON "PURPOSE"

COMPREHESIVE ADMINISTRATIVE TRAINING
MANUAL FOR 21ST-CENTURY MINISTRY LEADERS
(PART TWO COMING SOON)

FOR BLACKS ONLY: ID REQUIRED
"MAN-IMIZING THE PLAN & MAXIMIZING THE
MANDATE IN MODERN-DAY MADNESS

(COMING SOON)

For the latest information and up-to-date editions,
PLEASE PLACE YOUR BOOK ORDERS AT:

Author's Publisher: AuthorHouse
www.authorhouse.com
888-519-5121

BONUS OFFER:
If you are an aspiring author and would like to receive my personal,
COACHING TIPS for 1st -TIME AUTHORS,
visit my website and click on the "BONUS OFFER."

To contact the author, you may write to:

The Twin Ministries (T.T.M.)
Empowerment Network, Inc.

Attn: Karen D. Reid
P.O. Box 752613
Memphis, TN 38175
(901) 634-2667

Email address – www.thetwinministries@yahoo.com
www.karenreid.com

Printed in the United States
By Bookmasters